Henry M Davidson

Fourteen Months in Southern Prisons

Being a narrative of the treatment of federal prisoners of war in the rebel military prisons of Richmond, Danville, Andersonville, Savannah and Millen

Henry M Davidson

Fourteen Months in Southern Prisons
Being a narrative of the treatment of federal prisoners of war in the rebel military prisons of Richmond, Danville, Andersonville, Savannah and Millen

ISBN/EAN: 9783744755108

Printed in Europe, USA, Canada, Australia, Japan

Cover: Foto ©ninafisch / pixelio.de

More available books at **www.hansebooks.com**

FOURTEEN MONTHS

IN

SOUTHERN PRISONS;

BEING A

NARRATIVE OF THE TREATMENT OF FEDERAL PRISONERS OF WAR IN THE REBEL MILITARY PRISONS OF RICHMOND, DANVILLE, ANDERSONVILLE, SAVANNAH, AND MILLEN; DESCRIBING THE AUTHOR'S ESCAPE WITH TWO COMRADES, FROM ANDERSONVILLE AND THE BLOOD HOUNDS; HIS ADVENTURES DURING A FOURTEEN NIGHTS' MARCH IN THE SWAMPS OF WESTERN GEORGIA, AND HIS SUBSEQUENT RE-CAPTURE; TO WHICH IS ADDED A LARGE LIST OF THOSE WHO HAVE DIED IN VARIOUS PRISONS IN THE CONFEDERACY.

BY H. M. DAVIDSON,

Member Battery A., 1st O. V. L. A.

MILWAUKEE:
DAILY WISCONSIN PRINTING HOUSE.

1865.

Entered according to Act of Congress, in the year 1865, by

H. M. DAVIDSON,

in the Clerk's Office of the District Court of the United States, for the Northern District of Ohio.

INDEX.

CHAPTER I.

	PAGE.
Chickamauga Battle,	9
Hospital,	15
In the Enemy's hands,	17
The Wounded,	18
Want of Water,	20
Paroling Hospital Attendants,	21
The Field, seven days after Battle,	24
Arrival of United States Ambulances, with supplies for the wounded	27
Paroling the wounded, previous to passing through Federal lines,	28

CHAPTER II.

March to Chickamauga Station,	31
Tunnel Hill,	32
Dalton,	33
Resacca and Fortifications,	34
Pies and Cakes,	34
Marietta,	35
Arrival at Atlanta,	36
Trip to Augusta,	39
Branchville,	42
Raleigh,	43
Richmond,	44

CHAPTER III.

Smith Prison	47
Pemberton,	48
Scott,	48
Libby,	49
Prison Fare,	50
Incidents,	57
Newspaper Gossip,	60
Removal to Danville,	61

CHAPTER IV.

Danville,	66
Prisons Nos. 1, 2, 3, 4, 5 and 6,	66
Writing letters home,	74

	PAGE.
Occupation of time,	75
Small Pox,	76
Receipt of Rations and Clothing, by flag of truce,	77
How appropriated and issued,	79
Hospital,	81
Express boxes,	83
Tunneling,	88
Handicraft,	91
Incidents,	95
Newspaper reports,	98
Exchange,	101
Removal to Georgia,	102

CHAPTER V.

Andersonville Prison	109
Appearance of the Prisoners and the Pen,	111
The First Night,	118
The Morning,	120
Roll-Call,	121
Rations,	123
Cooking Utensils,	124
Wood and Axes,	125
Belle Islanders,	128
Prisoners from Cahawba and Plymouth,	131

CHAPTER VI.

Enlargement of the Stockade,	137
The Camp at Daylight,	141
Shelters,	142
Cooking,	148
Appearance of the Prisoners,	150
Roll-Call,	153
Sick-Call,	155
Market,	157
The Sutler,	160
Smugglers,	161
Manufacturers,	162
Gamblers,	163
Water,	164
Fortifying,	165
Raiders,	168
Six men hung	170
Police,	176
Petitions,	176
Writing letters,	178
Receiving Express boxes,	178
Incidents,	180

CHAPTER VII.

	PAGE.
Rations,	185
Cook-Houses,	186
Escapes,	190
Punishments,	197
Removal of Hospitals,	200
Sick-Call,	201
Hospitals,	218
The Dead,	228
The Burial,	233
General Winder,	235
Capt. Wirz,	237

CHAPTER VIII.

Atlanta taken by Sherman,	241
Order of Gen. Winder that 20,000 prisoners are to be exchanged,	242
The Author escapes with two comrades,	244
Avoiding the Dogs,	249
Encounter Hood's Scouts,	251
Hair-breadth Escapes,	292
In the midst of Hood's Army,	297
Surrounded and re-captured,	301

CHAPTER IX.

Rebel Headquarters,	307
Opeliki,	311
Columbus,	314
Plan of Escape detected,	316
Andersonville again,	319
Savannah,	321
Special Exchange of 10,000 sick,	325
Removal to Millen,	327
The Prison Pen,	328
Recruiting among the Prisoners,	334
Free,	337

CHAPTER X.

Paroled,	341
Rebel Truce Boats,	343
On Board Ship,	344
Homeward Bound,	345
Northern Soil,	346
Furloughed,	347
Views of the Prisoners,	348
Tables,	357
Conclusion,	368
Appendix,	383

PREFACE.

During my captivity in the South, it was a settled conviction among the prisoners, that if the Northern people were apprised of the condition in which we were placed, they would not cease to employ the most strenuous efforts to induce the Government to adopt measures whereby our terrible sufferings might be alleviated; and we pledged ourselves to each other, if any of our number should ever make his way to the North, to do all in his power to spread abroad a knowledge of our treatment, and arouse the sympathies of our friends to action in our behalf.

Upon my arrival at my home, by special exchange, in December, 1864, the following narrative was begun, in fulfillment of this pledge, with a view to its publication early in March following. Illustrations were to be furnished by a comrade who returned with me, and who, being an excellent artist, had sketched many scenes of prison life, and the work was to be printed by another comrade, who was a practical printer. Before the work was ready, we were separated,—the artist confined to his bed in New York, the printer at home in Michigan, and myself ordered to duty at the front, and consequently unable to attend to the passage of my book through the press; while the sudden close of the war, by releasing the prisoners has made it no longer of value for the purpose for which it was originally designed. A picture of the cruelties which the rebel leaders practiced, to gratify their private vengeance, when they felt themselves baffled in their attempt to cut loose from legitimate authority, and set at defiance the laws they had sworn to obey, may not be entirely devoid of usefulness; and the hope that a perusal of this book will awaken, in the mind of the reader, a deeper abhorrence of a rebellion, whose origin was in selfish ambition, and whose pretext was a stupendous lie,—is my apology for presenting it to the public at this time.

The work contains but one illustration—a ground plan of Andersonville, which is correct, except, it may be, in some o the greater distances. I am not insensible to the fact, that correct drawings add much to the interest of a narrative of this character; but, as I could procure no other than fancy sketches, I abandoned the item of cuts altogether.

It has been my design, in this work, to show that the treatment of Federal prisoners was the result of a deep laid plan to murder them by starvation, or at least to reduce them to such a point of weakness and disease as to prevent their ever again performing active service in the field. How far this may appear to be the case, I leave for the candid reader to judge. In the five different prisons in which I was incarcerated, the treatment was on the same general scheme, and differed only in the details—these being left to the several commanders of prison interiors.

I have endeavored to tell my tale as it appeared to us in prison, to add nothing for the sake of embellishment—to keep back nothing that would operate in favor of the men in charge of us. All the statements are the result of personal observation, except a few, which have been referred to their proper authorities. For their truth I pledge my veracity. The chapter devoted to my escape was inserted, because the difficulties and dangers I encountered do not differ materially from those which beset others who made similar attempts.

To paint the terrible sufferings of the starving, writhing, dying mass of human beings, confined in those narrow prisons, is beyond the power of language; a shadow only can be given in place of the dreadful reality. But if my pen shall have awakened one feeling of abhorrence against, or shall have quickened one pulse to a deeper hatred of a Rebellion that could sanction such barbarities against helpless prisoners; if I have added one leaf to the laurel wreath, woven for the brave and martyred men, whose sublime fortitude and steadfast love of country and right, enabled them to endure these inhuman tortures without a murmur or complaint, and whose only regret was that they could die but once in the holy cause, my task will not have been in vain.

         H. M. DAVIDSON,
          Battery A., 1st Reg. O. V. L. A.

GALLATIN, TENN., June, 1865.

FOURTEEN MONTHS
IN
SOUTHERN PRISONS.

CHAPTER I.

Chickamauga Battle—Hospital—In the Enemy's Hands—The Wounded—Paroling Hospital Attendants—Want of Water, Bandages and Medicines—The Field Seven Days after the Battle—Arrival of United States Ambulances with Supplies for the Wounded—Paroling the Wounded previous to their passing through the Federal Lines.

The marches and countermarches of the 20th army corps, Army of the Cumberland, under Gen. McCook, over Lookout Mountain, previous to the great battle of Chickamauga, will long be remembered by the survivors of the old "Second Division," commanded by Gen. Johnson. Three times was this division marched over this steep and rocky range, and the united strength of twelve horses was necessary to move one of our field pieces over the mountains. At a very late hour on Thursday evening, September 17th, 1863, after having made a forced march from early morning, with the exhausted horses dropping down in harness, we were formed in line of battle near Chickamauga Creek.

When daylight appeared on the following morning, the roads and fields showed evidences of a large body of troops in motion. News of the evacuation of the stronghold of Chattanooga, by the rebels, had just reached us ; and up to that time the belief prevailed that there would be no general battle at this point. The batteries, however, were picketed on the chief roads, to guard against surprise, as well as to prevent any advantage to the enemy, in case of sudden attack. But the day wore away so quietly that our previous impressions that there would be no general fight, seemed confirmed.

Before sunrise on Saturday, the 19th, orders were received which gave us notice to be ready to move in fifteen minutes. The division was immediately in motion, and swinging around to the left, found itself on a good road, *en route* for Chattanooga. Crawfish Springs were soon reached, and it was while halting here for rest and water, that the roaring of cannon in the distance announced to the soldier that he had not been summoned there for nought.

Thus far the glorious success of the Army of the

Cumberland, under "Rosey," all the way from Nashville to this point, had won the admiration of every man in the ranks. He had led them into the very heart of rebeldom; had confronted, attacked, and routed Bragg on his chosen ground at Murfreesboro: had driven the rebel army three hundred miles in their own country, and had maintained his communications over this long distance, intact. We had made one grand, triumphal march through the States of Kentucky and Tennessee, building bridges, and repairing railroads, so that the iron horse, with his long train of supplies, might keep pace with us as we advanced. Every true soldier, therefore, felt that the Army of the Cumberland, under its gallant leader was capable of marching any where it might please, in the Confederacy, and of routing any force which might be sent against it. Inspired by such confidence in its leader, and with such reliance upon itself, the booming of the distant guns, approaching nearer and nearer, brought no terror to our ranks; and as the sun approached its meridian, the near sound of cannon and the sharp rattle of musketry, told us that the tide of blood was rolling rapidly toward us. From a gentle knoll upon which we stood, the smoke and dust of the conflict might be distinctly seen, rising in billowy volumes, as if to shut out the fearful spectacle from the eye of Heaven.

Gen. Rosecrans and his staff hurried past us on their fleet chargers, straight forward to the scene of action, where, as it proved, his presence was most needed. It was just at this time, near ten o'clock in the morning, that the column filed off to the right of the road and hurried on to the rescue. The screaming shells passed over our heads, madly slashing through the tree tops, severing the largest limbs from their trunks, with the apparent ease of a thunderbolt; or taking a lower flight, dashed through the ranks, mowing down whole columns of men in their deadly career. In all directions men were lying with their limbs crushed and scattered, their bodies still warm and quivering. The scene was too horrible for description.

Our position was soon taken. Goodspeed's Battery, (Bat. A, 1st Ohio Light Artillery,) of which I am a member, held the center of the artillery of the Division. We had been transferred to the left of the whole line of battle, away from our usual position, which was on the extreme right. The afternoon was spent in firing leisurely at the enemy massed in our front, concealed by heavy timber, behind which they were apparently maneuvering around us in three fourths of a circle; and though they seemed maddened with desperation, and resolved to crush our line, by rolling in great waves upon one point at a time, yet with equal valor and determination, our forces met them, and with the point of the bayonet, pushed them back, inch by inch, over their chosen ground, during the whole of that dreadful afternoon. Among the trophies of our own Brigade, were five pieces of artillery and four caissons, which the Battery had the satisfaction of drawing off the field, under a terrific shower of bullets. At about eight o'clock in the evening, the enemy charged our line in front, advancing with their tremendous whoop, and delivering such a terrible and deadly fire, that for a moment the whole line trembled and reeled, and seemed about to be thrown into complete disorder, when Goodspeed's and Simonson's batteries swept the field with well aimed shell and cannister, causing the foe to fall back hastily and in total route.

Early in the evening the division was relieved and passed back to the rear of the reserve line, where, with fence rails for our pillows, and the ground for our beds, we passed the remainder of the night, as best we could; and there was not a man of the command that did not realise fully the fearful responsibilities of the next terrible day, as we lay in our position waiting the appearance of dawn. The reflection that if upon the morrow the enemy were successful, we should be driven back, broken and demoralized, to wander over three hundred miles of a hostile country, and subjected to all the tortures of starvation, cold and thirst, or be captured, to pass the weary months in rebel prisons, did more to nerve us for the coming crash of arms, than the presence of our officers or the glory of a hoped-for victory.

At early dawn on Sunday, the 20th of September, the whole line was astir. Entire trees were carried on the shoulders of the men to construct a line of temporary breast works, in anticipation of an attack at that point. These anticipations were soon realized, for before the works had reached completion, a rebel force, outnumbering ours two to one, massed in their front, prepared to carry them at the point of the bayonet. Successive charges made by them were repulsed with great slaughter. Our artillery, which had been placed about six hundred yards in the rear of the works, had not yet opened its fire. At last, after due preparation, the rebels advanced for a final charge. The signal was given and the thunder of cannon rolled along the whole line from one end to the other, in one terrible billow of sound. Hardly had the rising column of thick, sulphurous smoke lifted from the scene, before another wave of sound rushed along the line. The charge was repulsed on our front; but the enemy were suddenly descried, massed on our left, advancing with deadly resolve to crush our flank and turn our position. At the same time it was whispered that the hospitals in our rear were captured; that our center had been pierced, and that no communication could be had between the two wings of the army. Nothing daunted by this disheartening intelligence, we trained our guns to bear upon the nearer peril, and sent forth a volley of cannister to meet the advancing foe. On—on they pushed, heedless of their falling comrades, whom our gallant gunners at every shot were sweeping down by hundreds. Braver men never fought in any cause; but despite their iron courage, the carnage was too fearful for endurance. They waver, they halt, they turn,—a shout of victory and a volley of grape follow the retiring foe. The field is ours, but at a fearful sacrifice. Sixteen of our company fell: two killed and fourteen wounded. But the victory was won; and satisfied with the futility of any further attempt at storming our stronghold, the enemy retired and "let us alone," at that point, at least. Our fallen heroes were now assisted off the field. My services, among others, were offered in removing the wounded, and accepted. We carried our patients a mile or so to the rear, before we could find a hospital, owing to our entire ignorance of the direction in which it lay. We finally succeeded in reaching a log hut called Snodgrass Hospital, where we deposited our comrades. Meantime, the line of battle had changed so entirely, that the rebel skirmishers were stretching through the woods, across the track we had just passed over, and the battery was apparently cut off. Under the circumstances, it was thought by the Major of the battalion too hazardous to attempt reaching our comrades upon the field, at that time, and he ordered us to remain at the hospital until matters should assume a more favorable aspect. Acting under this order, we remained assisting the wounded and relieving their necessities to the utmost of our ability.

From this point it was impossible to judge which of the contending parties would hold the line of hills, which seemed to be the great stake fought for. The fighting continued with unabated severity during the entire afternoon. General Granger's corps came up late in the day, and their presence inspired those engaged, with new courage and vigor. As they moved to their position, solid shot and shells went crashing through the timber from the rebel guns. That corps in a short time was engaged and scattered in every direction. The firing was terrific. For the last few hours it was apparent that the enemy were stretching every nerve to get between us and Chattanooga; but at sundown, they had fallen back, and our forces took possession of their ground. It was now dark, and with the advice of the Major, we remained at the hospital during the night, hoping in the morning light to find our way back to our comrades.

Five or six ambulances now arrived, which were immediately filled and driven off for Chattanooga, expecting soon to return and remove the three hundred remaining, who were, with few exceptions, mortally wounded. But they never returned, for during the stillness of the night, broken only by the moans of the wounded, the enemy suddenly and stealthily advanced, took possession of the hospital, and informed us that we might consider ourselves prisoners of war.

This is properly the beginning of my story. Our army, for the safety of Chattanooga, had fallen back, under the cover of the darkness; a movement of which the hospital had not been notified until they were in the enemy's hands. A rebel guard was immediately placed around the hospital, and a picket line in front. To escape and return to our command was now entirely out of the question, for, to the uncertainty of running the enemy's pickets, was added a total ignorance of the position of our own army, and if we should succeed in escaping the vigilance of the former, we were by no means certain of reaching the latter. We were forced to accept the only chance that was left for us, and remain where we were. But had we known what was in store for us, or realized the terrible sufferings we were to undergo, there was not a man of us but would rather have periled all in an effort to escape from that hospital.

Morning came and showed us a sufficient field of labor. Three hundred men were lying in and around the old log house, with limbs shattered and broken, faint from loss of blood, and stiff from the cold dews of night. What could *we* do? we had no bandages, no medicines; no food of any sort was to be found; water could be had at no less distance than three fourths of a mile, and there were only a dozen canteens in which to bring it. With such utensils and such means little could be done to relieve the wants of the suffering. Soon after sunrise a strong line of battle was formed behind a rail fence in front of the hospital, and between us and Chattanooga, in the direction of which at intervals, cannonading could be distinctly heard. Roving bands of cavalry, commissioned officers of all grades, from General to Lieutenant, came to the hospital to inspect the spoils. A Colonel of a Tennessee Regiment rode up, and dismounting, called for the surgeon in charge of the hospital, with whom he held a long conversation on the state of the wounded, and their necessities, &c. When he had mounted his horse to depart, he said: "Boys, I am from Tennessee, and my residence and plantation are a few miles south of Nashville, on the

Franklin pike. I suppose you had a good time when you camped there feasting upon my chickens and turkeys. I hope you did, and I hope they did you good. But in less than three weeks, boys, my regiment shall camp there, and my house shall be my headquarters." We gave the Colonel, who was really a good natured fellow, our congratulations on the "good time" he would have before he reached there, in climbing over the mountains and the Federal bayonets. Generals Longstreet, Bragg, Hood, Lee and Preston, rode up to the hospital on very poor horses, and without escort. General Preston was the only one who had much to say to us. He is a very pleasant man to talk with, has a fine form, compactly built, and a heavy moustache. He wanted to know what battery that was, pointing in the direction of one which stood near. "I would like to know," said he, "for it did terrible mischief with one of my batteries that I ordered to silence it. I could count on that battery as number one, every time; it did splendid shooting." The other Generals said but little; but that little would have been a good deal, if it had happened to be true, for they told us that Gen. Bragg's army had captured ninety pieces of artillery, taken nearly one half of our army prisoners, killed and wounded the half of what remained, while the rest, dispirited and demoralized, were trying to cross the

Tennessee and retreat to Nashville; they also said they had no chance of reaching Nashville, for Forrest's cavalry were between Bridgeport and Murfreesboro, and had torn up and destroyed the Railroad for miles, &c., &c. Their fine stories did not alarm us, however, for the booming of the cannon told us that the conflict was still going on at no great distance.

The few canteens we had, were kept constantly in use, bringing water for the wounded; but with all our efforts we could not furnish enough to allay the thirst of the poor fellows, to say nothing of any to dress their wounds with. That terrible cry, "water! water!" coming from a hundred voices at once, haunted me for days after I had left the scene. Poor fellows! we did all we could for them with the limited means at our command, but while doing our best, we knew that we could not assuage that agonising thirst which the gun shot wound excites.

On the evening of the 22d, a Captain Reid of Bragg's staff, rode up, and ordered all that could walk to fall in, as he was going to send them all to Richmond. Some sixteen of us tied a red string around our arms and claimed to be regular hospital attendants, that we might stay and see the battle-field. One of our surgeons protested against leaving so few men to take care of the wounded, but his arguments were of no avail, the circumstances of the situation having no influence with the inexorable agent. Each of the well men that remained was furnished with a separate parole,* requiring him to report to the post commandant at Atlanta, as soon as his services should no longer be required at the hospital. Thus we remained. For three days and nights we were without food of any kind, and the only bandages we could procure were pieces torn from old shelter tents. The tasks of these volunteer nurses for the three days and nights, with no food, amid the dead and dying, inhaling the stench of gangrened wounds, and hearing the groans and complaints of the sufferers, who were asking us for aid, when we knew we could do nothing for them, were by no means light or agreeable. On the evening of the 24th of September, a rebel surgeon was sent us, who, possessing some humanity, upon seeing our situation, ordered a

---

* PAROLE—"I, H. M. Davidson, private of Company A, 1st Ohio Light Artillery Regiment of the United States army, captured at the battle of Chickamauga, Georgia, solemnly swear that I will not bear arms against the Confederate States Government, nor help, aid, or assist, either directly or indirectly, by assisting in any service of the United States Government, until regularly exchanged a prisoner of war. And that I will report to the commandant of the post at Atlanta, Georgia, as soon as the sick and wounded of the United States prisoners of war, whom I am only paroled to attend, shall no longer require my services.

HENRY M. DAVIDSON.

Subscribed and sworn to before me at the
Chickmauga, September, 22d, 1863.

WM. REID, Capt. and Ass't Pro. Marshal Gen."

bushel of corn meal to be sent to us the next morning. This supply, insufficient as it was, for three hundred men, who had tasted nothing for seventy-two hours, was all that was given us for the next two days. We were thankful, however, for so small a favor, and ate our meal with a great relish. The following morning he came again with a set of surgical instruments. Although kind enough about the corn meal, he proved to be a haughty, over-bearing man, whose high opinion of himself would have put the sceptre of empire into his own hands, if unfortunately he had not lacked the power to do so. His great weakness was his denying human emotions to any who were beneath him in rank; in consequence of which he exacted the utmost humility from all below him—a weakness unfortunately common to a large majority of officers in both the Federal and Rebel armies. He laid down this proposition, in his treatment of the wounded Federals;—that if they had all staid at home and let the Confederates alone, none of them would have been lying then and there, demanding his services; with which highly satisfactory theory he consoled the fortunate man who obtained those services in the amputation of a gangrened limb. He was not always in the amputating mood, and when the freak set in, no amount of solicitation could induce him to examine a wound; and many a poor fellow died from gangrene, whose life might have been saved by a timely application of the knife. My after experience taught me that it was no part of the design of the rebel government to save the life of a Federal prisoner, and that if they could not succeed in killing him, in open, manly warfare, they would at least capture and render him unfit for further service, by cruelties and neglect practiced upon him while helpless in their hands. I remember one instance of this cruelty of neglect. A man was taken to the table to have his leg amputated. His right leg was wounded; under the hot sun the wound had gangrened, become putrid—and his body near the wound was filled with maggots. The surgeon cast a hasty glance at him and ordered him removed. The sufferer had possession of all his senses and begged that the amputation might take place, but the surgeon was deaf to his entreaties, and the poor fellow was removed. He bore his sufferings like a hero and lived several days after this, although he knew that death could not be long delayed. The boys sang and prayed with him; he arranged his little affairs so that his wife and children might know that he died gloriously for his country, and that in death he remembered them. And so he died, the victim of neglect on the part of those whom every sentiment of humanity called upon to assist and care for him.

Seven days after the battle, in the company of a comrade, I made a tour over the field. I had long desired to inspect a battle ground, and, although I had taken part in several general engagements, being constantly with my command, I had never had the opportunity. So that from what I already knew of the matter from slight observation, I had an eager curiosity to examine this field. A mile's walk brought us to the scene of the hardest fighting on Sunday. Every tree in front of our line of works, taking the smallest as the average, contained sixty bullets, ranging all the way from a foot in hight to twenty. Trees from twelve to twenty inches in diameter, were twisted off and shivered as if a tornado had passed over them. The earth was furrowed in all directions with the solid shot and shell that were still lying about. Back of this line, and off to the right, in a strip of timber, our dead were lying unburied where they fell. Many of them had been divested of all their clothing, except a pair of drawers too much tattered and worn to be worth stealing. Everything that could be of service had been taken away by the men of Bragg's army. The appearance of these bodies, having lain upon the ground, exposed to the hot sun, for seven days, was too horrible for description. At intervals could be seen scores of artillery horses, piled up in heaps, by the bursting of shells, while dismounted guns and fragments of limbers and caissons, showed the fearful part played by the batteries in the terrible carnage of Sunday. In various parts of the field, little boys and old grey-haired men were seeking and gathering together loose cartridges and cartridge boxes, and anything else that came in their way, that could possibly be of service to their own army. Rich old planters with their wives and daughters, were roaming over the field, still red with gore, and rejoicing that there were so many "dead Yankees" bleaching upon the fields of the "sunny south." Where the dead were lying thickest, we met an intelligent citizen, and it being a very appropriate place to ask questions, he expressed a desire to talk with us in regard to the strength of Rosecrans' army and the war feeling at the North. Without any hesitation, he said he had the means of knowing the exact strength of Bragg's army. He told us that Bragg's old command numbered 40,000 men; that it had been reinforced by Johnston with 20,000, and by Longstreet with 20,000, swelling the list to 80,000 men, exclusive of the cavalry commands of Forrest and Wheeler; and that with such a force they would march triumphantly to the Ohio river. We replied that Rosecrans had sufficient force to hold Chattanooga against the whole Southern Confederacy. He said he thought the battle of Chicka-

3

mauga would teach the Northern people that the South could never be subjugated, and that a few more such lessons as we had had during the past two weeks, would convince us that we had better "let them alone," for they would all die before they would acknowledge themselves conquered, or give up the institution of slavery. We told him that the majority of the Northern people had never wavered in the prosecution of the war; that we did not wish to subjugate the South; that our mission would be ended, and hostilities would cease, when the rebels laid down their arms, surrendered back the *United States property* which they had *stolen*, and consented to live peaceably under the laws of our common country. We gave him to understand that the battle of Chickamauga was but an insignificant item in the grand total of carnage, unless the terms of unconditional surrender were accepted, and that if subjugation were the issue they made, we must accept it and subjugate them; for in that case there was no other way left of settling the matter. Satisfied that we were not loyal to *his* cause he left us, and we returned to the hospital.

On the 28th of September, the wounded were all moved to a general hospital a mile further up towards Chattanooga. It was located near a large spring of clear water, which furnished us with an abundance of that now invaluable article. The worst cases were moved upon stretchers, while those with comparatively slight wounds were transferred in army wagons. An arrangement was here made to parole and exchange all the wounded. One hundred and ninety-six ambulances arrived from our lines to receive them; which contained supplies enough to last till all were through the lines. The ambulances on reaching the lines had exchanged drivers, and in consequence nearly every box of hard bread had been broken open and a part of its contents abstracted. I knew this to be the fact because I saw the rebel drivers filling their haversacks from the boxes that had come to us under "flag of truce." What was left was put into a commissary tent, and a guard placed over it; but every guard embraced the opportunity to fill his haversack with sugar, coffee, dried fruit and hard bread. We complained to the chief surgeon in charge of the hospital, but he made no effort to have the matter corrected, though he had entire control of the medicines and supplies. He freely offered to the Confederate officers the hospital whisky and dainties that were designed for the exclusive use of the wounded. It is presumed that he thought by so doing to gain favor with the enemy, and anticipated a little more gentle treatment in return at their hands on his arrival in Richmond, whither he was soon to be sent as a prisoner. Such men deserve the condemnation of the whole world, and should receive a dishonorable dismissal from the United States service.

As soon as the ambulances arrived, the Confederate Surgeons commenced paroling the prisoners, and continued the work until its completion. Two trips were made before all could be taken away. The last train was loaded during a heavy thunder shower, the rain pouring down as it can pour only in the South. The men were completely drenched, but were too happy to escape from the hands of the rebels to mind it much. One of the boys who had two blankets gave them to me, as I had none, and would probably need them, while he was going where he could procure new ones. The ambulances were loaded, and as we saw our comrades start for home we envied the poor fellows their wounds which had proved to them a passport to better things. As soon as they were gone, we who remained were informed that the next day we were to start for Atlanta. Seeing the rebels making a general raid upon the supplies sent for our hospital, we made bold to appropriate a portion for our own use, and by this means laid in a quantity for our journey. It was well for us that we did this, for, as it proved, it was all we had furnished us till we reached Atlanta. Great promises were made us of excellent fare at that place, and our anticipations were raised high at the glowing accounts of the plenty and luxury those enjoyed who were so fortunate as to fall into the hands of the rebel government. Experience, it is unnecessary to add, soon taught us that the "plenty" they had so finely represented, existed, if at all, only in the imaginations of those who told about it. Certainly it was not our lot to partake of "plenty" at Atlanta, or at any other place in the Confederacy.

CHAPTER II.

March to Chickamauga Station—Tunnel Hill—Dalton—Kingston—Resaca and Fortifications—Pies and Cakes—Marietta—Scenery—Arrival at Atlanta—Trip to Augusta—Savannah River—Branchville, Kingsville, Columbia and Charlotte, N. C., Raleigh, via Salisbury and Greensboro—Goldsboro, Weldon and Petersburg—At rest in Richmond.

A little past noon on the 2d day of October, twelve days after the battle of Chickamauga, we were ordered to form in line for a march to Chickamauga Station, seven miles distant, and ten from Chattanooga. A guard, composed of citizens principally, armed with shot guns and old muskets, and various utensils for shooting, and facetiously denominated "cavalry," accompanied us. As regular soldiers, we felt humiliated in being obliged to submit to be guarded by these sneaking citizens, whose courage increased after the battle as rapidly as it had decreased before, and the most of whom no doubt possessed papers showing that they had already taken the oath of allegiance. We passed through a woody country, near Bragg's headquarters, where the reserve forces were drawn up in line of battle. Beyond this at a little distance

Chickamauga Creek confronted us. Reaching the ford, at which a large guard was stationed, we halted for ferriage. A small dug-out was after a time procured, and we were taken across in parties of eight at a time. While waiting our turn, the rebels flocked around us by hundreds to talk and trade with us; their old clothing formed the chief article of barter, and a liberal quantity of Confederate scrip was offered to make up balances. As our "personal property" consisted principally of our apparel, we were not inclined to "trade," and it was only by a persistent and vigorous defense of our personal rights that we succeeded in "holding our own." We did it, however, in spite of repeated orders to exchange, and threats of violence if we did not comply. Being across the creek we started for the Station, where we arrived in due time. A train of box cars was in waiting for us, and we proceeded to load ourselves therein. This being effected after some delay, owing to the crowded state of the cars, and the dislike manifested by the boys to lying more than two deep upon the bottom, we finally got under way about dark, and proceeded as far as Tunnel Hill, where we lay to till morning. A few houses were to be seen at this place, scattered here and there along the line of the Railroad, all presenting the same dilapidated appearance so characteristic of Southern villages. It is a place of no particular consequence, and except for the passage of the railroad through the mountain at that point, would be nameless. At sunrise the train passed through the tunnel on its way to Atlanta. Permission being given to ride upon the outside, I took up my position on the top of the car, both to escape the press and close air within, and to note the character of the country. When I entered the army it was with a determination to learn all I could, in whatever situation I might be placed. I knew that this part of Georgia would soon be the theatre of active military operations, and if it should happen to me to be exchanged and return over the same ground with our army, all the information I might be possessed of, might be turned to good account. For this purpose I took notes of the principal points of interest as far as I was able to do so, and from these notes the following narrative is compiled.

By eight o'clock the train reached Dalton, a connecting point of railroads leading to East and Middle Tennessee, a situation, which, if once in our possession and held, would prove of great damage to the Confederacy. We made but a brief call at this point, and passing on through a pleasant country reached Kingston, another railroad junction. Several hundred soldiers and officers and citizens were gathered at this point, apparently for no particular purpose.

A train of cars which had preceded us from Chickamauga, loaded with the debris of the battle field, halted here to let us pass. By ten o'clock we reached Resaca, afterwards the scene of a bloody fight between Sherman and Bragg's army. A large camp of State militia had been established here, and upon one of the adjacent eminences an earthwork was in process of erection. Small works had been thrown up near the railroad bridge, mounting some five pieces of artillery, and a line of breastworks constructed of sand, had been built on the south bank of the river. It was evident that Bragg's main reliance was upon the natural defences of the country about Chattanooga, and that he even doubted his ability to hold those. It occurred to us that these industrious "lads" had commenced their defences too far North, and would be obliged to vacate them and fall further back whenever Uncle Sam saw fit to advance again.

Making a short call at this place for wood and water, the train moved on again toward Atlanta, crossing the Etowah, near large iron works, situated at the right of the railroad. The country was very rough, and the train wound and coiled itself among the hills in graceful curves. At every station and water tank the women, girls and boys flocked around the train with "leather" pies and cakes for sale.

The pies were made apparently of sweet potatoes, (chickens were rare,) baked in a crust without any previous preparation, and formed a remarkably durable article of food. From the samples sold us on our route to Richmond, we concluded that a reformation was imperatively demanded in the *cuisine* of the "Southern Confederacy."

At Marietta we met a train load of Georgia militia on their way to join Bragg. They looked brave and heroic, (the battle had been fought,) and if words had been available for such an event, would have annihilated the whole of "Lincoln's horde" then and and there. Fortunately for us, words were not bullets and we were unscathed. A corpulent lieutenant, something of the Falstaff order of heroes, was particularly noticeable. He said that when his State was invaded by the foe, he could no longer remain peaceably at home, but felt it incumbent upon him to buckle on his sword and hurl back the invaders from the soil or bury them beneath it. "Boys," said he, protruding his Falstaffian proportions full toward us, "you started for the great city of Atlanta, and will probably arrive there sooner than you expected, and if you ever return to your friends at the North, tell them that when Georgia is invaded, one patriot on the soil can whip five of the puny Northmen, and bid them remember that the 'stag at bay is a dangerous foe.'" We consoled him somewhat by telling him that we were only the advance upon Atlanta, and that our friends were quietly coming that way, when he would have an opportunity of finishing any five of them he chose to select for that purpose. We intimated also that we did not doubt his courage in the least, at that distance from danger, after the battle had been fought, and sincerely hoped there might be no casualties so far from the scene of the action. The only friends we had here, as well as at most places through which we passed, were the negroes, and they, under the eye of their masters, were unable to lend us much assistance. From this we moved directly toward Atlanta, through a country, which in times of peace, and in the hands of any but the indolent Southern master, would be fruitful and beautiful beyond description. Coming gradually upon the town, we had opportunity briefly to notice something of its environs. The city is built upon a table land, and surrounded with parks, shaded walks and costly residences. Wealth, luxury and idleness abounded on all sides. Ladies, gaily dressed, promenaded the streets, and fine equipages, and gay " turnouts" met the eye in every direction. Many of these had gathered about the depot expecting a train load of wounded from the Chickamauga battle, but finding the " contemptible Yanks" instead, their expected pleasure changed suddenly into scorn and derision. I had heard much of the modesty and high breeding of Southern females and was prepared to see ladies of high accomplishments. After making all due allowances for patriotic devotion to their country, it would hardly seem consonant with refined female character to treat even enemies with so much contempt, as these high blooded women manifested for us. A true women never loses the character of a lady under any circumstances, much less will she descend to vile epithets or words of derision. On the whole, I prefer our Northern notions of refinement to anything I saw in the South. It may be an error in my early education, but "on general principles," one does not like to be spit upon even by rosy lips, and a Northern man is inclined to construe promiscuous salivation upon his own person into an affront.

We were not allowed to leave the cars until ordered to do so by the Provost Marshal—a young man of great proportions, no doubt, in Atlanta, and his own estimation. He formed us in two ranks and marched us through the principal streets of the city, the little boys throwing stones at us, meanwhile, and calling upon us by opprobrious epithets. The women in carriages waved flags, spit, and hurrahed for Gen. Bragg and his victory at Chickamauga. Under the circumstances we felt called upon to cheer for Rosey, and the streets of the rebel town rang with the loud hurrahs for our gallant commander and the Stars and Stripes. Previous to this we had borne their jeers and insults in silence, but we answered with louder cheers than they did and drowned them with our good Union noise. The pen into which we were marched was an enclosure of about half an acre in area, surrounded by a board fence twelve feet high, upon which was a parapet for the guard. Before entering the place, the column was halted, and our names taken, when the gates were thrown open and we entered. As the first man passed in he was halted by a commissioned officer and robbed of all his clothing, except what was necessary to cover him, together with his blanket. We knew that prisoners were robbed and sometimes stripped of their clothing by privates in the rebel army, those whose desire for pillage was superior to every sense of honor, but we did not anticipate robbery by *order* of the rebel authorities. We foolishly supposed them governed by the plainest rules of civilized warfare, which respect property of prisoners of war. No shelter or fire was provided for us, although the night air in Atlanta is very chilling even at this season of the year. At ten o'clock a dray load of bacon and hard bread was issued in the dark, for which every man scrambled;

and with this little episode to cheer us, we passed the night shivering with cold.

At an early hour we were all (some 500 in number) ordered to the Augusta depot. Our march was through a busy street, lined with ware-houses, stores and banks, and the scene was lively and bustling as in our Northern cities. Evidences of wealth and importance were on all hands. The devastating influence of war had not yet reached this fair city, and it reveled in its security. Fancy young men, gentlemen in Southern parlance, (snobs and dandies we call them at the North) perambulated the streets in broadcloth and jewels, superciliously looking upon us through costly eye glasses, which they had procured in New York and forgotton to pay for. From what we saw of these nice young men, we concluded that chivalry consisted mainly in ruffled shirts, fancy kids, jewelry and billingsgate; although we may not have seen the best of the South, and our eyes may have been prejudiced.

The train of box cars being ready, we stepped on board, the whistle sounded and we were off for Augusta. We passed slowly out of the city, by warehouses and stores, past the trains of cars loaded with iron and machinery, which had been run back to this point from Chattanooga, for safety; and the boys regaled themselves with the thought, that in the onward march of the Union armies, this place would feel the crushing heel of war upon its bosom, and repent the foul deeds it had sanctioned against such prisoners as had been unfortunate enough to be cast within its gates.

The train passed the base of Stone Mountain, which is a singular freak of nature; it stands in the midst of a rolling country, the only elevation of any extent within the scope of vision. It is half a mile in diameter at its base, and of solid rock. This was almost the only noticeable feature of the country through which we passed. Now and then a costly mansion of some aristocrat appeared, but in close proximity to it would be seen the hovels of the " poor trash." We rolled on monotonously to Augusta, at which point we arrived at half past five P. M., where we encountered a large crowd of citizens, negroes and soldiers, changing cars for Macon, Savannah, Charleston and Columbia. Like Atlanta, Augusta had not felt a touch of the war, and its busy streets gave evidence that it was thriving, while many of its sister cities were feeling the blight of treason. We stood in rank for a few minutes, awaiting orders to march, and were soon surrounded by women whose sympathizing looks plainly told us that had they dared, they would have lent us aid in our misfortune.

From the depot, we marched to a large vacant

warehouse and yard, where we remained two nights and a day. Those that could, stayed in the building, and when it was full, the remainder were compelled to lie in the yard. The nights were very cold, and the boys who lay in the yard were saturated with the heavy dews. Rations were scarce and our clothing was gone. Afterwards we became accustomed to this kind of treatment, and did not mind it very much, but our initiation was sudden and we felt it the more keenly.

While in Augusta, watermelons were smuggled among the prisoners by the guards, for which most exorbitant prices were paid. There was no hesitation manifested about taking greenbacks, which at that time had the same value as Confederate Scrip. On the morning of the 6th of October, at an early hour, we were aboard a train for Branchville, South Carolina. We crossed the bridge, a structure similar to the Railroad bridge at Nashville, where by some error in connecting trains, we remained until 4 P. M. The train at last got under way, and we flew rapidly on across a long stretch of swampy land, and through forests of birch from whose branches hung long, flowing bunches of grey moss. A dismal, weary ride it was, in our pent up boxes. To vary the monotony, the cars midway the train, uncoupled, and the engine with a few cars plunged on and left us. The engineer discovered his loss and backed up for the remainder, when we went on again. We arrived at Branchville some time during the night, the distance from which to Charleston, is sixty miles. The negroes here told us they often heard the heavy guns fired in Charleston harbor during the bombardment of that city. We halted only long enough to change cars, and pushed on for Charlotte, North Carolina, which place we reached in just twenty-four hours after leaving Augusta. The total distance between the two places by rail, is 248 miles. Charlotte seemed at that time to be an active, thriving little town. Whether its importance was owing to its natural advantages as a business center, we had no means of determining, but judging from its appearance, it was the most important place in the Confederacy. The streets were lined with teams, hacks, busses and express wagons, and along the sidewalks were huge piles of cotton bales, and bales of cotton cloth, awaiting transportation. We passed the dark stormy night following our arrival, in a grove outside the town. The rain poured down in torrents, and our clothes were saturated in a short time. We had been accustomed to rain and storm without shelter, but our blankets and overcoats had kept us in a comparatively dry state, and the inner man was fortified with plenty, to resist the elements. Here, however, we had neither food, fire, shelter, nor blanket, had ridden 250 miles in close cars, and were nearly famished. We accepted the condition, however, as an incident of war, and made the best we could of it.

Next morning we shipped for Raleigh, taking a Northeasterly direction, and passing through a barren, desolate country. At Salisbury we passed the officers' barracks, where, it was said Union officers were held in solitary confinement as hostages. We reached Raleigh at midnight, changed cars and proceeded through Goldsboro to Weldon, where we arrived at 3 p. m., of the same day. Here we halted for a few hours and received a ration consisting of three small crackers to each man—the first we had had to eat since leaving Augusta, on the fifth of the month, and it was now the ninth. The people here seemed possessed of a good deal of Union sentiment, and expressed a strong desire to be under the old flag again, with many curses against Jeff. Davis and his "bogus confederacy." One lad told us that he had secreted a hundred dollars in gold, which Jeff. would never get, though he expected himself soon to be conscripted. The citizens informed us that they were living under a complete despotism. The poorer classes were in a state of beggary and want, while the wealthier were obliged to contribute all they could spare, for the support of the Government, and receive in exchange Confederate scrip which was worthless.

After changing cars, we proceeded on towards Petersburg, across an extensive bridge which was strongly guarded, in anticipation of a cavalry raid upon it. The rolling stock of the road was in a very dilapidated condition, the cars being so worn that many of them were left behind, while the engines were so light that they could not move a full train upon an up grade. We arrived at Petersburg at midnight, and remained till the next morning, when we marched through the main street to the Richmond depot. Taking the cars here again we were soon on the last stage of our trip, in length about twenty-four miles. The country is gently rolling and strongly fortified through the whole extent. We reached the Confederate capital at sunrise on the morning of the 10th of October, 1863, and crossed the long, high bridge over the James river. The bed of this river seems to be solid rock, the bottom being covered with large loose boulders, against which the water plunges and dashes in its onward rush to the ocean. The bridge itself seems to be about half a mile in length and is a very solid and expensive structure. The cars carried us directly into the city, and the first building that caught our eye at the end of the bridge was the arsenal, at which a negro was unloading a dray load of 64 pound shell. Opposite the arsenal was the "Tredegar Iron Works," the main dependence of the rebels for their car and locomotive work, north of Charleston and Columbia. A line of guards was stationed here, extending from the railroad to the notorious Castle Thunder, of which every one North and South has heard so much since the breaking out of the war. This prison consists simply of an old tobacco warehouse two and a half stories high, with all the windows knocked out;—a place where the Richmond authorities put all their deserters, runaway negroes, and men sentenced to death. If a Yankee prisoner escaped and was retaken, he had a choice cell in the filthy tenement.

Arrived and unloaded, we were marched to an old warehouse opposite Castle Thunder, a hole in every respect the counterpart of the castle. After being here a couple of hours or more, a Major Turner came into the building and ordered us to fall into four ranks, when he informed us that he wanted our money. If it had been in the street and he had had a pistol instead of a sword, we should have supposed him to be a highwayman. He informed us that if we came forward and freely gave up our money, it would be refunded to us on our being paroled or exchanged, but if we refused, he would cause our clothing to be searched, and all money found upon us would be confiscated. The men finding themselves in the hands of thieves and seeing no way out of their unfortunate dilemma, determined that it was best to deliver their money upon the rascal's promise of refunding. The whole amount thus collected was not less than $30,000 from the squad of men in our party. This was in sums varying from $1,500 to $50. This was an unexpected manner of effecting a forced loan, and one which none but Jeff. Davis and his friends would ever have invented. Not one dollar of this money was ever returned. After our robbery, we were marched to Smith Prison, a few rods from the famous "Libby," where our officers were confined, and inducted into Prison Life in earnest.

CHAPTER III.

ßmith Prison—Pemberton—Scott—Libby Prison fare—Incidents—
Newspaper Gossip—Exchange—Removal to Danville.

Smith prison lies Northeast of Libby, on a street running nearly North and South, and meeting the street upon which the Libby stands, at right angles. This building was originally designed, and previous to the war, used as a tobacco warehouse and factory. It is sixty feet long by forty wide, three stories and a half high, and contained four full floors, although the upper one was very low, being directly beneath the roof. The three upper floors were already filled upon our arrival, with prisoners captured at Chickamauga, who had been sent forward before us, so that our detachment, numbering nearly 500, was crowded together upon a basement floor. The room contained just twenty-four hundred square feet of space, and this including what was occupied by thirty-one large tobacco presses, which were stored in it, divided equally among us, would give to each man less than five feet in which to " spread himself," counting out the space occupied by the presses, there were not more than four feet of room to each. If we reckon the hight of the room to be eight feet, there would be a total of 19,200 cubic feet of air in the apartment, or about 40 to a man. A healthy man is estimated to consume 500 cubic inches of air in one night. The only ventilation was by means of the crevices of the walls, the windows not being allowed to be raised, except as they were occasionally slipped up an inch or two, when the guard was not particularly attentive. The privies were constructed in the Northeast corner of each room, without doors, and were entered through an open window. Water was furnished through pipes and facets from the James river. The stench from the privies, which came constantly into the room, together with the dampness caused by water drizzling from the wash sink, and from the cups, into which it was drawn to be drank, and our crowded state, filled the air with poison, and rendered our physical systems doubly susceptible of diseases and contagion.

The Pemberton prison was likewise a tobacco warehouse just south of the Smith, and fronting upon the same street, its end being on the Libby street. There was just room enough between the Smith and Pemberton for the guard to walk. Opposite to the Smith was the Scott prison, also a tobacco warehouse. These buildings were so high and so near each other as totally to exclude the light and heat of the sun, for the greater part of the day, from the prisoners confined upon the first floor.

From the southwest windows of the Smith, where our party was confined, the Libby prison, in which our officers were kept, could easily be seen. It is a large building with four floors, including the basement. The two floors on which prisoners were at that time confined, fronted on a street running parallel with the canal on the bank of the James, and extended back to the canal itself. On the Northwest corner was a sign which read "Libby and Son, Ship Chandlers and Grocers." There were forty windows visible to us, in front, some of which were secured with iron bars, while others were tightly boarded up. Across a few old blankets had been stretched, but there were several that were open to the winds and storms. Of the interior economy of this prison we had no opportunity of informing ourselves; we knew our officers to be confined there, from seeing them occasionally at the windows in their uniform; their pale, haggard faces indicated that their fare was none of the most sumptuous, while it was a common report that they were confined in dungeons for the most trifling offences.

The cooking for the prisoners was all performed in

the lower rooms of the Libby. From each of the twenty messes, into which the men on our floor were divided, one man was daily detailed to go to the Libby for rations. In going there we passed directly under the end windows of the prison, and our officers frequently dropped a Richmond paper among us, enclosing a letter directed to their friends at home, to be carried North by the first one of our number who might chance to be exchanged. In this manner a letter containing particulars, would sometimes be smuggled through the lines, when, if sent by flag of truce, it would have been destroyed. If the guards detected an officer dropping such papers to the men and recognized him, he was at once placed in confinement on half the usual rations.

Our rations were issued to us at very irregular intervals of time. They consisted of half a loaf of wheat bread and a small piece of yellow bacon, in which the worms were holding high carnival. Though so unfit for eating, our appetites had become sharpened by the small supply until we devoured this living food with the greed of wolves. In place of the bacon we sometimes received beef. According to the Richmond Examiner, seventy-five bullocks were daily slaughtered for the use of the prisoners. This seems a large amount of meat to be consumed, but according to the rebel estimate, there were 14,000 prisoners in Richmond at that time, and allowing 250 pounds as the average weight of a bullock, and that the meat was served regularly once in three days, instead of daily, as was actually the case, it would give a daily allowance of less than four ounces per man. But this is an over estimate. The author previous to entering the service was accustomed from boyhood to weigh meat in a retail market, and hence might be considered a competent judge of the weight of a quantity of beef, whether in a large or small piece, and he would solemnly aver that he never receeived as a three days' ration, more than two ounces; and his fare was not more stinted than that of his fellow prisoners. The loaves of bread weighed 18 ounces short, half of one of these was the allowance for one day. Our rations, then, were 9 ounces of bread and 2-3 of an ounce of beef daily; this fare, when followed up for weeks and months, certainly had no tendency to excite corpulency among us.

Our first exercise in the morning was the roll call which was performed by a fussy, conceeited individual from New York, named Ross. After roll call, we were formed in four ranks and counted to make sure that no one had escaped. If the number was found all right, the exercise was soon over, but if by chance the roll-call man made a mistake in counting, which he was quite likely to do, or if any one had escaped, we were compelled to stand in line until the whole prison had been searched and all the prisoners recounted, a process requiring usually about six hours. If after all, the missing man could not be found, our rations were cut off for a day or two, to compel us to divulge the manner of the escape, of which, in most cases, the majority was totally ignorant. It seemed rather hard treatment to be compelled to fast two days for our inability to communicate what we knew nothing about.

Of course we were all under the necessity of practising the closest economy in our food, and in the occupancy of the floor also. In this latter particular, our four square feet of room led us to exercise the greatest regularity in all our movements. We formed five columns lengthwise of the floor, when we all, at the word, proceeded to lie down in line, our feet and legs webbed or woven in with those in the next column, and so closely together that it was impossible to stir without disturbing our neighbor. When one moved, *all* moved. All in the same file were obliged to lie on the same side, and when they became tired and wished to change, the order was given "to the right, or left, over—turn." It was impossible to lie upon our backs at all; there was not room enough. Considering that we had no blankets to put under or over us, and that the floor was usually damp from the frequent washings we were compelled by the guard to give it,—there being no heat, either natural or artificial to dry it, meantime, it will readily be seen that our sleeping arrangements were none of the most comfortable. In fact, we slept under the greatest difficulties.

A regular daily skirmish was kept up with the vermin of the place. In less than a week after our arrival, these parasites made such hostile demonstrations, that it required the very best of Generalship to maintain the mastery of the situation. They rallied by squads, companies and regiments, and charged our lines in whole corps. By dint of perseverance and constant watchfulness we kept their numbers so reduced that no one was captured, though many were severely wounded. If the Confederacy could re-inforce their armies as rapidly as these vermin increased, the Yankees would soon be overwhelmed and the Stars and Stripes go down forever.

The ravages of vermin, filth and hunger soon began to appear, and, as if to tantalize us still more, our thoughts could run upon nothing but food. The strength of a hungry man's imagination is wonderful. The finest dishes which a French cook, *par excellence*, could invent, were garbage compared with the fancy *cuisine* of those famished men. We had beef roast and steak, for substantials, oysters, lobster, &c., for side dishes, and the pastry which we conjured up, was beyond all comprehension, wonderful. After all had retired to our floor board for the night, the hours, till midnight, were spent in contemplation of the luxuries we would have had for supper, if we had been at home, and many and hot were the discussions we held over these imaginary repasts. There is no torture equal in intensity to this fierce longing for food. It consumed our strength; we became dizzy-headed; there was a hollow ringing in our ears; our voices became weak and husky; our motions slow and monotonous; our eyes glassy, and faces sallow and sharp; while the vulture within gnawed remorsely at our vitals. We could not stand, sit, or lie down with any cessation of this terrible craving, and we were fain to scramble and quarrel over the very crumbs that fell from our scanty food upon the dirty floor, as ravenous wolves battle over the last morsel of flesh left upon a bone they have picked.

Our only hope was in release. The exact state of the exchange question, we did not fully understand, but previous to our capture, we knew that there was some difficulty growing out of the employment of the negro regiments; and we had been told that until all Federal prisoners irrespective of color, could be exchanged upon equal terms, the United States authorities had refused to continue the exchange upon the old cartel. We had faith enough in our government to believe that it would not let us suffer if it could honorably prevent it; and we also had faith enough in its *honor* to believe that, once enlisted, under inducements of protection, in our army, the government would insist upon the negro prisoner being treated as well as a white man under the same circumstances. There was of course a difference of opinion among the prisoners in regard to the propriety or policy of enlisting the negro in the first instance, but no man caviled at his being protected after he had become a soldier. We should have felt that we could not trust our rulers at all, if they had left the captive colored soldier to the mercies of the enemy, and expended all their care and protection upon us.

We usually managed to obtain the Richmond dailies, but they were barren of news. Shut up in this den, with nothing to do or to read, we were forming habits the very reverse of the active Yankee character. The impulse to do something was still strong, and, in the absence of all other means of employing our time, we organized a debating society, with its President, Secretary, &c., and made speeches by Confederate gas-light. The subjects of discussion were as various as numerous. War schemes, plans of attack upon Richmond, the origin of the war, its probable duration, the status of the rebellious States when the war should be ended; foreign and domestic

policy, abolition, Jeff. Davis, and a thousand and one
topics, were considered and gravely decided, upon
"merits" and "weight of argument." Many of the
predictions by these private prophets have since been
verified, though most, alas! of those who made them,
lie beneath the turf at Andersonville. Occasionally
the debates were omitted, and lectures and extem-
poraneous speeches substituted in their place. Mr.
John Smith of the 1st O. V. I., gave us a fine off-hand
lecture on moral culture, and I had the honor one
evening "to define my position" upon the best methods of cultivating bees. Others chose political topics,
while others still, lectured upon matters connected
with science or art. But like all things in Southern
Prisons, except misery, our intellectual growth was
stopped, the guard having orders to prohibit further
discussion, and we abandoned these "feasts of reason" as we had already abandoned those of a grosser
kind. This forced us back upon the exchange question again, and wherever there was a group, there
the words "exchange" and "parole" were the most
used. The 1st of November was argued by the sanguine, as the limit of our imprisonment, and the guard
confirmed the prophecy. The Richmond papers,
however, announced that 10,000 of the prisoners were
soon to be sent to Lynchburg and Danville, where
provisions were more easily to be obtained. We

hesitated to believe this, as it looked suspiciously towards a long winter's campaign, and that we did not wish to "believe in."

One day we had an episode to relieve the tedium and monotony of our hungry existence. Some of the "boys" in prying into one of the tobacco presses, discovered a box of choice pressed tobacco, which had evidently been forgotten by the owners in the hurry of evacuating the premises. By loosening a screw in the press, the treasure lay revealed. The news soon spread through the apartment, and the boys "went for it." They surrounded the box in swarms, each man clutching the precious waif, if he could reach it, or snatching it from the hand of a more successful competitor. Light men climbed upon the shoulders of stronger ones and plunged fiercely forward toward the box; but the tobacco was so tightly pressed that all their efforts were unsuccessful. The scramble continued for an hour or more with none but the most barren results, when a compromise was agreed upon, and an orderly sergeant was selected to divide the treasure equally among the men. The matter was thus amicably settled and the division accordingly made.

On one occasion, we opened a door that had been nailed up, for the purpose of getting a little fresh air, when a Richmond stripling in broadcloth and with an air of simpering importance, came in and ordered the door fastened again, at the same time threatening us with rations of bread and water for two weeks, if we ever dared re-open it. We gravely informed him that his threat was useless, for we had become so accustomed to that diet, that an addition of a little more of the same sort would be thankfully received. He evidently had not sufficient brains to appreciate the jest, though at the same time he could see evidences of bread and water diet all around him. The door was not again disturbed, and we saw his face no more.

Two men in our prison, managed to trade with the guard for suits of gray clothing, which they put on after dark, one evening, and assuming an air of great importance, went to the door and announced themselves as members of the police, claiming a right to pass out. The guard allowed them to go out, and they departed on their way rejoicing. Whether they succeeded in making their escape we never knew.

In the early part of November, the prisoners confined in the Pemberton building, cut a hole through the walls and floor of the prison and opened communication with a cellar, in which a large quantity of commissary stores, consisting of sugar and salt, had been placed. After dark a regular detail was made, each man of the detail taking a bag or haversack and packing it full before returning. The utmost caution was observed lest by making a noise, the attention of the guard might be called to the fact. For a number of nights these foraging expeditions were carried on successfully, and so much had accumulated upon the hands of the prisoners, that they opened a contraband trade with the guard, receiving tobacco and bread in exchange for sugar and salt. The guards knew very well, from the first, where the sugar and salt came from, but so long as they could drive a good bargain, they did not divulge the secret. The "business" was, however, accidentally discovered by an outsider, but not until some $35,000 worth had been abstracted. All kinds of reports were then put in circulation relative to the punishment to be inflicted upon the perpetrators of this "outrage;" among others that all the money taken from us on our arrival in Richmond would be confiscated; that enough would be deducted from our rations to make payment; that we would be the very last to be exchanged, &c., &c. Nothing, however, came of it, as far as I knew.

The small pox broke out among us a few days after our arrival in Richmond. It made its first appearance upon the person of one of our men who had been infected with it, by a Confederate soldier, passing through Atlanta, and it soon spread with great rapidity.

Not being acquainted with the symptoms of this disease, none of us knew at the time what it was. In a few days a dozen or more were taken to the hospital. They never returned, and we knew not whether they recovered or died. It was currently reported among us, that the Rebels took care that those who were confined in the hospital should never recover; but this, like many other stories afloat, was undoubtedly false. It served, however, to excite a dread of hospitals, and nerved the men to suffer in silence rather than expose themselves to the danger of removal, in consequence of which they were not taken away from prison, until too far gone with the disease to recover from it. A few pills were occasionally left with the "sergeant of the floor" to be distributed among those who desired to take medicine. They were seldom called for by the men, and of course were in no way beneficial.

Being debarred from all open communication with the world, we of course knew nothing of what was transpiring outside of our prison-walls, except when we could fall secretly upon a Richmond paper. These gave us, on our arrival, glowing accounts of the wonderful and brilliant victory at Chickamauga, and some time afterwards, mentioned the nice "little affair at Missionary Ridge," in which they conceded superior generalship on the part of the "Yankee commander." Nearly every paper had some remarks to make upon the treatment of the prisoners, and particularly recommended that all the meat allowed them, be withdrawn, in order that the citizens might obtain it, at lower figures in the market. In one of the papers was quite a lengthy article upon the general appearance, &c., of the prisoners. It seemed that some Baltimorean of riotous memory, had been paying us a visit, and airing his opinions of us. From his knowledge of the groveling nature of the Yankee, he was prepared to find the Federals dirty, filthy and lazy, too lazy to keep their persons clean, or to clean their rooms. He did not mention whether in his experience of Yankee character, they became hungry on three ounces of bread a day, or were of that peculiarly filthy nature, that can keep itself clean without soap. Undoubtedly the nice Baltimorean would have been the same exquisitely nice man in a mud puddle, but all men, and among them Yankees, not being of gentle blood, could not keep themselves clean without some means of doing so.

Just about daylight on the morning of the 14th of November, we were formed in rank and counted; the door was unbolted, and we passed out, each man as he stepped into the street receiving a small loaf of heavy corn bread. Guards were stretched on either side of the street through which we marched to the

Danville Railroad bridge, near which the head of the column halted, for the last of the men to get out of the building, and "close up." We knew nothing of our destination, until we reached the Danville depot. All were expecting that we were *en route* for City Point. The train awaited us and we were soon aboard in readiness for another ride through the Southern Confederacy at the public expense. Our train was long and heavy, the engine light, and the grade ascending. In consequence the train was soon at a stand still, and a messenger sent back to Richmond for help. We could plainly see Belle Island with its tents and prisoners. This island was then used as a place of punishment for Federal prisoners, who had been guilty of various petty offenses as well as for the unpardonable crime of attempting to escape starvation in the regular Confederate way. A more extended notice of this place of horrors will be given hereafter.

The Railroad from Richmond to Danville runs through a gently rolling country, and was in a fine condition. Petersburg junction is the largest place on the line, and that is of no importance except as a Railroad junction. Previous to our leaving Richmond, and as soon as we had learned it was probable that we should be sent either to Lynchburg or Danville, I constructed a map of the country between

Richmond and those two places, and also a map including the rivers and mountains between East Tennessee and those points; and a third, between those points and Gauley Bridge. This was a precaution necessary in any attempt to escape, in fact, indispensible in the undertaking. There seemed to be no Confederate troops stationed along the railroad, and the authorities evidently regarded them safe from raids. The distance to Danville is one hundred and forty miles, and ought to have been made before sundown, but owing to the heavy grades in the road, and the inadequacy of the locomotive, only about half the distance had been passed over, at that hour. At dusk it commenced to rain, and by eight o'clock it poured down in torrents, continuing until near morning, and growing much colder all the time. When the cars were within six miles of Danville, the train was again "stalled," and was compelled to stop two or three hours. While standing here, I went to the door, found the guards half asleep, and passed out upon the ground. It was very dark and the rain was yet pouring. I debated for some time whether it were best to attempt my escape here or not. My first thought was to run for my liberty, but upon reflection I abandoned the project. I was very weak and suffering from disease and close confinement; it was raining very heavily, the streams were swollen, the roads muddy, the fields and grass wet; the cold weather had just set in and I had no clothing to protect me except the blouse and pants I wore. The nearest point to our lines was two hundred miles, through the enemy's country, totally unknown to me. I had maps but no compass. If I tried to escape I wished to be successful, for I dreaded being caught, and returned to Castle Thunder. It would have been an easy matter to get ten or fifteen miles away, but beyond that all was dark and doubtful; I therefore returned quietly to the car. Several of my comrades attempted to escape that night, but owing to the severity of the rain, they were all re-taken and brought back. We reached Danville on the morning of the 15th of November, having been just twenty-four hours on our trip from Richmond.

CHAPTER IV.

Danville—Prisons Nos. 1, 2, 3, 4, 5 and 6—Writing Letters Home—Occupation of Time—Small Pox—Receipt of Rations and Clothing by Flag of Truce—How Appropriated and Issued—Hospital—Express Boxes—Tunneling—Handicraft—Incidents—Newspaper Reports—Exchange—Removal to Georgia.

Danville is a fine town situated on the south bank of the Dan river, near the boundary line between Virginia and North Carolina, a little northeast of Greensboro, in the latter State. It is a place of some two thousand inhabitants, contains a Female Seminary, a Cotton and Woolen Factory, a Foundry, Arsenal, several Saw and Grist Mills, and a large number of fine brick residences. The river closely resembles the James in some important features, being both wide and rapid—and, from the latter circumstance, furnishing excellent water power. It is spanned by a long, covered bridge to accommodate highway travel, and also by a railroad bridge. The country gradually rises into considerable hight from the river banks on either side, and the village stands upon a hill sloping Northeastwardly to the river.

Appearances indicated that, at some previous time, Danville had been a place of considerable business importance, in which the staple product of Virginia constituted the chief article of traffic. A great number of extensive warehouses were here built for the storage and manufacture of tobacco. But with the war business declined, and at the time of our imprisonment, the village presented an appearance of general desolation.

The Richmond papers had announced to us that great preparations had been made at Danville for our reception, but we discovered upon our arrival, that so far from this being true, not even rations were provided. The tobacco warehouses were the only provision visible, and to these we were in due time presented. One train load of prisoners had been forwarded on the 14th, and were stationed in a large brick warehouse near the foundry and the river, called prison No. 1. Our party was placed in a wooden structure on the opposite side of the street—also a tobacco warehouse, and named prison No. 2. No. 3, a short distance West of No. 2, was next filled, then Nos. 4 and 5. No. 6 was subsequently occupied by prisoners from No. 2, which was vacated to accommodate the guard, being in a more central position and consequently of more importance in case of an outbreak. I shall limit myself to an account of the prison in which I was confined, but as in essentials they will not differ materially, a description of one prison will equally apply to all.

We were marched into prison No. 2 on the morning of Sunday, Nov. 15th, 1863. As soon as the ranks were broken and we were at liberty to wander at will, after selecting my "place" and depositing my bed, which consisted of an old dirty haversack without a crumb in it, near the Southwest corner of the second floor, beneath a window, where I might obtain a sufficient supply of air and light, I carefully reconnoitered the "position." The building was found to consist of three full floors and a garret, the latter of considerable importance as the event proved. Nothing of particular moment, however, developed itself except the dirt and dust which had accumulated, and the only advantage of this consisted in the fact that until it became trodden down, it helped to soften the rigorous hardness of the boards on which we were to sleep. The "establishment" being noted, I next took a survey of the town and surroundings from the window. Upon the Northeast the Dan river with its long bridges, the mills situated upon its banks and their lazy wheels moving monotonously, could be seen. Beyond the stream was a fine cottage, apparently the abode of affluence and happiness, and it was pleasant in the long lonesome days, to sit at the window and look out upon that cottage and fancy the comforts and luxuries of its inmates, so strongly contrasted with the dirt and starvation around in our midst.

The prison was not furnished with either stoves or fireplaces,—a deprivation little noticed, however, from the fact that no fuel was given us. We had been promised both fuel and stoves sufficient to warm the rooms, but that part of the programme was not carried out; and it had never been the design to do so, as subsequent events fully proved. A few minutes after the door was closed, while standing on the first floor, near a front window which had been boarded up, I overheard two of the rebel commissioned officers, who were slowly passing the spot, conversing upon prison matters, when one of them said to the other, "WE NOW HAVE THEM, WHERE, WITH THE SEVERITY OF THE CLIMATE AND HARSH TREATMENT, NATURE WILL DO ITS WORK FASTER THAN THE BULLET." This fearful announcement made my blood run cold; but I tried to quiet my apprehensions, by reflecting that these were but subordinate officers, and, like too many of that class, gave utterance to their own feelings, instead of expressing the views of the government under which they held their commissions. The inhuman treatment we afterwards received, however, showed that they were quoting the Richmond authorities, whose deliberate plan it was to render such as unfortunately fell into their hands unfit for further service, and to attempt to throw the responsibility therefore upon natural agencies. We had received no food since leaving Smith prison, two days before, and many of the men were so nearly famished that upon drawing their last ration in Richmond, without looking to their future needs, they had devoured it all upon the spot. Two days of total abstinence from food, will not affect a well fed man with any great degree of inconvenience; but to one who has been kept upon less than quarter rations for many weeks, the consequences of a deprivation of all nourishment for forty-eight hours, are indescribable. Here we were, however, locked in with bolts and bars, and guarded with rebel bayonets, in a helpless condition, and if they chose to starve us, they had the power to do so. About 9 o'clock in the evening, a small half-baked loaf of what purported to be wheat bread was given to every two men. To live long on such an allowance was utterly impossible, and rather than die by inches in this most horrible of forms, we determined that it would be better to break down the prison doors and rush out upon the guard, even though every man should perish. The choice lay between a short pang and a prolonged agony—the end would be the same. We concluded to defer the desperate project for a few days, hoping that in the meantime our fare would be improved, since suitable preparation might not have been made for our reception, because we arrived upon Sunday, and our numbers were somewhat uncertain. No improvement having taken place for the three days following, on the evening of November 19th, we organized three squads of twenty-five strong men each, to break prison, overpower the small guard, and push with all speed for East Tennessee or Gauley Bridge.

During the day one of the boards of the first floor was removed, and an opening made into the cellar, in which were stored several tobacco presses and some twenty hogsheads of stem tobacco, and holes were chiseled through the brick partition walls which separated the ells of the building from the main part. The apartments beneath these ells, like those of the main cellar, were used for storing machinery for tobacco manufacture; each of which contained a door opening inward. Between the two ells on the Northeast side was a door leading into the street. We removed all the screws from the lock, except one, which was left to hold the door in its place until we were ready to go out. It had been loosed so that no difficulty might be occasioned in its removal after dark. Nine P. M. was the hour appointed for us to be in readiness. Twenty-five men were posted at each of the two front entrances, and twenty-five at the cellar door. I was stationed below with a squad of ten to be in readiness for any emergency. One of the front entrances was a door secured by a cross bar, and when this was removed the door, being a double one, was readily swung inward; the lock had been removed from the other door, as previously described. The signal for the outbreak was to be the call of the sentinel, "Nine o'clock, and all's well." The break from the three doors was to be made simultaneously, and the six guards seized and secured; when a rush was to be made for the guard-house, a short distance off, and the reserve guard with their arms to be captured. But the man who volunteered to remove the cross-bar, either through carelessness or fright, dropped the bar, making so loud a noise that the sentinels became alarmed, and an additional guard was ordered out, when the idea of escape at that time, was considered impracticable and the project abandoned.

I then thought that it would be impossible successfully to conduct any enterprise requiring secrecy, among a mixed number of prisoners, especially where it involved an extensive plan of operations; since where all entered upon the undertaking voluntarily, no one would have authority to compel each to perform his part, if necessary in spite of all personal risks; and I determined that I would never again engage in any general plan of escape. But I firmly believe, if I had escaped that night, the weather was so favorable for the succeeding two weeks, that I could have reached our lines at Gauley Bridge or in East Tennessee, in safety.

On the morning of the 20th, the first Federal prisoner died in Danville. He was reduced to a skeleton. His last words were, "Boys, if I only could have something to eat, I could live."

For a few days after this, our bread rations improved slightly and beef was added to the mess, but like everything rebellious, it was "too good to last." We soon returned to our scanty and ill-cooked food. Incredible as it may appear, I have divided among sixteen men a piece of meat containing not more than eight cubic inches, for a day's ration. Such a piece would not weigh more than half a pound. Our wheat bread lasted for a short time, when a kind of black, bitter stuff, made of what was called Richmond middlings, was substituted. This was so badly baked and so sour, that it made many of the prisoners ill, inducing dysentery and nausea. Our appetites sharpened with the scantiness of the fare, and we were fortunate if we could catch a rat for food. A hogshead of old wheat bran was found in the cellar and greedily devoured by the famishing men.

Such was the liberality of a people fighting for sacred rights, as they call them, towards prisoners taken in a war which they claim to have conducted purely upon Christian principles!

In addition to these discomforts, we were compelled to avoid all approach to the windows by the recklessness of the guard outside the prison, who, upon the slightest indication of a man at them, fired recklessly into the building. Our windows were riddled by the balls thus fired at us, and the beams and timbers of the several apartments, filled with them. This piece of tyranny was uncalled for and unnecessary, for no one, in his senses, would have had the temerity to attempt escape through a window, in daylight and in full view of the guard. One poor fellow in number five, opened a window in the upper room and thrust his head out to breathe a little fresh air after his confinement during the night in the close apartment, and not hearing the warning of the guard to draw back, was fired upon and instantly killed, being shot through the head. Very few casualties occurred from this firing, the "boys," when they perceived the sentinels making ready to fire, calling out "lie down," when all would fall upon the floor and the balls passed harmlessly over their heads.

About this time, a new roll of our names was made, after which we were searched and our case knives, pocket knives, spoons, scissors, watches, gold and silver rings—everything in short that could be found, possessing any value, except our clothes, were taken from us. Many of the watches were hidden in the ceiling, previous to the search, and saved. Some saved a few greenbacks by rolling them tightly and placing them in the bowl of their pipes, and covering them with tobacco which was then lighted. Others packed their bills in their blouse buttons which they opened for the purpose. But the rebels could not rob us of much money after we had been once searched. The " Yanks " were generally sharp enough for them, so far as they had tools to work with. Had we known that our case knives and spoons were to be taken from us, we could have secreted them, also ; but we supposed that they were safe from " confiscation," otherwise how could we be expected to be able to cut and prepare our meat ration ? we were completely out-generaled in this respect here. But it seemed from what followed that their plan was too deep for our penetration ; for after this, the quantity of meat served to each man, was so small that no knife was necessary to cut it into proper dimensions for eating—a strategic point in economy we were not able then to foresee.

Soon after this, permission was given us to send letters to our friends, by flag of truce. Many improved the opportunity to send for boxes of provisions, while some, distrusting the Confederate Authorities, preferred that their friends at the North should keep their "good things," rather than that they should fall into our enemy's hands. It was, however, some satisfaction to be permitted to correspond with our friends, even though we could only describe our health, in the briefest possible manner.

Being deprived of our conveniencies for eating, necessity, the reputed mother of invention, soon called out the ingenuity of the Yankee mind. Before the officials discovered it, we had torn in pieces the tobacco presses and the hogsheads, using the bolts, sheet-iron and tin of the former for hammers, punches, saws, cups, pails and plates, while seats and firewood were made of the staves of the latter. It was too late to rectify the evil when the authorities discovered what we had been doing; they, therefore, made the best of a bad matter and let us go on. The sound of clinking iron could be heard from early morn till sunset, in manufacturing the various articles which the boys busied themselves about.

The old practice of "skirmishing," which had been carried on at Richmond, soon had to be incorporated with the daily tactics at this place. The water we used came from the Dan River, in small quantities, such as could be brought in pails, by a detail, which performed its duties as often as they were permitted by the guard, but in insufficient quantities for any but drinking purposes. In consequence our clothes were unwashed. My own, which were a fair sample of the rest, were not cleansed for one hundred and fifty days, because I could procure neither soap nor water to wash them with; and even if we could have washed, we had no fires by which to dry them, and no change to put on while they could dry in the air—the sun did not shine in prison No. 2—and if we once wet them, there was no alternative but to dry them upon our persons. This process would have been uncomfortable and dangerous, in a December atmosphere in a room without fires. The Richmond papers seemed to make a jest of our filthy condition, and the moral which they drew from our *personnel* was, " the naturally groveling tendency of the Yankee race."

About this time the small pox broke out. But little notice was at first taken of the fact by the authorities, and I have known as many as eighteen patients lying helpless upon the filth and dirt of the bare prison floor, without medicine, without food, without blankets, till their flesh dropped in decayed lumps from their bodies; while no effort was made to remove them, or alleviate their sufferings. And all this time the other prisoners were in constant contact with them, sleeping side by side with them, and inhaling the vile stench of this loathsome disease. In consequence, all who could be infected, were more or less severely attacked, while many who had been vaccinated were brought down with varioloid. About the first of January, I was promoted to the position of hospital attendant, and had charge to some extent of the sick and medicines of our prison. A small pox hospital was meanwhile established, and a detail of men who had had the disease, was made to nurse the sick. By giving strict attention to each case as fast as it appeared, and removing the infected at once to the hospital, the disease was finally suppressed, and did not make its appearance again in our prison after the fifth of January, although it was still raging in the others. This was the only contagious disease among the prisoners to which our diet was favorable. We received no fat meat and no salt, and in these two particulars our treatment by the rebels was highly sanitary, whether it was by design or accident.

While on the train from Richmond, I read in a paper of the 14th November, that fourteen tons of clothing and rations had been received at City Point by flag of truce, from the U. S. Sanitary Commission, for distribution among the prisoners. The clothing, it was stated, consisted of 12,000 complete uniforms which would be distributed immediately. It was now the 1st of December, and the weather was extremely cold. We had no blankets, and our clothing was thin and nearly worn out. We all looked forward to the issue of our thick, comfortable, *clean* clothes with the greatest eagerness, although our ardor was somewhat dampened by the foreboding that the supply of new clothes intimated a distant day of exchange. Yet we could not quite make up our minds that we were to be left in our present condition, and hoped at least that our Government would force an early exchange. The authorities trifled away three precious weeks, after the clothing was received by them before any of it was issued—three long, anxious weeks to us who were nightly chilled in our fireless pen. There were at this time some 4,200 prisoners at Danville,—prisons Nos. 3, 4 and 5 having been filled. There was, as had been intended, an entire new suit for each man; and if these had been properly distributed there would still have been enough left to clothe the entire guard set over us. But without waiting to issue to us our share first, the guard proceeded to help themselves; and sometime before anything was given to us, the rebel soldiers were seen wearing the great coats, pants and shoes intended for the prisoners, either with or without the complicity of the rebel authorities; but certainly with their knowledge, for no attempt was made to conceal the fact. Among the number of our guard were several who had participated in the mob attack upon our soldiers as they passed through Baltimore in April, 1861, apparently selected as our overseers, on account of their known infamous character; and these were the first to set the example of plunder from the Sanitary stores. Richie Brady, and one or two others, will long be remembered by those who suffered under their barbarous treatment during that fearful winter of 1863-4. The clothing was issued to our prison on the 24th of December, but without any reference to the necessities of the recipients, for many who already had passable clothes received full suits, while others whose uniforms were in tatters obtained only partial ones in their place. It is not too much to say that out of the 12,000 full suits sent to us, not over one half of the 4,200 prisoners obtained one complete; the balance receiving one or two pieces, according to the whim of the distributing officer. We were extremely grateful for what we did get, however.

In the afternoon of this day, the occupants of prison No. 2 were transferred to No. 6. This prison was a tobacco warehouse one hundred feet long by forty wide, containing four full floors, built of brick and not very pleasantly situated, being further back from the river than the other prisons. Here each of us received our Christmas dinner, which consisted of eight small pieces of hard bread per man, besides the usual rations of black bread and beef. On one other occasion we received a ration of hard bread, some mess pork and white beans, and this was all we ever received of the 300,000 rations reported to have been sent to us, by flag of truce. Of the presence of sugar, coffee, kraut and vinegar we had no occular demonstration. The other prisons received about the same quantity, and those returned from the hospital reported a similar state of things there. What became of the balance is not definitely known; the presumption is that none of it was allowed to spoil.

As soon as the clothing was distributed a sutler was sent into the prisons with rice, salt and tobacco, to barter for the prisoners' clothing. The table of prices he employed in the exchange of his goods was as follows:

Articles (new).	Gov't Price.	Sutler's Price.
Pants	$4 60	15 pounds Rice.
Blouse	3 00	3 " "
Overcoat	10 00	20 " "
Blanket	3 60	18 " "

Taking advantage of our necessities, this army vampire succeeded in wheedling their new clothing away from some of the thoughtless and imprudent prisoners, who preferred gratifying their present cravings to providing for future comforts. They were without doubt induced to exchange their clothing for food, by the prospect of a speedy release, a hope too often disappointed to be indulged in by any but the most sanguine. Through this want of foresight, many a brave fellow now lies in a prisoner's grave, who, by saving his clothing might have saved his life; for subsequent exposure to sun and storm at Andersonville bent many an unprotected form in death. I believe I am safe in stating that two thirds of the clothing and rations sent us from the North, found its way ultimately into the hands of the Confederate authorities, either by direct stealing, or through the agency of their sutlers.

In each of the prisons, a steward was appointed, whose duty it was to inspect every room daily and make a list of the sick who required medical treatment, at the same time ascertaining, as nearly as possible, the nature of the disease. The next morning, he reported the list to the surgeon, bringing out to the door of the prison for examination those whose disorder he could not determine, and receiving medicines to be given to those who remained. If upon examination, any were found too ill to be returned to the prison, they were placed in an army wagon, which accompanied the surgeon for the purpose, and conveyed to the Hospital. The Hospital barracks were situated upon an eminence South of the town;

they were constructed for the use of the prisoners, were warmed by stoves, and contained good bunks for sleeping upon. When the sick arrived there they received as good treatment as could be expected under the circumstances; clean clothes, plenty of water and soap for bathing were furnished, and their food consisted of light wheat bread, with a hash made of Irish or sweet potatoes and beef; their rations were cooked by prisoners detailed for the purpose. Upon the whole the authorities seemed to do all they could for the sick, and every one appeared satisfied with the attention bestowed upon them. It is pleasant to look back upon this, the almost only bright spot, in the gloom of the fourteen weary months I spent in their hands.

About this time, we received an addition of soup to our daily rations of black bread. This was prepared under the supervision of a rebel Sergeant called Irish Pete. The cook house over which he presided was located in a little wing on the North side of Prison No. 1. The establishment contained four large potash kettles of about two barrels capacity. The soup was made by boiling black cow peas or musty rice in a liquor of meat, with sometimes, though seldom, a little cabbage thrown in. The prisoners were divided into messes of from sixteen to twenty each. One man from each of these messes, went under guard, to the cook house with two pails for the soup. When all the soup carriers had collected before the kettles, they were marched to the river, where each one was required to fill his pails with water, after which he was marshaled back to the cook house. The first man in the line was then required to pour the freezing water into one of the kettles, whereupon his then empty pails were filled with the compound, when he fell back a few steps; the next man then went through the same process, and thus the rations were served out through the whole line. The quality of the last mess was decidedly thin, after undergoing so many dilutions; and there is no doubt that the addition of some eighty pailfulls of cold river water, detracted somewhat from its flavor. The four original kettles served for four thousand men; or two barrels of water flavored with a decoction of buggy black peas or musty rice, constituted a good part of one day's rations for one thousand hungry men. Truly here was fine pointed economy.

About the latter part of January the boys began to receive replies to the letters they had sent to their friends, and soon after came the boxes of "good things." These boxes were first taken to the commissary rooms where they were subjected to search, lest anything contraband of prison regulations might be concealed in them. This was a necessary precaution, but unfortunately the authorities, after taking all the articles from the boxes and examining them critically, omitted to put back such trifling matters as the tea, coffee, sugar, canned fruit and clothing, which they contained; an oversight for which, if there had been any efficacy in prisoners' oaths of condemnation, they would have been sent to fraternize with certain other rebels of whom mention is frequently made in Holy Writ. We were required to receipt for everything the boxes originally contained, and these receipts were returned to the authorities at Washington; and thus conclusive evidence was filed, of the strict performance of their duty by the Confederates. By this means they possessed themselves of the receipts for our boxes and their contents also : a shrewd piece of diplomacy, and a kind in which these lovers of freedom, the " nigger and the last ditch" have excelled for many years. They began by borrowing money and repudiating their debts; is it any wonder that they should sink to the profound meanness of robbing prisoners of war of the little gifts of friends, designed to alleviate their wretchedness and encourage their hopefulness, by the knowledge that they were remembered at home. Nearly all the boxes sent us, were examined and delivered in this manner, except those that were not delivered at all.

Petitions had frequently been sent to the officer in command of the prisons to furnish us with firewood; but they were disregarded, and we were forced to remain in our cold apartments, during the months of February and March, with no fire except on two or three occasions. In each of these months a load of tough oak wood was hauled us, in logs ten or twelve feet long. For a long time, no axes were furnished us with which to cut it into proper dimensions for burning, and we had no saws. It is presumed that the rebels supposed us to have iron fingers and muscles to pull the logs in pieces with. Our mother wit came to our aid here as on many other occasions. From the iron bolts of the tobacco presses, we manufactured wedges with which, and a great deal of perseverance, we succeeded in working up the wood into fine splinters. By means of a piece of plate iron, boiler thickness, we constructed a fire place, by simply laying the iron, which was a follower in a press, upon bricks, to prevent burning the floor; while for a chimney we had the whole room. Of course when our fires were burning, we suffered from the smoke; but the heat was comfortable. The effect of so much smoke was to create sore eyes, and we were finally obliged to abandon the project of artificial heat altogether, and to return to the simpler method of forming a column of two ranks and marching about the room until the old building shook again; after which exercise, we would lie down as snugly as possible and try to sleep, renewing the exercise whenever during the night we became too cold to lie down longer. This performance was attended with only one disadvantage; it increased the demands of nature upon the commissary, and heightened the cravings of the hunger already famishing us.

The early part of February brought us encouraging news of a speedy release. The Richmond papers announced a special exchange already made, and predicted a return at once to the old cartel. This was the first exchange that had been made since our capture, and we clung to this forlorn plank—the only one we had upon which to place a hope of salvation,—with the tenacity of a drowning man. But about the middle of the month, news of a contrary character came. The papers told us that "Beast Butler" had been appointed commissioner of exchange, with plenary powers, and that in consequence of this appointment the plan was virtually abandoned; for the Confederate authorities would never consent to treat with the "Brute." Bombastic threats of horrible treatment of the Federal prisoners were made, unless he were removed; they were to be shipped to the scorching climate of Southern Georgia, where amid the marshes and swamps of that low country, the heat and miasma would accomplish the fatal work faster than the bullet at the front; that the United States Government would find itself mistaken if it thought it could force them to exchange a negro for a white man; and that howmuchsoever they loved their friends, who were pining in the military dungeons of the North, they would let them rot there before they would submit to the dictations of the "Beast." The article closed by stating that it was now a question of time as to which Government would soonest yield, with much more to the same effect. The news filled us with the deepest gloom, for we came to the conclusion that if our Government had fixed upon a course of policy, it would "fight it out on that line," even if we were all sacrificed.

The date of our release was now entirely beyond conjecture, and we made up our minds that the only way left to escape death was to escape from prison. All our thoughts were turned in this direction, and every method which ingenuity could suggest, was immediately canvassed, and its merits duly weighed. On the evening of the 15th of January, a young man, named Williamson, had made good his escape from No. 6, by climbing down the high board fence that enclosed the prison yard, the cross pieces of which formed a kind of ladder on the outside. As he reached the ground he was challenged by the guard, but by a few vigorous leaps, he was soon out of sight in the darkness. The guard exploded a cap at him, but by good fortune his piece was not discharged. His less fortunate companion, however, was captured as soon as he reached the ground. This success encouraged us to follow the example, and nearly every day a man was missing at roll call; the secrecy and adroitness with which these escapes were effected, baffled every effort of the authorities to discover the means that were adopted, in making them. They even nailed two inch planks to within a few inches of the tops of the windows of the first, second and third floor, in their anxiety to prevent the boys from getting away from them.

At the time of the escape of the officers from the Libby at Richmond, a tunnel was being dug under Prison No. 5, which was subsequently completed and some seventy made their escape through it, nearly all of whom reached our lines in safety. In digging these tunnels, many precautions were necessary, as our prisons were frequently examined, and unfortunately we had among us some men, who, for an extra ration, would divulge the secret to the guards. The whole enterprise, therefore, was known to but few. Another precaution was necessary in disposing of the earth removed, so as to leave no trace of it in sight. A corner of the prison was selected where a board was removed from the floor, so that the operators could pass up and down without attracting observation. Case knives, which had been secreted at the time of the grand search, and escaped " confiscation," were used for picks, and half canteens, for shovels; these, together with small boxes for conveying away the earth, constituted the implements for these engineering enterprises. The loose earth was thrown back under the floors between the sleepers and crosspieces.

The "hole" was dug of the proper size, a little inclined until so deep, (generally four or six feet below the surface,) that the thickness of the earth might be sufficiently strong to support any burden that might cross it in the street above. It was then carried far enough horizontally to pass beyond the guard line and into some street or field convenient for escape. The tunnels were of various sizes, according to the diligence and perseverance of the operators. That dug by the prisoners of No. 4 was wide and deep enough for two men to walk abreast in it. Prisons No. 3, 4 and 6, had begun similar tunnels at about the same time. Those of 3 and 6 were nearly completed and that of 4, entirely so. The prisoners were waiting for a favorable night for escape, when some traitor in No. 6 reported to the authorities, and they immediately put an end to farther proceedings in that direction. The discovery in No. 6 led to the immediate examination of the other prisons, when all were disclosed. The prisoners were driven from the first floor at once, (it was midnight when they made examination), and a guard was put at the stairway. A general hauling-up of the first floors ensued, and the whole of our mining operations exposed. The discovery of these excavations created no little excitement in Danville; the papers gave them the name of "Morgan tunnels," claiming that we had borrowed the idea from Gen. Morgan, who had recently escaped from the Ohio Penitentiary. They gave us credit for being very industrious and persevering, and counseled the closest watching over the "Yankees." But in spite of all their precautions, men daily made their escape. One way in which this was effected, was as follows: the wells in the prison yards became dry, and it was necessary for a detail to go, under guard, for water to the river, some twenty rods distant; in going to which, we had to pass over a stone culvert. If by straggling behind, or slipping suddenly to one side, one of the "boys" could evade the guard, he concealed himself in this culvert until night, when he went on his way rejoicing. A very few who had money, bought their way out through the guards. These guards were the North Carolina Militia, and many of them would have been good Union men, if they had dared. They often expressed to me their abhorrence of the treatment we suffered, and would have done something to alleviate our distress, but were so closely watched by military detectives, that they were compelled to be very cautious both in what they did and said. They frequently asserted a lack of faith in their ability to gain their independence, and many declared that they could not enjoy a greater degree of liberty, even if the "Confederacy" should be established, than they had always enjoyed under the old flag. The boxes we had received by express, contained Cincinnati papers, which we were at a little pains to distribute among them, and they read with surprise the accounts of the prosperity of Northern cities; for they had not been accustomed to see any papers but their own, which, of course, contained nothing favorable to our side of the question.

One of the worst enemies we had to contend with was idleness. To persons who have been all their lives accustomed to active labor, there can be nothing more wearisome than continual inaction. We had no physical exercise and nothing to read; the little stock of stories,—tales of our experience in our several campaigns, and eventful, or humorous incidents in our lives,—was soon exhausted. Nothing new transpired to attract our attention and furnish food for conversation and thought from day to day; for each day's events were but a recurrence of those of the preceding; and the time dragged itself monotonously along. This monotony at length became more horrible than our imprisonment, and it often seemed that death would be a welcome change; so utterly exhausted were we with this prostrating *ennui*. I would infinitely rather have been confined in the Ohio Penitentiary, for the same offence, where I could have been occupied, than have remained in the situation I was placed in. Many of the prisoners were excellent mechanics; in fact, representatives of all classes of society were among us, and under the influence of the monotony of our life, the ingenuity of each class began to develop itself. It has before been stated that we had made many kinds of tools for various purposes. A more particular account of the methods adopted in constructing these tools, may not be uninteresting. Our "raw material" was the old tobacco presses which were found in the cellar. We made saws of sheet iron, bolts and case knives. The teeth of the saws were cut with cold chisels, that were hammered out of bolts; and were then hardened to a proper degree, by heating and cooling. Drills were made of sewing and darning needles; an upright wooden shaft was first fastened securely upon the top of the needle; upon this, and at right angles with it, were arms attached immoveably. The drill was put in motion by means of a bar through which the shaft was passed, in such a manner that it moved freely in a vertical direction; to the ends of this bar a string was tied and fastened firmly to the top of the axis, about which it then was coiled. The operator then, by pressing down upon the bar, uncoiled the string at the same time, causing the drill to revolve; when the string was all uncoiled, sufficient momentum was imparted to the instrument to cause it to re-wind in the opposite direction. By alternately bearing down and raising the bar, the drill was kept in constant motion, as long as the operator might desire. Files were constructed of bolts by means of the cold chisel; and although the tools were made in a primitive manner, they were finished quite nicely, and were certainly very serviceable. These, with bits of glass, the pocket knives that escaped "confiscation" and bricks, used for polishing, constituted our chest of tools; and the articles that were fashioned with their aid, were really very curious and very highly finished. No prisoner after his experience in Southern prisons can ever doubt the veracity of Robinson Crusoe's narrative.

With trinkets that we had manufactured we bought of the guard an article called Laurel root. It is the root of a shrub that grows upon high places in various parts of the South, and when dried becomes very hard and susceptible of a high polish; the bones of the beef which was given us for rations, and which were carefully preserved, together with the Laurel, formed the stock out of which were manufactured a great variety of articles.

Every man now turned "tinker," and continued his labors as long as we remained in Danville. In passing from prison No. 6 to the soup-house, the noise in the other prisons reminded one of the busy hum of an extensive machine shop, so constant and untiring were the labors of those within. A person inside could not be heard, unless he spoke at the top of his voice, and the loud shouts, mingled with the click of hammers and the buzzing of saws were a Babel of discordant sounds. Of the articles manufactured, the majority were finger rings, books, shirt studs, needles, toothpicks, spoons, buttons, pipes and pocket-knives, together with a great number of things engraved with war scenes and their mementos. The pocket-knives were made entirely of bone, except the rivets. The Laurel pipes were ingeniously and laboriously carved, and many of the designs were extremely intricate, requiring weeks for their completion. Time was of secondary importance, and the more of it that could be spent upon one article, the better pleased the mechanic would be. Many a pipe was made that was very valuable as a work of art. The figures were all wrought in relief, and many of them, representing human faces, dogs, buildings, battle scenes &c., exhibited marked features of artistic skill.

After the men were all driven from the first story, some eight hundred were crowded together on the three uppermost floors, in each building. This was packing us pretty closely, but thus cramped, we remained until sent away from Danville to the South. To add to our sufferings only six out of these eight hundred were allowed to pass below at one time. Those who desired to go, were obliged to form in line and wait their turn, and he who was so unfortunate, either by accident, or from those crowding behind, as to step over the line in front, was immediately fired upon by the guard. Several were killed or maimed in this manner, and a window at the top of the stair case was completely riddled with bullets, fired at these innocent offenders. The filth and stench arising from our rooms, pent up as we were like cattle, with no means of egress, and more than half of us sick with that scourge of the soldier—the chronic diarrhea—was beyond description. The order for this worse than brutal treatment, came from Major Moffit, a deserter from our regular army, who had command of the post at Danville. If but one half the enormities practised upon helpless prisoners, under his orders, could be told with decency, the vile odors of those Danville stables where we were kept, would be fragrance to the stench of his memory.

In prison No. 6 was nearly a whole company of the 35th Indiana Infantry. They were bold, rough, determined, dare-devil fellows, whom nothing could daunt or discourage. Fuel not being furnished us, they began tearing up the garret floor for fire-wood. A guard came up and ordered them to desist, under penalty of terrible punishment. The floor remained unmolested until one morning, just after the rations had been issued, the boys, being out of wood, commenced another raid upon it. The boards cracked and flew in splinters in every direction; the guards of the prison, hearing the noise, called the Lieutenant, who immediately ran up the stairs and ordered them to stop. But his orders were ineffectual to stay the work of destruction; every board of the floor was torn up and broken in pieces. When this was done the stairs leading to the garret were pulled down and and in like manner destroyed. After the work had been finished, which it required but a few minutes to do, about twenty of the guard came up, with bayonets fixed. They trembled with fear; for there was visible on the faces of the prisoners a determination to avenge any violent act upon themselves. But not even an arrest was made; the guard was marched back again, and the men, each with his trophy piled up at the head of his sleeping place, left to enjoy his victory unmolested. But the victory was not yet won. About ten o'clock "Irish Pete" and the commissary brought the meat ration to the prison and ordered the Sergeant of the prison to divide it only among those, who had had no part in despoiling the garret floor. The tidings of this proposed division soon reached the Indiana boys, and they at once made a claim for their share, which the Sergeant could not do otherwise than refuse to grant them. Thereupon they seized the pails of meat, which had been divided into parts for the different rooms, and upsetting them, each laid hold of a portion of their contents and hurried to his quarters. "Irish Pete" and the long, lean Commissary, immediately followed them up the stairs with their heavy hickory canes, to re-capture the spoils. Reaching the third floor, the "men in authority" at once identified the "thieves," as they, in their indignation termed them, by the pieces of meat still in their hands; whereupon "Pete" commenced to belabor one of them over the shoulders with his "shillalah." A young Irishman, named Carter, seeing his "erring brother" thus exercising his favorite method of correction, immediately called out: "Boys, that won't do, let's go for 'em." In an instant, the whole 'floor' rallied with such weapons as first came to hand. They failed in cutting off the enemy's retreat down the stairway, but charging in the rear, they pursued them with oaths, bolts and brick bats, down the first flight of stairs, across the room to the next flight where they halted. The retreating foe sprang wildly down the last stairs, their coat tails bearing horizontally and their staring eyes hanging out of their heads, exclaiming: "where's the kays! where's the kays! open the door! open the door!" at the top of their voices. Having about ten feet the start, they made good their retreat, escaping with two or three slight bruises. It was lucky for "Irish Pete" that his retreat was not cut off, for had he been caught, the enraged boys would undoubtedly have killed him on the spot. He had made himself unpopular among the prisoners by several times striking them with his "schtick," and no one would have interfered to save him being torn piecemeal. No punishment followed this daring act; on the contrary, it seemed to have a good effect upon Major Moffit, for he immediately promoted Carter to the office of Sergeant of the prison, and for sometime afterward, our supplies of wood for cooking, were both frequent and in sufficient quantities, and an ax with which to cut it, was furnished us.

Near the last of March, another plan of escape was formed. News from Richmond gave accounts of

Kilpatrick's raid upon that city, and hundreds of citizens flocked into Danville to secure a safe retreat in case the city should be captured. This news encouraged us to hope that, if we could once break through the guard at Danville, we could reach the lines of Kilpatrick's force, which was reported as striking towards the Railroads, between us and Richmond. By means of prisoners on parole at the cook house, we were able to communicate with the different prisons, and thus, to arrange the details of a plan for a general escapade. In spite of all precautions, Prison No. 5 had constructed another tunnel by opening their floor into an unoccupied room on the first story, and seventy men had escaped. This caused closer watching over us, and so careful did the scrutiny become, that it was next to impossible for any one to escape by the ordinary means. The plan was, therefore, a desperate one, and involved no less than a release of all the prisoners in Danville, with the seizure of the railroads and telegraphs. Each prison was to organize itself in companies of 60 men each, with proper officers, and these companies formed again into battallions, whose officers in like manner were to be elected. This organization, if completed, would form an effective force of some 4,000 men—a truly formidable array, if properly officered and reduced to discipline. The expected attack upon Richmond had caused a withdrawal of a large part of the prison guards, which never had been very strong; so that only a feeble resistance to us, was apprehended at first. When all should be organized, at a favorable moment, a chosen body was to rush upon the three guards in each prison, seize and secure their arms, then to burst open the doors and windows, and overpower the street guards before they could re-load, after the first discharge of their pieces. Meantime, a large force was to proceed to the central guard house, attack and capture it—a thing easily done with a slight loss of life;—No. 6 was to make an onset upon the arsenal and try and capture it, with its contents, which consisted of large quantities of small arms with ammunition, and a battery of artillery. The suddenness of the attack and the total want of preparation on the part of the guard, were thought sufficient to ensure success. The plot was undoubtedly feasible from its desperation; no commander would have been able to foresee and make preparation against, so daring an act. But the most difficult part was yet to be performed. Telegraph communication could at once be made with Richmond, and all places along our intended route where troops were stationed. Having control of the Railroads, the Rebel Government, upon the receipt of news of our escape, could forward a brigade of well armed troops to head off and re-capture us. It was true that we could cut the wires at Danville, and take possession of the Railroad at that point, but this would only have given us a few hours longer respite, for couriers would have been sent to the nearest telegraph station, long before we could have intercepted them. In any event, if we had succeeded in getting a day's march ahead of our pursuers, how were we to subsist so large a force, without a commissary department, in an enemy's country and with no officers of experience, or authority to compel obedience and direct our march? There were nine chances for failure to one for success in the enterprise. Yet desperate as it was, it was firmly resolved upon, and several of the Prisons had perfected their organizations, when unexpected news from Richmond and subsequent events, put an end to the scheme.

On the 12th of April, a daily paper, just from a Richmond press, was brought into the prison by Old Charley, who called the daily roll, containing intelligence so gratifying to him, that after roll-call he read it aloud for our information. The article intended for our ears, commenced, in heavy capitals: "GLORIOUS NEWS. THE OLD CARTEL TO BE RESUMED."— It then proceeded to announce to the Southern people that their friends who were "pining away in Northern dungeons," were soon to be released; that all Federal prisoners were to be exchanged; that a heavy burden of expense would soon be lifted from their shoulders, and a general exchange effected upon a basis highly satisfactory and honorable to all parties, &c., &c.

On hearing these glad tidings, every one was on tip-toe with delight; our hearts beat high with hope; the joy of the prisoners exceeded all bounds. We danced, shouted, sung at the top of our voices, making the old warehouses tremble with our jubilees. Danville prisoners were to be released as soon as those in Richmond had been disposed of, and we were assured that the paroling and exchanging at that place were far on towards completion. Many were so certain of speedy release, that they even bought, for various articles of manufacture, and sometimes for money, their "first chance" for City Point. No. 5 Prisoners were to be forwarded first, and No. 6 next, the others in such order as should be agreed upon.

On the morning of the 13th April, No. 5 left for Richmond; our turn would come the next day. That one day "dragged its slow length along," so tardily that it seemed almost an eternity. Our impatience would burst the bounds of time and hasten the lazy hours apace. The morning of the 14th came at length, with orders to us to be ready to march to the depot. After receiving three days' rations,—a liberal supply for a journey to City Point—we were marshaled to the cars and loaded. Our apprehensions excited by the liberality of the commissary, were quieted with the information that a recent freshet had carried off the bridges between Danville and Richmond, and that the James was so swollen and filled with drift wood that the Flag of Truce boat experienced great difficulty in ascending that river. As the train started we raised one loud shout of joy,—our farewell to the late scene of our sufferings,—little thinking that to this lowest depth of misery, the Confederate authorities could find a lower still. The fresh, pure air filled our lungs once more and sent the hot blood glowing through our veins; and we felt that we were soon to stand again beneath the starry emblem of our National liberty, free men. By ten o'clock we reached the Staunton River, the bridge over which had been swept away; but by making a detour of half a mile, we found an old log bridge over which we crossed in safety. On the opposite side stood a train of cars awaiting our arrival; aboard which we were soon placed, and hastened on our way in the direction of Richmond. We reached the Petersburg junction of the South Side Railroad just at sundown, and were still sixty miles from the end of our journey. While stopping here to change cars, a citizen informed us that we were fortunate in being so far advanced, as this train load was all that was now to be exchanged; for new difficulties had arisen and exchange was to be stopped immediately. But the train proceeding on, cut short our conversation with him, and we ceased to think of what he had told us, or this intelligence would have increased the misgivings excited by our three days' rations. We arrived at Petersburg about four o'clock in the morning, where we were again unloaded to change cars, for the last time, as we supposed, before reaching City Point. Marching along the streets, we instantly recognized the various buildings we had passed on our route to the South in October. Here our misgivings were again aroused, for we knew that City Point did not lie in that direction; and something of our true destination flashed upon our minds. Arriving at the depot, we found a train of cars awaiting us. The locomotive had not been brought out, and it became a matter of deepest interest to us, to which end of the train it would be attached; if to the North end, we were all right, and a speedy exchange with home and friends, awaited us; if to the South end, we knew not what might be in store. The engine soon came puffing from a Southern direction, was coupled to the cars at the South end of the train, and we started. How eagerly we watched the road for a curve to the

Northeast, each holding his breath in the anxious suspense with which we looked through the crevices in the cars, for a favorable turn in our affairs. The train kept straight on, turning neither right nor left, bearing almost due South. Slowly and gloomily we allowed the conviction to settle upon our minds that we were now bound for the long threatened swamps of Georgia, there amid the heat and miasma, to die. A few tried to console themselves with the thought that Congress, knowing our sufferings so well, would make every effort for our exchange, and that Savannah was the point toward which we were moving, for that purpose. Many murmured at the seeming indifference to our fate, thus exhibited by our Government, but with our limited knowledge of the reasons for such a course, we could come to no conclusion, other than that a sacrifice was demanded for some purpose, and we were the designated victims.

During the afternoon we reached Gaston, where we exchanged both guard and cars, and proceeded towards Raleigh. Arriving within four miles of that place, shortly after dark, we halted and camped in the woods for the night. A train was backed down to us from Raleigh early next morning, and we commenced our journey for the far-famed Andersonville prison-pen.

Little of interest transpired on our trip to the South,

except the insignificant accident of three of the cars being thrown from the track and completely wrecked, doing damage to no one, however. Our route lay through Raleigh, Charlotte, Columbia, Augusta, and Macon. These towns bore the same dilapidated appearance, exhibited the same quiet, grass-grown streets, the same lazy, listless air, which characterizes so many cities of the South. At Augusta, a prisoner, having by some means procured a rebel uniform, put it on, and while walking around among us was ordered away. Complying with the order, he stepped aside and falling in with a regiment that was going to Atlanta, he joined it, and commenced his "trip" to the North. He was, however, betrayed by a man who informed him that a ferry, which he wished to cross, was unguarded; on reaching which, he found that the statement was false, and he was retaken and sent to Andersonville. He afterwards effected his escape from that place, by passing through the gates as a sick man, and was never *re-taken*.

The train rolled slowly on, reaching Macon at daylight, where we halted for a couple of hours, waiting for the road in our front to be cleared of trains, which were coming up from the South. From the cars, we had a near view of the extensive iron works located at this place; and for a time, nearly forgot the fact that we were prisoners, while watching the workmen as they plied their busy craft. Here were old locomotives, placed *hors de combat* in some disaster, waiting to have broken arms disjointed and new ones put in their place. Scattered over the ground and lying about in confused heaps, were pieces of iron guns that had burst, old rails, bar and pig iron, brought here to be wrought into articles of service. The train finally moved on, in a South-west direction, past the Confederate States Chemical Labratory, wherein most of the medicines were manufactured for their army, reaching Andersonville station, sixty-five miles distant, about noon of the 20th April, 1864, where we halted and disembarked.

CHAPTER V.

Andersonville Prison—Admitted—Appearance of the Prisoners and the Pen—The First Night—The Morning—Search for Water—Roll Call—Rations—Cooking Utensils—Wood and Axes—Belle Island—Prisoners from Cahawba and Plymouth.

As soon as we had been removed from the cars, we were placed in charge of Captain Wirz, the commandant of the prison, who rode up and ordered us all to form into four ranks; he then passed along the line dividing the whole column into detachments of two hundred and seventy men each; these detachments were then subdivided into three divisions of ninety men, and three Sergeants appointed to take charge of them. This process required about two hours in the performance, and while we were waiting, standing in the broiling sun, we took a bird's eye view of our future place of confinement. The cars had halted upon a gentle knoll, sloping Southwardly to a swampy creek, and in a Northern direction for a short distance, leaving us upon a semicircular ridge, from which we had a good view of the surrounding country. About half a mile in our front, as we faced the East, we descried the "buildings" which were to constitute our abode, and which consisted of what appeared to be a fence of logs set upright in the ground, enclosing a long, narrow area. We had been told that here we were to be furnished with comfortable houses, both numerous and roomy, in which there would be no more crowding together, as at Richmond and Danville; and that as much liberty would be allowed us, as was compatible with security against our escape. We, therefore, strained our eyes to catch a glimpse of those "comfortable houses," and not seeing them, concluded they must be so low as not to be visible outside the enclosure, and that the fence was the limit of the yard in which we were to take the "plenty of exercise" promised us. Beyond the prison and stretching out on all sides of us, was a vast forest of pine, whose heavy dark foliage hanging from the tall and limbless trunks, seemed like a funereal canopy spread over the gloomy scene. A little to our right, was a small sluggish stream, bending slightly to the North, and terminating in a narrow, marshy belt, just as it reached the prison walls; this we presumed was to supply us with water. Near the walls of the prison, on the North side of the stream, stood a building in process of construction, the skeleton of the roof being all that was visible. The whole presented a dismal appearance of desolation, which can be felt only by those who witnessed it.

The preliminaries being finally settled to the satisfaction of the Commandant, the column moved forward upon the main road, until it reached the vicinity of the stream, where it separated into two nearly equal parts, the advance continuing directly forward to the main entrance of the yard, while the rear turned to the right, and crossed the stream, entering by the South gate. The detachment to which I belonged was in the van, and when we reached the gate, we halted; the guard with loaded muskets and with bayonets fixed, was drawn up in line of battle; the massive double doors swung open, disclosing a horrible and heart-rending spectacle. The prisoners had gathered in a disorderly crowd upon either side of the main street, opposite to the entrance, to receive us, and to recognize any acquaintances or friends that might be in our company; their faces and hands and naked feet were black with smoke from the pine fires; their clothing hung in tattered strips from their limbs and bodies; their hair, long and matted with tar and dirt, fell in ropes over their eyes, which glared fearfully upon us, as we marched between these living walls. It was like entering the borders of hell, where the gathered demons had crowded to the passage, to bid us welcome to their infernal abodes. These men, who had been heroes upon many a well contested field, were now shorn of their strength, and stood helpless beside us; their black skin drawn tight upon their fleshless frames, their bony arms trembling with weakness. Some were without hats, some without coats or shirts; others had no pants, and nearly all were destitute of any covering for the feet. They more resembled fiends than human beings; to such a fearful pass had the brutality of their jailors brought them. From this moment, hope forsook us; we felt that this was, indeed, "the last of earth;" that we had been brought here into dreary forests and swamps, far from home, and beyond the reach of friends, to die. True foreboding, alas! to how many of us.

The prison at Andersonville is a roofless enclosure containing, at the time of our arrival, about fifteen acres in area, being nearly sixty rods in length by forty in width. The site was selected by Captain Winder, a son of General John H. Winder, who was sent from Richmond for that purpose, some time in the latter part of December, 1863. It is located upon both sides of the little creek, (it had become a swamp at this point) which we had noted, while standing at the Railroad station, sloping gradually down to it, from both sides. The walls of the stockade were of pitch pine timbers, hewn about twelve inches in thickness, and as wide as the trees from which they were cut, would admit. The timbers were about twenty feet long; they had been set in a trench some five feet in depth, into which the earth had been thrown, holding them firmly in position. It was said to have been built under the superintendence of Capt. Winder, who had impressed a sufficient number of negroes for the purpose, and was a fine specimen of stockade architecture. At intervals of about a hundred feet, sentry boxes were constructed, six feet in length by four in width, and of sufficient hight that when the sentry stood erect, the top of the wall was on a level with his breast; they were reached from the outside by long ladders, and were covered with boards for shelter against the sun and storms.

Within the enclosure, about eighteen feet from them was a railing some four feet in hight, running parallel with the prison walls; it was formed by nailing scantling upon posts driven at regular intervals into the ground. This constituted the mark between life and death—the limit of the prisoners' ramble— the dead line. Any man, sick or well, sane or demented, found on the inside of that line, was fired upon, without a word of warning, and, if the aim of the guard was good, shot dead. Many a time, as the author afterwards saw, the guard fired and missed their mark, hitting and killing men peaceably walking about in the area, far from the dead line;—so carelessly and recklessly did they discharge their muskets among the prisoners. On one occasion, a "Sergeant of Division" doing duty, in bringing the sick to the place for examination by the Surgeon, was pushed beyond this line by the crowd behind him; the guard fired without warning, and the ball passed completely through both arms and his body; he lived about two hours after this. It was currently reported that for every Yankee shot, the fortunate sentinel received a furlough of thirty days.

Scattered about in various parts of the area were the "houses" of the prisoners; these consisted of pieces of shelter tents, or remnants of blankets stretched upon boughs of pine trees; but few of the prisoners possessed these accommodations, and the majority were either with no covering at all, or had dug holes in the ground into which they crawled for shelter. In looking over this field, there could be seen nothing of interest to attract the eye, or engage the attention of the beholder. Turn in which way we would, the same dismal scene of wretchedness confronted us; the same squalid forms crawled past; the same sullen look of despair was on every face. Around us were the high, gray walls, upon whose top stood the relentless sentry, ready and eager to destroy us, at the first motion beyond the limit fixed; the gloomy pines, upon whose dark tops the blue smoke of our pit had settled down, in ominous clouds, stretched far off on every hand; it was only when we looked upward to the sky that we saw faint rays of light in the mild blue eye of Heaven, beaming pityingly down upon us; there, from the presence of the God above us, we gathered new strength, new inspiration, well knowing that only by keeping our hearts strong, and our courage true, could we survive the terrible scenes we knew must shortly follow.

In the Northeast and Southeast corners, were spaces about eight rods in length by four in width, in which white canvas was stretched, in the form of wedges, with the sharp edge uppermost; the tops of these contrivances were about five feet high, while the bottoms were fastened to wooden pins, some six inches from the ground; the floor was the bare earth, uncarpeted with grass or straw. This constituted the "Hospitals" of Camp Sumter, and were excellently designed for the purpose of baking the unfortunate victims of disease, who might chance to crawl into them. Destructive as these ovens were, they were crowded with sick men, who lay moaning upon the naked bed, sweltering in the glowing heat of the Southern sun, which, even at this time of the year, was pouring down torrents of fire.

The only unoccupied space in the enclosure North of the swamp, was a narrow strip fifty feet wide, reaching quite across the East side of the pen, from North to South. Into this we were ushered in due form, and turned loose, to shift for ourselves. In this confined space, we were permitted to select our position, and the right to it, when selected, was based upon the principle of Squatter Sovereignty; if the fortunate occupant of the soil, however, was too weak to maintain his right, he was subject to be ousted at any time, by his stronger neighbor. Generally, each detachment had a portion of soil assigned by the authorities, as we afterwards learned, where it was required to "locate," for purposes of roll-call, sick-call, and the issuing of rations; but the men were not obliged to remain there at any other time, or for any other purposes.

Having been admitted to this den, with but little trouble on our part, we threw down our "traps" and waited for further developments. In the army, it had been the custom for two congenial spirits to put their few articles of food, their blankets, and cooking utensils, together, forming a partnership concern, from which both derived equal benefit. My "partner" and I tried to do something of this kind here, but the scheme was mostly a failure, for the common stock did not extend beyond a couple of dirty haversacks, a piece of tin which we had "gobbled" from the top of one of the cars, that had been wrecked on our trip, two tin cups, and a couple of pieces of dirty blanket, which had survived the winter at Danville. By a piece of good luck, we had halted near a stump about four or five inches high, and as soon as we were permitted to break ranks, we stepped upon it and proclaimed our possession. Here was our home, and having laid our worldly goods upon it, we gravely sat down to consider what next was to be done.

Our last rations had been issued at Augusta, and consisted of a *pone* and a small piece of shoulder bacon. The *pone* proper was a mixture of corn meal, salt and water, baked in the form of a roll twisted to a point at both ends, and weighing about a pound, although at Andersonville, any irregular piece of corn bread was known by that name. We had already fasted for thirty-six hours, and traveled more than two hundred miles, but were told, upon inquiry of the older prisoners, that we should draw no rations until the next day. It was now about the middle of the afternoon; the scorching sun was burning and blistering us, unaccustomed as we had been to exposure to its rays, in the warehouses of Danville; we knew that our fate was in our own hands; that if we became despondent and gave way to the horrors of our situation, we should inevitably grow sick, and sickness and death were synonymous.

Nothing but discouragement met us at every turn;

we were not even safe from the depredations of the prisoners themselves. We were cautioned particularly against the "raiders," a class of depredators with which every army abounds and of which no military prison is ever free, who under cover of darkness, were wont to search the camp and steal such few useful articles as they could take unobserved from their fellows. We were assured that we must keep the strictest guard over our effects at all times, or the raiders would get them, and we be left destitute; the prison authorities furnished us material, which we were expected to cook, if we did not wish to eat it raw; but our cooking utensils must be such as our own ingenuity could devise, for nothing of the kind was ever issued.

Too tired with our long journey to venture out and explore our prison, in minute detail, we threw ourselves upon the ground and waited patiently for the darkness to shut the miserable scene from our sight. The sun went down at last; the prisoners sought their beds; and silence, broken only by the feverish moan of some dying sufferer, as he rolled upon the earth, which was soon to open and receive him into its bosom; the "all's well" of the sentry, as he called the hour to his fellows; or the occasional cry of "raiders," settled down upon the camp. The dismal strangeness of the scene banished slumber from our eyes, and thoughts of our situation came strong and rapid upon us. If we had been sentenced to die at the stake upon the coming morrow we could not have been more gloomy and despairing. Until now we had not believed that the Government we had voluntarily joined in protecting, could abandon us, after faithful service, to the tender mercies of our enraged and barbarous enemies. But it was the 20th of April; we had passed six months amid the horrors of Richmond and Danville, and we were now brought here, a thousand miles beyond the reach or hope of succor, into a region of wilderness and swamps, sick, starving, naked,—to die. A few square feet of earth were ours; sacred to our use and our cherishing care; over us was the canopy of Heaven, the roof of our mansion; our couch was the cold, damp soil; our earthly possessions were at our feet; there was no day of exchange to look forward to,—nothing to hope for. We had left the world behind when we entered this spot; the great gate had swung into its place and shut us in, how many of us, forever. We dared not look forward, for a contemplation of the future was too appalling; we had fallen into a deep gulf, where our own kind, fallen before us, had changed into hideous specters, that threatened to torture and destroy us. And thus the first long night at Andersonville passed away.

Morning broke at last, and rising from the couch on which we had in vain sought repose, we rolled together our blankets, wet with the chilling shower of dew which had fallen copiously during the night, and fastening our cooking utensils to the bundle, left them with a friend, while we set out in search of water. Taking the direction of a belt of fog, which had settled down about half way between our situation and the south end of the stockade, we found, on reaching it, a black, boggy swamp, that appeared to be about eighty yards in width, through the center of which flowed a muddy stream of water, winding its sluggish way along till it passed between the timbers of the stockade, slightly scored off for the purpose, on the East side. The swamp contained about three acres of land, or nearly one fifth the territory assigned us; along the borders of the stream, and extending back to either edge of the morass, were frequent bogs, in which the stagnant water, oozing up through the loose earth, had formed in little pools, and was covered with a thick, dark scum, which gave out a sickening stench when it was disturbed. At its eastern extremity, where the water made its exit, the prison sinks were located; although, from the weakness of the sick men, the lower part of the stream, for the distance of several rods, was used for this purpose. The water was warm and disagreeable; it had a boggy, earthy taste, and was, in its purest state, of a dark, reddish-brown color; yet, if all the arrangements for our imprisonment had been as good as this we should never have murmured. On the west side, near the dead line, was a bridge of loose boards, upon which communication could be had with the opposite side of the swamp. Above this, a place had been scooped out directly beneath the dead line, where water for drinking and cooking purposes, was dipped up in cups; below, the water was reserved for bathing and washing clothes. These arrangements, however, had been made by common consent of the prisoners, the authorities having nothing to do with it; there was nothing to prevent the evil-disposed from disturbing the water and rendering it unfit for use, except the moral influence of camp.

Having bathed our hands and faces, we returned to our "lodging," just as the men were lighting their little cook-fires preparatory to the morning meal. Having nothing to cook, we sat down upon our stump and waited, looking hungrily on, until the brief repast of the others had terminated. At eight o'clock came the roll-call. For this purpose the drum beat the assembly at the south gate, and the men formed in four ranks, by divisions and detachments, to be counted. Sergeants had been appointed to take charge of their respective divisions, to receive and distribute rations; to superintend the men in foraging for wood outside the stockade; to form them in column for roll-call, and to attend to such other business of a public nature as occasion might require. The "roll-call man" was usually a Confederate non-commissioned officer, who had charge of several detachments, which were counted in regular order. He was accompanied through each division by its sergeant, and counted the men by fours. If the division was full, the time employed at roll-call was brief; but if one man was missing the sergeant was called upon to report what had become of him; when, if he could be found, the division was reported full, and at once broke ranks, going wherever the men pleased. It was only when a man was missed and could not be found, that the roll-call became an oppression. On the morning after such an event was discovered, all the prisoners were placed in four ranks, and required to stand in their places, in the hot sun, until every man in the stockade could be counted; a process requiring about six hours for its completion. By this means any one out of his place in the ranks, could be found, if he were still in the stockade; but if he had escaped, and no trace of him was discovered, the entire division to which he belonged, was put upon two-thirds the usual meat ration, unless some of its members would divulge the manner in which the escape had been made; which punishment was continued according to the whim of the commandant, or until the man was re-caught. The sergeant of division was required to report every absentee to the "roll-call man," as soon as he came upon the ground; if he neglected to do this, he was subjected to punishment in the standing stocks for twenty-four or forty-eight hours, after which a ball and chain was attached to his leg, and he was turned loose into the stockade again. Occasionally a man who made his escape, arranged with a friend, who belonged to another division than himself, to fill his place for a short time, until he could get far enough away to avoid re-capture; this would be done by the friend taking his place in his own division, until it had been counted, when he would quietly slip into the division of the other man, thus making it full. The deception was ultimately discovered, of course, but generally not till the runaway was beyond pursuit. To prevent the divisions breaking ranks, while the long search continued, the sentinels were trebled in the sentry boxes, with orders to fire into the first squad that attempted it.

Sometime in the afternoon the ration wagon drove into the stockade laden with corn meal, bacon and salt, which were thrown down into a heap, in an open space about midway the enclosure. It was a horrible sight to witness the haggard crowd, gathered about this precious pile, while the Commissary superintended its division, among the squad sergeants; gazing, meanwhile, with wolfish eyes upon the little heap as it diminished, or following their sergeant commissary back to his quarters, as famished swine follow clamorously the footsteps of their master, as he carries their food to the accustomed trough. The rations were distributed by the division-sergeant to the mess-sergeant, who then divided them among the men. To avoid quarreling, during the last distribution, it was the custom among all the messes, for the mess-sergeant to separate the rations into as many small parcels, as there were men in the mess; one man of the mess, was placed a short distance off, with his back toward the parcels, in such position that he could not see them; the mess-sergeant then pointed to one, with the words: "Who has this," to which the man replied, announcing the name of the recipient, when it was given to him. In this manner the whole number was gone through with, with satisfaction to all.

Iron bake pans, like those used by the Confederate soldiers, had been issued to the prisoners, who first arrived at this place, in which to bake their meal and fry their bacon; but nothing of the kind was ever given out afterwards, to my knowledge. The United States soldiers, as is well known, were never provided with other cooking utensils than mess kettles and mess pans, both too large to be transported in any other way than upon army wagons. At the time of our capture, in numerous instances, the tin cups and plates which we had, were taken from us; our knives, it will be remembered, were confiscated at Danville; nothing, therefore, was left in our possession with which to cook our raw food, after it was given us. How to accomplish this necessary feat was a grave question. We made shift, however, with chips, half canteens, tin cups, that had escaped confiscation, and pieces of sheet iron, to bake one side of the stuff, while the other was scarcely warmed through. The solder of the tin, melting and mingling with the bread, added another to our almost innumerable hardships. But with all our care and labor, the rations were at last devoured in a half-cooked state—a fact which aided in the increase of the frightful misery, that subsequently occurred, quite as much as the small quantity that was issued. A more extended account of the quantity as well as of the quality of our food, will be given hereafter.

A few tops of the pine trees, which had been left within the stockade, by the Confederate authorities, when the interior was cleared, together with the greater part of the stumps, had been used by the first detachments, and an adequate supply of wood was never afterwards provided, although just outside of the prison walls, millions of tons, apparently worthless in that country, were growing; and we would have gladly gathered it, and brought it in upon our shoulders if we had been allowed to do so. Such permission was not granted, except for a few times, when a squad from each division was sent under guard to forage for dead limbs and sticks; the practice being brought to an end, by one of the "details" seizing the guard, and marching Northward with him. After this circumstance took place, Capt. Wirz devised a kind of parole, or obligation, which the boys agreed to before going out, wherein they agreed to make no attempt at escape, while foraging; but even this was not respected, and the plan was dropped in a short time. During all the time, in which the men were allowed to go out of the stockade, any one with sufficient money or other valuables, was permitted to hire a guard, if he could find one unemployed and willing to be hired, and with him to go into the woods to gather up such dead wood and loose twigs as were lying upon the ground. No axes or any tools for cutting wood, were ever furnished by the authorities, except a few issued when the first prisoners were confined there. Some of the boys, however, had bought axes of the sentinels, who had purloined them from the Quartermaster or their regiment; and after wood was brought into the prison by the Commissary the owner of these tools often made an extra fuel ration, by loaning them to those who had no other means of cutting it. The quantity of this wood was extremely small, so small indeed, that I hesitate to make an estimate of it, lest I should be disbelieved; but it is safe to assert that no more than one fourth of a cord was ever given to a detachment for one day; this divided equally among two hundred and seventy men, would give to each a little more than one ninth of a foot, or, to reduce it still farther, it was equal to a green pine board one inch in thickness, twelve inches long, by five wide. This was the maximum; the minimum was no wood at all, which was frequently the case. This wood was drawn to us in various conditions; being mostly the tops of trees that had been felled to obtain the stockade timbers; it consisted of large and small sticks varying from a foot to an inch in diameter, and from two to twenty feet in length. To reduce this to proper dimensions required the aid of tools, and these consisted principally of iron spikes, which had been picked up, upon the railroad, while the boys were being transported hither, and wooden wedges, which had been whittled out with jack-knives. With these implements, we could reduce the wood to splinters of sufficient dimensions for cooking purposes; but it required the closest economy in the using. Little holes were dug in the earth, in which the fires were built; and over these our tins, if we had them, were hung, in which we heated water for scalding our meal preparatory to baking it; and at the same time, toasting our morsel of bacon, to economize the heat.

It becomes necessary to introduce at this point, a brief account of the treatment experienced by the prisoners at Belle Island, previous to their being brought to Andersonville, in order that a full appreciation may be had, of the misery endured by them at the latter place, as well as to account for the frightful mortality which subsequently occurred among them; although the tale is presented at second hand, it was told the author by a relative, in whose narrative full confidence can be placed, corroborated, as it was, by the statements of hundreds of living witnesses, with whom the author conversed.

One day soon after our arrival, as I was returning from the creek, I saw a young man before me, whom I thought I recognized. Approaching and calling him by name, he responded, and here, indeed, was a cousin whom I had not seen for several years; but so changed was he, that it was only by his peculiar gait that I remembered him at all. Cold and starvation had reduced the bluff, hearty man of one hundred and sixty pounds, to a meager skeleton that I could easily raise in my arms.

He was captured soon after the Battle of Gettysburg, while on a scouting expedition, (he belonged to the Cavalry branch of the service,) and taken to Belle Island, in the James River, above the Railroad bridges at Richmond. The river, at this point, is nearly half a mile in width, and quite deep, and the chilly Northwest winds sweep pitilessly down from the neighboring mountains, across this cheerless spot. The island contained a large rolling mill, but at that time, was otherwise unprovided with shelter or enclosure; batteries of artillery were planted upon the surrounding hills, in position to throw shell or canister into the camp, at the least appearance of disorder among the prisoners. The first ten detachments, some three thousand men in all, arrived in February and the early part of March, to inaugurate the Andersonville prison, from the prisons of Richmond and Belle Isle. Those who had been upon the Island had suffered during the fall upon that desolate spot, without proper clothing, shelterless, and with no firewood, save what was furnished in scanty measure for cooking purposes. The daily allowance of food was so meager, that, pinched by hunger and want, they caught rats, and devoured them with greed. One day, a dog belonging to the roll call Sergeant, followed him to the island, and the prisoners, by a little "engineering," caught, killed and ate him. The dog being missed, he was inquired for, and his whereabouts ascertained; when the man who killed the brute, was sought and found, and for punishment, was compelled to eat raw dog for two days; a punishment, which, my informant told me, would gladly have been shared by every man on the island. This story getting abroad among the Northern papers, by some means, the Richmond editors came out with what they denominated the "facts in the case," namely: that the prisoners did kill a dog, and having dressed it, offered it for sale as rabbit meat; and out of this circumstance originated the dog-meat story; but they did not mention the punishment inflicted for killing the animal. When the cold weather came, a few tents were provided, but they were totally inadequate to the wants of the men. Furnaces were constructed in these tents, and chimneys carried up outside, built of gravel and sand, in order to economise the heat of the scanty fuel. The chimneys retaining their heat imparted a welcome warmth to the men who were destitute of blankets, who gathered closely around, hugging them with their freezing limbs. The number of the destitute was so great that all could not do this, and the rest packed themselves together in ditches and low places, striving thus to keep alive the vital spark, by cherishing it in common. After living through this frost and famine, surviving the treatment which was inflicted upon them at Belle Isle they had been brought to Georgia to be further experimented upon, where the majority found a grave. The cold was less disastrous in its effects than the sun, because by exercise the blood could be kept sufficiently warm to continue in circulation; but, under the fervid heat of the summer sun, they were powerless to save themselves. Occasionally, one had a piece of ragged blanket which he stretched upon sticks and sought shelter beneath its protection; but by far the greater portion had not even a hat to shield their heads at noonday. The nights, too, were chilly and oftentimes frosty; and two or three blankets were hardly sufficient to ensure warmth. And thus, by alternate melting and freezing, with an occasional rain through which to pass the day and night, and with constant starvation, is it any wonder that these men died daily by scores? Is it not rather a wonder that any of them survived so long as they did?

In the early part of May, some five hundred Tennesseans, who had been captured by Forrest, and wintered at Selma and Cahawba, Alabama, arrived among us; the most of whom were hatless, bootless and shoeless, without coats, pants and blankets. On leaving those places, the authorities had told them that they were going to be exchanged—a shrewd piece of "strategy," with which rebel officers duped the unsuspecting prisoners, upon all occasions of removal, to avoid increasing the number of the guard that accompanied them. They were wholly destitute of cups, plates, spoons, and dishes of every kind, as well as of all means of purchasing them; they having been stripped of these things by their captors. In their destitute condition, they were turned into the stockade and left to shift for themselves in the best manner they could. To borrow cups of their fellow prisoners, was an impossibility, for no one could be expected to lend what, if it were not returned, would be the means of his own destruction, particularly when the borrower was an utter stranger; there was nothing left for them but to bake their raw meal and bacon upon stones and chips, eat it without moisture, and afterwards to go to the brook like beasts, to quench their thirst. To keep themselves from the cold during the night, they scooped out shallow places in the earth with their hands, and lying down side by side in these, with their bare heads and naked feet resting upon the surface of the ground, and their unprotected bodies wet with dews and storms, the wretched men trembled and shivered till morning.

There was no hope of bettering their condition, for, having no money they could buy nothing; nothing would be given them by their fellows or by the authorities; they could do nothing by which to earn even worn out apparel; they were utterly helpless to benefit themselves; and yet these men were kept here for many months and lived.

Soon afterward came two thousand more, who had been recently captured at Plymouth, N. C. These men came to Andersonville with better provisions than any that had before arrived. By the terms of surrender, they were allowed to retain their money, knapsacks and extra clothing; together with certain articles pertaining to culinary uses. These "things" were private property, bought and paid for by each man, and by all law and decency, should have been preserved to him without stipulation; but such was not generally the case. It was a matter of the greatest surprise to us, that the Rebel authorities respected these terms after they had been made with them, yet by some oversight doubtless, on their part, they were respected; but they knew full well that such articles as could be of use to their army, would just as surely find their way ultimately into their possession, for trifling returns, as if they had taken them by force. A few days before the capture of these men, they had been enlisted as veterans, and received pay as such. Each man had consequently, quite a large amount of money—some as many as three hundred dollars—and nearly every one had an overcoat, extra pants, shirts, drawers and blankets. It was pleasant to look upon them, to see their noble forms arrayed in the comfortable uniforms of our loved country; but, while we were glad to find them so well provided with materials for their comfort, we were by no means rejoiced to see them among us; for we knew too well by our own experience, that their present good cheer could not last. They were, as a general thing, noble-minded and intelligent, with a high sense of honor and integrity, men whose associations had evidently been of the best charater; they had enlisted and periled their lives to save that of the nation, because they felt it to be a duty. It was sad to think how soon they would be brought low, their courage gone,—and squalid want and misery claim them for their victims. They brought us some news on the exchange question, and like all prisoners who had been but recently captured, indulged in flattering anticipations of speedy release; and being animated with this hope, they spent their money freely, buying such things of the older prisoners as they could induce them to part with, and paying exorbitant prices therefor. Like all new prisoners, who had had no previous experience in the kind of life we were leading, they were horror-stricken with our appearance; but they attributed it entirely to our indolent habits, for they could not believe that men professing to be Christians, could be so totally devoid of humanity as to reduce the helpless beings in their power to such a terrible condition of wretchedness. They accordingly charged us with being the cause of our dirty appearance, and jeered at us, when we told them we were powerless to prevent or improve it. We, knowing full well that they would soon learn the true state of affairs, forebore to reply to their taunts.

In a brief time, they had wasted their money, and, when it was gone, they could endure the climate and the fare no better than we; as soon as the soap they had brought with them, was exhausted, their appearance was no cleanlier than ours. The pine smoke penetrated their skin, as it had done ours, and ground itself into their flesh; frequent and copious ablutions would not remove it from them; the soft soap they received once in three or four weeks, whitened their skins or cleansed their hands no more than it did ours; and their clothing rapidly became filthy and worn; in a few weeks they mingled undistinguishably, with their fellows. They soon began to decline under the horrible treatment, and in a short time, hundreds of them were placed in the grave. The money they put in circulation, doubtless saved many a man's life, for it often fell into the hands of those who, after an experience of eight months of prison life, knew how to economise their little funds. The thousands of dollars spent by them, while they added a few comforts to others, proved of brief advantage to themselves, and in the end they were the means of hastening their unhappy fate; for they could not easily assimilate to the habits of the other prisoners, and died before they could become inured to the climate and fare of the prison. I believe I state the truth in saying that, before that fatal summer was past, two in three of those two thousand strong, robust, healthy men, that came among us, flushed with spirit and hope, slept their last sleep in the prisoners' grave at Andersonville and Millen.

CHAPTER VI.

Enlargement of the Stockade—The Camp at Daylight—Shelters—Cooking—Appearance of the Prisoners—Roll-Call—Sick-Call—Market—The Sutler—Smugglers—Manufacturers—Gamblers—Water—Fortifying—"Raiders"—Six Men Hung—Police—Petitions—Writing Letters—Receiving Express Boxes—Incidents.

In the preceding Chapter an attempt has been made to introduce the reader to the stockade, and to relate the extent of the preparations made for our maintenance there, by the officers having charge of the prison; in the present, it will be the author's aim to show the methods adopted by the prisoners themselves to subsist upon the scanty means afforded them; together with other matters pertaining to the stockade itself. The next Chapter will show some of the results of our treatment.

In the early part of the month of June, the number of the prisoners had increased to nearly twenty thousand men. These were crowded into an area containing less than eleven acres, after deducting the spaces included in the swamp and dead line; and a further allowance being made for the various streets and paths, there will be left to each man a plat containing twenty-four square feet, or six feet in length by four in width. As the number was almost daily increasing, under an order from the War Department at Richmond, that all the prisoners East of the Mississippi should be concentrated at this point, it became necessary to enlarge the dimensions of the stockade. It had been proposed to the prisoners to do this sometime in the latter part of May, but they had refused to comply with the request, preferring to remain in their crowded state to aiding their enemies in any manner, fearing, among other objections, that such an act would be construed to their disadvantage by their own Government; they also hoped that the rebels, knowing this objection to taking part in the work, would enlarge the enclosure for humanity's sake; how far the humanity of the rebels could be confided in, will be amply illustrated during the progress of this narrative. Finding, however, that their numbers were constantly increasing, and Gen. Winder's order to Capt. Wirz "to pile the d——d lazy vagabonds three deep if they held out longer," being reported to them, they finally consented to perform the labor.

Some thirty men were selected for the purpose, each of whom gave a verbal parole to make no attempt to escape while on this duty; they were then provided with axes and spades, and set at work. The enlargement was made upon the North end of the old stockade, and extended some forty rods in length; and, if this estimate be correct, the addition would include some ten acres of land. The whole work was concluded about the 1st of July, having continued two weeks.

When all was completed, a few feet of the old wall, which was still standing between the two portions of the pen, was taken down, making an opening ten or twelve feet in width, through which the living tide soon began to pour its filthy current. The number of detachments at this time, was ninety, one half of which, from the forty-fifth upward, was to be transferred to the new ground. At ten o'clock the moving commenced, and it continued until the sun had long gone down. More than ten thousand men passed through the narrow opening; all eager to rush in and inspect their new quarters. The crowd was so great that the sick, falling down in the press, were trodden upon and killed; strong men became wedged in between the moving mass and the standing timbers and were crushed; men, carrying all their earthly goods, wretched though they were, yet precious to them, dropped a little cup or a piece of ragged blanket, and stooping to pick it up and preserve it, were overthrown, trampled upon by the hurrying feet that could not turn aside, and left a shapeless, hideous mass of broken limbs, bathed in blood. How many were thus killed outright is not known, but a large number, both of the strong and weak, were so injured that they never recovered. It is painful to contemplate this miserable scene, which a little foresight might have prevented. Had the officers of the prison taken the charge of the removal in hand, as they were bound in virtue of their office to do, the frightful tragedy would never have occurred; and many a man, who dated from the fatigue and the injuries received upon that day, the disease which terminated in the grave, might have survived to be finally exchanged. Had the Cofenderate authorities ordered the detachments through the opening, one by one, assigning to each its place in the new ground as it entered, the whole might have moved harmoniously, and the work would have been completed in a few hours at most, without hurry, confusion or disaster.

The whole area now occupied by the prisoners included twenty-five acres, and was spacious enough for all necessary purposes. The tops of the few trees which had been cut down within the new enclosure were left upon the ground, and the partition wall torn away by the men for their own use; for a time there was much improvement among us, but, when the wood was gone, which had been thus furnished, and the constant trampling of feet had beaten down the grass, the new stockade became like the old one, and the inmates of each undistinguishable.

The better to understand and appreciate the horrors of the situation in which we were placed, I will take the liberty to introduce the reader into the interior of the stockade, and point out to him, the daily routine of the place, together with the appearance of its inmates. Let him not shrink from the terrible sight; for here he will witness how a noble spirit can overcome the weakness of the body, with its strength; how the brave heart battles with the slow, steady, but certain approach of the dreaded foe, who conquers all at last; and will learn a lesson of patient endurance, of calm, yet fearful suffering, of sublime courage, that will raise his faith in humanity, and arouse his deepest sympathies with men that can suffer all this, buoyed up and sustained by an ardent love for that country, upon whose altar they offer themselves a sacrifice.

We obtain our passes from Capt. Wirz, and present them at the south gate, where they are examined by the officer in charge of it, who pronounces them all right and turns us over to the sergeant, with orders for our admission; he thereupon opens a little wicket and we enter. Passing hurriedly down the wagon road, we cross the dead-line, without halting, lest the sentry may mistake us for prisoners and fire upon us, where we come to a halt and take a brief survey of the scene. It is early morning, and the first gray streaks of dawn are lighting up the sky; but the bright rays of the sun, itself still below the horizon, seem to pass far over our heads, as if to avoid a contact with the loathsome objects around; as birds are said to fly high above the sea in whose bosom the cities of the plain lie engulfed. Before us are the "huts" of the prisoners, looking like little irregular heaps of black rags, strewn thickly and in inextricable confusion over the ground, lying beside which are human forms, stretched at full length upon the sand, their upturned faces black with grime, and their naked bodies wet with dew; they lie in this unsheltered manner, because they have nothing to protect them against the night. Two tall trees stand in the corner, off to our right, looking grimly down upon the piteous spectacle. Turning round to our left our eye passes rapidly over the low, white belt of fog that stretches across the pen from west to east, where lies the swamp from which those sleeping beings draw their water, to quench their burning thirst, or cleanse their filthy garments; beyond the fog, we can faintly see a continuation of the irregular heaps which had attracted our attention at first, and the dim outline, of the wall, upon whose top the sentry stands with sleepless eye, his long musket gleaming in the breaking light, like a bar of polished silver. In the dim perspective we descry the skeleton roof of a long low building, in the Northwest extremity of the yard, but its outline is too faint to be examined from this point. Within the walls, a strip of unoccupied ground, a few yards in width, stretches around the whole; the enclosure made by the dead line, and to tread upon it is death. The damp morning mist rises upon the place, as the air grows warmer from the ascending sun; and the view is shut out from our eyes.

Treading lightly, lest we disturb these slumbering beings, whom it would be cruel to bring back to misery, from the blissful unconsciousness into which they have sunk, let us examine the huts before us. The first that meets our eye is formed by fastening long stripes of cloth together, with wooden pins, which is then stretched across a couple of poles, that are placed with one end upon the ground, the other resting upon a bank of sand laborously raised a few feet high, by the hands; it is open like trellis-work, and black with smoke and dirt, and affords a covering only in spots to the wretched beings lying beneath it. Further on is another style of habitation,—for these things contain all the household goods of two or three men ;—this consists of but two parts, a short pole set upright in the earth and a piece of blanket stretched over it. Next to this is a hole scooped out in the sand, in which the owner while lying upon his side, can have a support for his back, and here half a dozen, nearly naked men are lying, with their faces turned from each other like pigs; but into it the rain sometimes settles, and drives the unfortunate occupant, into the pelting storm. Another form of the burrow is an improvement upon this primitive habitation; three or four have joined together in excavating beneath the surface, first digging a hole some three feet in depth, of the size of their bodies, and afterwards scooping out the sand at right angles to it; into these they crawl and are protected against the heat and storm; but the fine particles of which the roof is composed, becoming detached upon the lightest jar, drop down in their faces, threatening to smother them in their sleep. Here we find another hut; this has been built with adobe, formed from a bluish clay that was found near the swamp; with much labor and patience, the poor fellows have moulded the materials with their hands and dried them in the sun; three walls have been built, three or four feet high and slightly inclining towards the center, over which they have stretched an old shirt, which can be made of more service here than upon the owner's shoulders.

But some of these shelters are of a higher grade of comfort, and are inhabited by the acknowledged "aristocracy" of the prison. They are constructed of slabs, split from pine logs, which they had brought in from the surrounding forest, during the time when the prisoners were permitted to hire a guard to go there with them. They are of sufficient size to accommodate six or seven men, and form a complete protection against the weather. They are high enough to allow the occupant to stand erect; little slabs are placed around for seats, pegs and shelves are arranged upon the walls; bunks of "pine straw" are made upon the ground; and a door shuts out the beating storms. The last structure which we will examine is formed by placing several poles parallel to each other, over which two blankets sewed together are thrown, forming a burrow some eighteen inches high, and as long and wide as the blankets will allow. Its inmates must crawl beneath it, and when in, are quite well protected. Very many of the men, those whom we see lying about us on the surface, are unfurnished with any "shanty," either dug in the ground or built upon it. They are mostly late arrivals, who have not yet been initiated into prison life, and are waiting to learn how to take advantage of the few conveniences that are furnished them. If we were allowed to go out into the woods we could all be provided with cabins; for we are willing to help ourselves in every way possible; or if fear of our taking advantage of the brief liberty, to make our escape, prevents that, let the authorities bring us logs and furnish axes for us, and we will do the rest; or supposing that to involve too great expense to the Confederate government, let us draw upon the money of which they have robbed us, and we will purchase the materials and hire them brought to us. It is not the fault of these men that they are destitute, for they are utterly helpless in the hands of their enemies; and these, unfortunately for us, are too little inclined to pity, to assist us, and too brutal to allow us to help ourselves.

While we have been inspecting these novel shelters, the sun has risen above the horizon, and the prisoners begin to appear; for in the middle of the day, the heat is too fervid to admit of much activity, and all the little "chores," which are necessary to be performed, must be completed during the cool of the morning. The half naked, squalid wretches, black with smoke and dirt, feebly drag their emaciated forms from the holes into which they had crawled the preceding night, and begin their preparations for the coming day. Passing quietly across the swamp, we hasten up the rising ground on the North side of the stockade, where a full view of the scene may be had at a glance. Taking our station at the summit, we watch the tattered forms, as they creep slowly by, making their way to the creek for water; they approach the little stream, some carrying tin cups, or pails made of empty fruit cans, into which they have inserted strings or wires, to serve the purpose of handles; some bearing small buckets or wooden pails which they have fashioned with their pocket knives from pine sticks, or occasionally one of larger dimensions, formed with staves and hoops; while others bear old boot legs tightly sewed together, and many, very many go empty handed, having been unable to procure anything in which to carry the liquid. There is here every variety of dress, too, from the apparel of Adam before the fall, to a ragged coat and pants; and these seem to have grown upon their forms, like bark upon a tree, so black and dirty have they become. There are men with one legged pants, and with no pants at all; men with coats of which one of the sleeves has been torn away for bandages, leaving the bare arm exposed; men with no covering but a pair of dirty drawers, too much torn and worn to be decently described; men without socks and shoes, or with one expiring shoe, the sole being upon the point of departure; hatless men, their long locks glued together with pitch and rolled up like ropes, hanging over their sunken eyes.

They gather into a sort of file, when they reach the swamp and pass upon the planks to the creek, each stooping down in turn to dip his little cup into the water, and turning back to seek his quarters again. Five thousand men at this hour in the morning, daily visit this spot to get water for breakfast, while the partner of each remains behind to watch their common " effects." But behind this press that *walks* to the water side, come other men, who cannot walk; they creep upon hands and knees, or crawl upon their breasts, pulling their bodies along by burying their elbows in the sand; these miserable beings, the victims of starvation, and the consequent diseases, writhe and twist themselves to the stream; but they come not all back; for, overcome with the fatigue of their laborious effort, they creep to one side of the path and die.

Presently little fires spring up upon every hand, sending out wreaths of smoke which rise a short distance above the pen and hover there in a dark cloud, through which the sun looks red. Let us approach these fires and examine the culinary department of the prison. Here are three miserable looking beings gathered around a few bits of blazing pine, which they have placed in a hole, to economize the heat; their hands, faces and garments are black with soot and dirt, and their Saxon features alone distinguish them from the negro. They mix the little ration of meal with water and a few grains of salt; this mixture they knead upon a chip, using the utmost care that no particle of the meal be lost, and place the dough upon another green pine chip and hold it before the smoking fire. It is painful to look upon them during this operation; to see the greed in their hollow eyes, while they watch the crumbs that occasionally drop from the narrow chip, as the compound, partially dried, is shaken by their trembling hands; and to note how anxiously they seek each tiny morsel among the dirt and ashes, and carefully replace it, when found. The bacon is toasted before the fire upon a stick, and when cooked, has an oily, smoky taste. The mystery of their black appearance is easily solved; pass your hand slowly through the smoke that rises from their fire, and the oily particles of soot, cling tightly to it; water will not dissolve it, and they have no soap to act the part of the " mutual friend " and bring the opposing elements into harmony. If you rub your hand upon your clothes, or your face, the black stain is left, and continuing the operation for a few moments, you have the same general look as the prisoners.

This is a fair specimen of the manner in which the bread is prepared for eating; yet there are other improved methods, while there are those that are even worse. Sometimes a *pone* is made by those who have bake-pans; others again make mush, upon which a little sorghum is spread; some fry the dough in fat saved from the bacon; and yet others make dumplings, or rather little round balls—in short, every change that hungry men can devise with the few conveniences they have for the purpose, is rung upon the pittance of corn meal allowed them. But it remains corn meal in the end, notwithstanding the thousand devices to render it palatable.

Crossing the narrow paths that wind tortuously among the "shanties," trodden here and there without method, by the weary feet of these wretched men, let us pause before this strip of black blanket that is stretched over a couple of poles. Stooping low down we discover a soldier stretched out at full length upon the bare ground. He is literally "alone in the world," and we learn upon questioning him that his comrade, but a day or two ago, died by his side, and has been carried out. He is too feeble to rise, as he tells us, and expects soon to be borne away in his turn. His face is begrimmed with dirt, his hair is long and matted, the dark skin upon his hands and feet is drawn tightly over their skeleton frames, shrunken, calloused, dried, as it were, to the bone. He makes feeble replies to our inquiries, but we learn that he passed the long, dreary winter on

Belle Island, where the starvation and exposure to the severe cold sowed the seeds of disease in his system, whose speedy end will be an obscure death and an unknown grave. He is hopeless, racked with pain; he knows that a few days at most will end his misery; but he complains not of his hard fate, and expresses his willingness to suffer on, if necessary, or the love of that country, whose life he has tried to save.

A few steps to the right we find a hideous object, ying in a hole, which his hands have scooped out in the sand. The tattered rags that partially cover him, cannot conceal the bones that gleam through the skin; his eyes move fearfully in his head, his hands clench tightly together, his limbs are drawn up, in horrible contortions, by the cramp. The only motion of which his body is capable, is a slow rolling from side to side upon his back as a pivot, and the vermin crawl in vast armies over his wretched person. He takes no notice of passing objects, unless particularly addressed, for the world is rapidly going out to him. Placing our ear to his lips, we gather from his fain whispers, that but a short time before, he had left some New England College, flushed with hope and courage, to battle for liberty and right. A fond mother pressed her lips to his brow, as, with tearful eyes she bade him farewell; a kind sister in cheering words urged him on to duty; a brother's hand wrapped the garb of his country's defenders about his form; and, in the field he had performed deeds of valor. He was captured, and—even while we linger beside him, a faint shudder passes through his frame, and all is over. He too, will soon be borne away to a nameless grave; and his loved ones shall seek in vain to distinguish him from the thousands that sleep by his side.

Just in front of us, we see a throng gathered about an object, which, in other places than this, would draw tears of sympathy from the hardest heart, but scenes of horror are so frequent here, that this excites but a passing interest. It is a young soldier, born and reared in a fertile township in Ohio; his early life had been passed among the pleasant vales of that noble State; every kindness which parental love could bestow, had been lavished upon him, and he had ranked high among the promising and intelligent youth of his country—a man of talent, of literary attainments, of noble instincts. But reason is now dethroned, and he tears his tattered rags from his emaciated form, in his frenzy, gnashing his teeth and foaming with rage; but the paroxysm is momentary; his strength is exhausted; he falls to the ground helpless as infancy, and is borne away by his comrades.

There is one form of disease which is almost too horrible to be witnessed, yet we cannot understand the wretchedness of the prison without looking upon it. This is not a solitary case, but we shall find numerous similar ones, before we leave this living charnel house. We instinctively pause as we reach the awful sight before us, holding our breath lest we inhale the terrible stench that arises from it. Here is a living being, who has become so exhausted from exposure that he is unable to rise from the ground, suffering with diarrhea, in its last and worst form. He is covered with his own faeces; the vermin crawl and riot upon his flesh, tumbling undisturbed into his eyes and ears and open mouth; the worms are feeding beneath his skin, burying themselves, where his limbs, swollen with scurvy, have burst open in running sores; they have even found their way into his intestines, and form a living, writhing mass within him. His case has been represented to the Surgeons, but they have pronounced him incurable, and he is left here in his misery; in which he will linger for three or four days more. Proper care and treatment would have saved him, long ago; but not now,—and his comrades abandon him to death.

While we are gazing upon this sickening spectacle, the drum beats at the South gate, and the prisoners, dropping their half-cooked food, hasten to form themselves in ranks, preparatory to being counted. Being arranged in irregular lines, the strong men standing for the most part, with uncovered heads,—having no hats,—the weak sitting or lying upon the ground, the Sergeant passes carefully around to see if all the ranks are full, and searches among the huts for those that are unable to crawl to the line. Raising our eyes, we observe that each sentry box contains two additional men, and that they grasp their muskets with a firm hand; the prisoners observe it also, and they know well that some of their comrades were missed at the last roll-call, and that the sentinels are there to fire upon any division that breaks ranks, before the camp has been thoroughly searched. The officer comes forward, hastily passes from the head to the rear of the column, counting the standing men; the Sergeant leads him to the sick that still remain in their hovels, unable to creep out, and to the dead, and the complement is filled; he sets the division down as full and passes on, the men still remaining in line. Let us also pass on with the officer, till he comes to the division to which the missing man belonged. It is drawn up in line like the others; the Sergeant reports his number present; the officer examines his book and finds that one is gone. The Sergeant shakes his head when asked what has become of him; the men in rank are interrogated, but no reply is obtained.

A sick man lying upon the ground, points to a hole near by; the officer goes in the direction, stoops down and looks beneath the thin shell of earth; and there, in the bosom of his Mother,—the Mother of us all— the missed one lies, dead; dead, unknown to his comrades,—to all, but the God who saw his dying struggle, and who will bring him in the last day, a living witness against the fiends that doomed him to such a fate.

The lost man found, the extra sentinels are relieved, the men break ranks and resume their occupations; but the Sergeant has work yet to do, for the sick of his division are to be gathered up, the helpless upon blankets, those able to walk, in squads; and all must report at the South gate to receive their medicines. We pass over to this gate and cast a casual glance upon the mass of wretchedness gathered there. Nay shrink not, there are worse spectacles than this in this horrible pit; there are sights here to freeze the blood, scenes of suffering with which the most frightful pictures of the horrors of hell, bear no parallel.

Gathered here from all parts of the Stockade, and crowded in the small space, is half an acre of human beings, suffering in every form of disease. Some are lying upon the blankets, upon which they have been brought; some are prone upon the earth, where they were laid by their comrades; some have crawled hither upon their hands and knees; and here they must remain for many long hours, in this broiling sun, without shelter or protection, waiting,—waiting, till their turn shall come to be served; yet, fourteen surgeons are busily working in yonder little enclosure, and each has his assistant, who can prescribe for most of the cases.

Here are to be seen the ravages of scurvy and diarrhea, of dysentery and fevers, of hunger and exposure; and as we stand looking upon the putrid mass, writhing in hideous contortions, a sickening stench arises from it, that penetrates, for miles, it is said, around the prison. We see men upon whom scorbutic sores have been long at work, and great holes are eaten in their faces; their limbs are black and swollen, or like rotten flesh, discharging a yellowish matter that emits this most offensive odor; in some the eye has been destroyed and they grope blindly about in the crowd. And here, too, are emaciated forms, too weak to walk, and they turn their hollow eyes pleadingly upon us; they are the victims of diarrhea; their fleshless arms hang languidly by their sides, and their hollow cheeks are livid with leanness. But few of these men can be benefitted now by the Surgeon's skill, many will call for it, but a little while; even while we stand here, some have felt the last agony, and expired.

We turn horror-stricken away from this scene of misery, and, crossing the swamp upon loose boards, reach the street leading back from the North gate. Here is the grand business center of the Stockade; for it is said that the "Universal Yankee" to support life, must trade, and that no two of that enterprising race ever met without " swapping " something.— Whether this " unappeasable hankering " for trade had anything to do with the origin of these hucksters' stands or not, it is unnecessary to inquire ; it is sufficient to know that here are gathered some thirty thousand Yankees, and that a regular daily market has been established, at which the owners realize what are to them great profits; for many of them can more than double the prison ration daily, besides providing themselves with clothing and comfortable shelter, through this constant interchange of articles of food.

Going upon the street and facing East, we advance through the line of stands upon the North side, noting, by the way, the various articles of traffic. Here are booths arranged in fancy style ; a rough slab split from a log that had been brought in for the purpose, or purchased at a figure which would appal a tradesman in our cities, and covered with a clean rag, or sometimes a strip of paper, cut in various patterns, forms the counter, and upon it, is spread the stock

in trade, in such a manner as to attract the attention
of the passer by; over the whole is stretched a wretched piece of blanket, an old coat, or a shirt, for an
awning. There are others, consisting of nothing but
a rough board which is fastened upon four stakes
driven into the ground; the most common kind, however, is wicker work formed of pine splinters, woven
together with considerable skill and taste. But by
far the greater number of tradesmen are those who
have no stands, and who carry on their "little business"
upon the street. These men generally have but one
or two articles for sale, and carry them in their hands;
or, if they have nothing but meat, by impaling it upon
a stick and hawking it about the stockade. First and
foremost of these traders are those who deal in the
necessaries of life,—as peas, pones, wheat-flour and
biscuit, corn-bread, corn-meal, soup, potatoes, rice,
meat and salt. These articles are of course held at
almost fabulous prices, owing to the difficulty with
which they are obtained, and only those who are flush
in funds can afford to purchase them. In addition to
these, are articles of luxury,—tobacco, onions, eggs,
soda, red peppers, gingerbread, soap, taffy, sour beer,
tea, apples, peaches, watermelons, pails, wooden
dishes, thread, buttons, &c. &c. In exchange for
these a great variety of things are taken,—as money,
gold and silver watches, and rings, shrewdly secre-

ted from the lynx-eyed officials, during the search prior to admission to the prison. In default of these things, the purchaser gives an old pocket-knife, a mug carved from wood, in making which he has spent much patient labor; rings made from bones that formed a part of the meat ration, and laurel pipe-bowls; all of which are readily taken, because they can be disposed of to the guard. Upon inquiring the price of some of these " goods " in greenbacks, we are told that wheat-flour sells to-day for one dollar per pint; peas for thirty cents; corn-meal, fifteen cents per pint; soup, five cents per half canteen; salt, twenty-five cents per table spoonful. If we wish for luxuries, we are informed that for a peach we must pay fifty cents, for an apple, the same. Tobacco is one dollar and twenty-five cents a plug; a plug is nine or ten inches in length, by three in width, and is the cheapest luxury the market affords; while for soap we must pay one dollar and a half per bar, or go unwashed. The itinerant traders, like all of that ilk, the world over, are the most noisy and persistent; having little to sell, and that of a poor quality, they try to make up for their lack of importance in this respect, by crying their wares at the top of their voices. "Who has this nice ration of beef, for ten cents, only ten cents?" "Who has this dish of rice soup, well seasoned with salt and pepper, warranted the best on the ground?" "Here you can buy your cheap onions, only seventy-five cents apiece." "Who has this nice pail, warranted not to leak?" "Who is the next lucky man for a plate of rich, bean soup, nicely peppered and salted? try it before you buy, and if you don't like it, you needn't take it." "Roll up, gentlemen, and get a glass of sour-beer, quick, it's nearly gone." " Sour-beer! sour-beer! t'will cure the scurvy in twenty-four hours, and will not intoxicate," &c.

It is a matter of much curiosity how these articles are procured for sale, and if we can gain the confidence of one of the heaviest of the merchants, he will inform us that they ostensibly come through the prison sutler, but in reality the most of them are smuggled in by the guards. This sutler is one of the tools of Winder, Wirz and Quartermaster Humes, and it is his mission to parade his wares temptingly before the famished men, and wheedle them out of the articles of value, which could not be found when they were robbed, giving a mere pittance in return. It is reported that he has been authorized by the Richmond Government to trade for greenbacks, as a special favor to the Federal prisoners, it being treason for any one owing allegiance to the Southern Confederacy, to traffic in the I. O. U's of Uncle Sam., without a permit; but it is understood that these greenbacks fall, ultimately, into the hands of the prison officers, who store them up, or put them in circulation among the farmers in the vicinity. To preserve a monopoly of trade for themselves, the officers have issued an order, making it a great offence against the peace and dignity of the Confederate States of America, for any citizen or soldier, save and except the sutler aforesaid, to offer for sale, sell, barter, or exchange, any article of food or luxury with the prisoners in Camp Sumter confined, under the pain and penalty, if the offender be a soldier, of long and rigorous confinement in the block house; and if it be a citizen, of punishment by fine.

But all these punishments do not prevent a contraband trade being kept up between the sentinels and the prisoners; for, upon dark nights, when the keen-eyed military spies, (called detectives, for dignity's sake) can not see, at a preconcerted signal the sentry throws a stone, to which two long strings are attached, across the dead line; one of these strings has a loop ring at the end, and is so arranged that it readily slides upon the main cord; to this the prisoner attaches the article which he wishes to dispose of, and the guard carefully draws it up to the box, for examination; if it is satisfactory, he returns the particular commodity agreed upon, and the "trade" is completed. In this manner, a heavy contraband business is almost nightly carried on, resulting in great advantage to both sides—the prisoner saving his life, perhaps, and the sentry obtaining a gold watch for which he exchanges flour, peas, &c.; besides, the "raw material" can be purchased much cheaper of the smuggler than through the regularly authorized trader; while the presence of the latter accounts to the officers for the appearance of articles unknown to prisoners' rations, and turns suspicion away from the former.

Besides these markets, we find various manufactories, "tinker shops" and barber shops, where the busy workman labors all day "to turn an honest penny," or to pass away the time, and gain an extra ration. Here wooden buckets are made by the whilom cooper, with pine staves and hoops; rings of bone, and pipes of laurel, by the jeweller, who also cleans and repairs your watch, if you have one; here, also, the brewer prepares his sour-beer, by putting a pint of corn-meal into a pailful of water, adding a little sorghum molasses, or a red pepper if he has it, and letting it stand in the sun till it ferments, when the liquor is decanted. This "sour-beer" has a ready sale, for it is a really valuable remedy for the scurvy, being, as its name imports, acidulous, and tasting like newly fermented cider. We also find the bakeries in this locality, which consist merely of an oven, monitor-shaped; the "monitor" is made by first placing a layer of the mud found near the swamp, upon the ground for the bottom, upon which a heap of sand is raised, of the desired shape and dimensions; over this a layer of mud is then placed, with an opening for the mouth and chimney, and it is left to dry in the sun. When it is thoroughly dried, the oven is heated, and the dough or meat baked. The "monitor" is generally a partnership concern, one of the firm remaining at home in the capacity of cook, while the other disposes of the articles on the market; they also take in the raw material and bake it on shares, and thus turn their labor into food. Here, again, we shall find brokers' offices, where Confederate scrip is exchanged for greenbacks, for gold and silver coin, and watches, rings, &c., and where the broker sits the entire morning, changing money of all kinds and descriptions; making his premiums by the difference in value between the Confederate Blue,—and the United States Greenback. In fact we can find almost every kind of industry within this den, wherein men engage to keep their thoughts away from the misery around them.

But there are places, also, where the vices are nurtured,—gamblers' stands, where men sit all day over cards and dice, tempting fortune, cheating, fighting, lying, swearing. Here are chuck-a-luck boards, three card monte, seven up and "seven over," faro banks, and all the simpler devices, by which men are wheedled out of their money and valuables by tricksters, under pretence of an appeal to the fickle Goddess. It is not strange that men who have little to lose, should venture it all, in the attempt to increase it; for to lose is but to hasten the evil time by a few days at most, while to win may be salvation. Therefore, even gamblers have their share of patronage, and some of them do a thriving trade.

Leaving this busy scene, we walk around among the prisoners and examine their facilities for procuring water. The main reservoir is the creek, which passes through the swamp; but it also runs through the camp of the prison guard, and along the base of the cook house, outside the walls, receiving the refuse and garbage of both of these; the prisoners within have dug holes in various parts of the enclosure, laboriously excavating the earth with their hands and pieces of canteens, and drawing the dirt to the surface in old boot-legs. We shall find perhaps fifty of these water holes, but the fluid so obtained, is pure and cool, and amply repays the patient toil, required in their excavation. Near the Northern extremity of the swamp, is a spring, bubbling up from the marshy ground, which has been scooped out to a slight depth; and just outside the dead line, is another, a living stream, flowing through a spout, fixed there by some daring prisoner in the darkness of night, or, mayhap, by some officer, more humane than his fellows; but it is beyond the reach of the hand, and the prisoners tie their little cups upon a long stick, and angle, as it were, for the cooling liquid.

Having examined this pen thus hastily, let us pass out again, where we came in, leaving these wretched beings, starving and dying, under the burning rays of this terrible sun; and if you have been able, in this brief view, to understand the thousandth part of the misery here endured; to realize anything of the horror by which you have been surrounded; or, on the other hand, if you can call up one thought of pity for the beings in authority over us, who have allowed their humanity to be all swallowed up in their vengeful passions, and who delight in nothing so much as in torturing us,—then your visit has not been in vain.

Some time in the latter part of July, Gen. Stoneman made his famous, but unfortunate raid upon Macon, the effect of which was felt at Andersonville, by both prisoner and jailor. There were, at that time, about thirty thousand men confined at this place, and it was greatly feared that Gen. Stoneman would ride suddenly down upon us, open the prison doors and set us free. The valiant Captain Wirz was greatly "exercised" at the prospect of his experiment of gradually reducing the rations, until he should ascertain, with infinitesimal exactness, the precise amount of food a Yankee would require to support life—being interfered with, when it was so near its solution; he therefore, under Gen. Winder's order, commenced fortifying the place. For this purpose a large force of negroes was conscripted, and immediately set at work. A strong earth-work was thrown up, some thirty rods from the Southwest corner of the stockade, mounting nine light guns, five of which were trained to bear diagonally across that enclosure, to guard against an uprising of the prisoners in case of attack; about twenty-five rods from the North gate, and a little to the North of it, another earth-work was constructed, of smaller dimensions than the first, shaped like a parallelogram, and mounting five guns three of which also bore upon the prison pen. Two lines of stockade were built around the whole enclosure, about sixteen feet apart, the inner one being fifty yards from the wall of the prison pen. An earth-work was then raised on each corner of the new stockades, except on the Southwest corner. A low intrenchment was then thrown up around the North end of the whole, which extended from the main road on the West side to the swamp on the East, and was arranged with angles so as to enfilade every approach from the North, East and West. If it is remembered that the stockade was built upon two opposite elevations, it will be seen by reference to the ground plan, that an attack from any direction upon the force guarding us, would be an attack against us also; for a gun fired from any point would either be instantly silenced by the artillery in the fortifications, or its shot must be thrown towards the stockade, with nine chances in ten of its falling among the prisoners themselves;—a method of release by no means gratifying to them, however well pleased they would have been to be taken out by their friends. Nor could the place have been taken by seige, for in that event we must inevitably have starved to death, for the temper of both Gen. Winder and Capt. Wirz was such that they would have taken away all our rations for the use of the garrison, and reduced us to the last extremity, before they would have yielded the place. The prisoners were thus made the chief part of their own security.

Had Kilpatrick made a raid upon Andersonville at any time before the fortifying of the place, with a force of five thousand men, and an equal number of extra horses, with arms and equipments, ten thousand able bodied men would have mounted the walls with a cheer that would have made the Heavens ring. Indeed, it was currently reported and believed, among the prisoners, that an exchange had been postponed, in order that our Government might re-capture us; and bright hopes of speedy release animated our hearts. For days the poor fellows cast their eyes Northward and Westward, straining every nerve to catch sight of the liberating host, or hear their heavy tramp in the adjacent forest. The sick stretched out their bony arms to receive the expected succor; the strong nerved themselves to fight bravely for the coming freedom. It was a piteous sight to see them sink back, day by day, and the old look of despondency creeping over them, as the bright hope grew fainter and fainter, and a deeper gloom settled down upon them, when the last flickering lamp expired. Had the War Department been advised of the true state of the defences, it might, with little difficulty, have released us all, at that time; but after they were erected, the place could not have been taken without exterminating us.

In the early part of the summer, the camp was infested by gangs of thieves and marauders, who committed their depredations upon the peaceably disposed, both in the open light of day and in the darkness of the night. Men were robbed of money, watches, rings and blankets, openly and by stealth; some, who were known to have money, disappeared mysteriously and were never heard of afterwards; assaults were frequently made in the streets, the victim knocked down and terribly beaten with clubs, and his pockets rifled of their contents; it became necessary for the prisoners, in lying down to sleep, to attach their valuables to themselves, in such a manner that they could not be taken, without arousing the slumberer; and to such a pitch of confidence and desperation did the ruffians reach, that no one felt secure in retaining anything of value upon his person, either by day or by night. These villains were called Mosby's Raiders, Mosby's Gang, or more frequently "Raiders;" they seemed to have a regular organization, with leaders and subordinate officers; and single resistance to their assaults was useless, for the gang was always ready to support any of its members when occasion required. Occasionally a raider was caught by a strong force of the prisoners, and "bucked" or gagged; but this punishment was little regarded, and the criminal after being released, signalized his repentance by knocking down and robbing the first man that came in his way. They had means of knowing and marking the man who had money; and secretly arranging their plans, waylaid him when he was off his guard, or picked his pockets in the crowd upon the market, or while at the creek for water; but the more usual method by which they operated, was by open assault; in these cases, the place where the intended victim concealed his money, was first discovered, when he was surrounded by the gang, one of whom seized him by the throat, to prevent his crying out, while the remainder relieved him of his treasure. For a long time no notice of these enormities was taken by the prison authorities; in fact, had they been disposed to take the matter in hand for correction, they would undoubtedly have failed in accomplishing any good result, on account of the difficulty of identifying the miscreants.

Some time during the latter part of June, their villainies reached a climax; one afternoon, a man was assailed by the gang, knocked down, beaten with clubs until he was covered with blood; his bones were broken, deep cuts made upon his body with the bludgeons, and his watch and sixty dollars in money taken from him. This brutal act aroused the whole camp, for if such atrocities were longer permitted to pass unpunished, every man was liable to similar treatment, at any time; a number of the prisoners, among them the victim himself, represented the facts to Gen. Winder, and appealed to him for protection; but he refused to do anything more in the matter, than sanction any action the prisoners themselves might adopt. At the request of the latter, a force of Confederate soldiers was sent into the prison and eighty-six men were arrested, taken out and placed under a strong guard. The prisoners within the stockade, demanded a trial by jury for these men, and their demand was acceded to by Gen. Winder. For this purpose, Capt. Wirz summoned all the Sergeants of detachments and divisions, laid the matter before them, and proposed that they request each of their respective divisions to select one man to represent it. This was accordingly done, when these representatives chose twelve of the most unprejudiced from among the men in the stockade to act as a jury, selecting for the purpose, those who had but recently arrived, and had, for that reason, seen but few of the raiders' operations; a presiding officer was appointed; counsel assigned both for the prosecution and the defence; and a clerk, or Secretary designated to record the proceedings in full.

When all the preliminaries were perfected, the accused were separately tried; the assault upon the man as described above, being the particular crime in question. The trial was held in the little enclosure around the North gate, and continued about a week; men were summoned from the stockade as witnesses, and closely and rigidly examined by the counsel for the defence, who had been an Attorney before entering the army; and every precaution was adopted in sifting the evidence, so as to ensure a fair hearing for the accused. When all the witnesses had been examined, the judge summed up the evidence, and presented it to the jury, who, after duly considering it, found six men guilty of robbery and murder, and eighty not guilty, upon the specifications presented at the trial. The six convicted men were, thereupon, sentenced to be hung, and the 11th day of July named for their execution. When the trial was completed, the criminals were placed in the "laying down stocks" and under strong guard to prevent their escape, where they were retained until the day of the execution. Meanwhile, the prisoners in the stockade, had procured lumber of the prison commander, and about midway the South section of the enclosure, and a little South of the wagon road, had erected a scaffold of sufficient hight, that all within could witness the execution, and ropes were formed by splicing cords belonging to shelter tents, and such other things as could be adapted to the purpose. When all was in readiness, the criminals were brought in and delivered into the hands of the prisoners, by Capt. Wirz, with these words: "Here, men, I bring you back the prisoners in as good condition as I received them; you can take them and do as you please with them, and may God help you." They were then taken in charge by the prisoners and conducted to the scaffold, where they were placed upon the drop, their hands and feet fastened in the usual manner, a cap drawn over their faces and the noose slipped over their heads. At the signal, the trap door was sprung, and five of the guilty men, swung off into eternity. The rope of the sixth broke, and falling to the earth he made an effort to escape, but he was soon re-taken and securely suspended by the side of his fellow criminals. The bodies remained hanging for half an hour, when they were taken down and placed in the "dead house," from which they were soon conveyed to the grave-yard, and buried. A full account of the proceedings from the beginning of the trial to the burial, was written by the Clerk of the Court, and transmitted by flag of truce to the Government at Washington.

It is painful to record this event, to contemplate these men, who disgraced the colors they wore, by their atrocious deeds; but justice to the prisoners themselves requires that a full statement of the case be published. Some of the prisoners within the stockade, disapproved of the proceedings, considering that they had no right to interfere, to the extent of depriving their fellow-men of life; the criminals themselves threw their principal defence upon this point, although each asserted his innocence to the last moment. There is no doubt that this terrible retribution was both just and necessary. Their lawless depredations had spread a complete terrorism throughout the stockade; no one felt secure at any time, either in his treasure or his life, either by day, or by night; they had prosecuted their villainous calling so long, and with such impunity, that they seemed to have abandoned all precautions for concealment in their operations. It was a matter of necessity that condign punishment should be inflicted upon the guilty parties, in order that the peaceably disposed might enjoy the limited rights allowed them, unmolested. There was surely no reason why this additional horror should be added to the already overwhelming wretchedness we were forced to endure; and the inalienable right of self-preservation, secured to us alike by natural and human law, demanded the infliction of the punishment these guilty men suffered.

There is no doubt that these men were guilty of the crime of which they were convicted. The evidence before the jury was both voluminous and explicit; they were impartial men who had not suffered in any manner from their depradations. They had ample time to consider and weigh the testimony; and more than all, some of the ill-gotted gains were found in the posession of the accused, and identified by those from whom it had been taken. A less complete chain of circumstances has often led to the conviction of murderers in Courts of Justice.

Of the character of these men, little need be said; that they were ruffians before entering the army, was evident from the ease and method with which they entered upon their career of crime, at Andersonville, and the entire absence of all restraint against a full and free indulgence in their vicious propensities, left an open field for their operations. The ease with which they effected their crimes and the good living consequent upon their possession of ready means, with which to patronize the sutler and the markets, were allurements which they neither tried nor wished, to resist. The consequences of their wickedness fell upon their own heads, and the justice of their sentence is vindicated by the necessities of the case.

The course pursued by the Confederate authorities in the matter, is also deserving of credit. It was well known to them as it was felt by the prisoners, that light or temporary punishment would not answer the purpose; and they did not wish to bear the responsibility of inflicting a severe one. They therefore, turned the accused men over to trial and punishment by their fellows, only placing within their reach such facilities as were necessary for carrying out the sentence, whatever it might be. The names of the men who were executed, are in my possession, but consideration for their friends, if any such remain, induces me to withhold them; a fuller statement than this, can be found among the papers in the War Department at Washington.

After the execution of the raiders, quiet and security prevailed among the prisoners. Little acts of petty larceny occurred, as is usual in all camps, however well regulated, but nothing of particular value was stolen, and no more brutal assaults were made for the purpose of robbing the victim. A police or vigilance committee, was organized, or rather organized irself, among the prisoners, for the preservation of order in the camp. The purpose for which it was designed was good, but there were acts of meanness perpetrated by these policemen, that deserve the severest censure; for many a poor fellow, unable to help himself, was unmercifully beaten by them, without any reason for their so doing. Yet on the whole, they performed their disagreeable duty with as much leniency, perhaps, as could be expected, although sometimes failing to discriminate between the innocent and the guilty. In virtue of their office they received an extra ration, daily.

Sometime in July, permission was obtained from the Confederate government, for a number of men to proceed North, for the purpose of carrying to our Government, a statement of the situation in which we were placed, together with petitions for relief. These men were to be paroled on reaching a flag of truce point, provided a like number of rebel prisoners were also paroled by the United States authorities; otherwise they were to return immediately. A mild statement was drawn up, setting forth the fact that we were without shelter and clothing; that the long confinement we had endured and the suffering and disease incident to it, to which we were exposed was fast reducing our numbers, &c., &c. The terrible crime practised against us, by depriving us of food, and the appalling sickness and mortality among the prisoners, were not mentioned, or hinted at; to this were attached petitions for our speedy release, expressed in as strong terms as our jailors would permit, and signed by a large number of the members of the several divisions. The papers were forwarded, according to the permission granted, the men reached our lines successfully and were paroled. But no good resulted from this, except to the men who carried the papers, and were set at liberty; for the statements were drawn in such a manner as to awaken no further sympathy for us, than the Government would naturally feel for its children, who were deprived of their liberty; and it was treated as the complainings of men who were unhappy in being thus restricted. Could the real state of the Andersonville prisoners have been known, something would undoubtedly have been done to relieve our sufferings; but it was only the most sanguine that anticipated any good results from this mission, and they only were disappointed in the event.

The messengers bore many letters to our friends at home, but as is well known, a prisoners letter contains no intelligence bearing upon the manner of his treatment, in short, nothing except the fact that he is still alive and hopes soon to be released. This meager news is doubtless gratifying to our friends, but at the same time, we would like to unburden our minds of the horrors with which they are filled, and receive their sympathy. But this is of course denied us, and we must suffer on in silence.

Express boxes were occasionally received by some of the prisoners, but as at Danville, they had been subjected to search by the authorities, and after leaving their hands, contained nothing more than a loaf of mouldy cake, unfit for eating: all articles of value, either for eating or wearing, had been confiscated. Packages of letters, also, came to the prison by flag of truce; but under the regulations of Capt. Wirz, every prisoner was compelled to pay the Capt. ten cents, *in silver* before receiving his letter. It was very seldom that the villain's exchequer was benefited by this extortion; for very few men in Andersonville possessed any money of any kind, much less in coin. The Capt. knew very well that the greater number of men had no money at all, and that those who were so fortunate as to possess Greenbacks, must buy their silver of his sutler, paying therefor an enormous premium. These letters had been prepaid, and bore a worthless photograph of Jeff. Davis; but this made no difference, the Capt. must have hard cash, or he would keep the letters. And he kept them. And thus this puerile scoundrel, this sneaking thieving, cowardly whipper of black women and helpless men, sought to gratify, at the same time, his avarice and his spite; to torment the wretched prisoners, already overwhelmed with disease and starvation, the result of his own barbarity. These letters were valueless to him, but priceless to their rightful owner; and many a famished man would have bargained his day's rations, though his life depended upon them, for the precious missive, bearing tidings of sympathy and love from home. No physical torture could equal in intensity, this deprivation; the poor fellows who had stood in the stocks for four and twenty hours, under a broiling sun, who had endured exposure and famine for months, without a murmur, wept like children, when they knew that kind words from loved and loving ones, had come so near, and were withheld; yet this man gloated over their misery and became profane with delight at their tears; he carried the letters to his office and experienced a devilish joy in reading and burning them, with no one to look on but himself.

A few incidents may not be without interest to the reader, although there was very little variation in the dull monotony of our existence; but there was sometimes an occurrence which raised a ghastly smile on our cadaverous faces, even though it was at misery itself.

A lieutenant of the guard came into the stockade, one day, to purchase buttons of the kind used by staff officers. Some of the men had cut such buttons from old uniforms found on the field, and preserved them. While he was chaffering with some of the men, one of them quietly slipped behind the officer and cut the buttons from his coat, and bringing them forward, offered them for sale. The Lieutenant looked at them, said they were just the kind he wanted, and paid the price demanded, and soon after went out, where he was informed of his loss. The truth flashed suddenly upon him, and he went back into the stockade in search of the thief; but he had mingled with the crowd and could not be found. He did not trade with the Yankees again for buttons.

Soon after the arrival of the negro prisoners from Florida, Capt. Wirz sent them out to work on the fortifications, giving them an extra ration for their labor. Seeing "how the thing worked," a white man blacked himself, so as to resemble a son of Ham, and when in the morning the negroes were ordered to "fall in for work," he joined the party. He had been out but a short time, however, before the cheat was discovered, when Capt. Wirz commanded him to be put into the standing stocks, and afterwards to receive fifty lashes, and sent back to the stockade. "He played nigger;" said the Captain, "I serve him nigger fare." It was a rich joke for the old tyrant, but the unfortunate culprit did not so interpret it.

It was a standing order, whenever a new lot of prisoners was admitted, that a heavy guard be drawn up in line of battle, in such a manner as to flank the gate; and the guns in the ports were shotted, so as to guard against an outbreak of the prisoners. Taking a hint from this circumstance, some wag with an air of the greatest secrecy, conveyed intelligence to Capt. Wirz, that he had just discovered an extensive plot for an immediate outbreak. It was a broiling hot afternoon, and the doughty Captain fretted and swore at his raw Georgia Militia; for half an hour, trying to get them into something like a line of battle. When all were ready, he stood sword in hand, at the head of his brave followers, swimming in perspiration, and cursing the "d—d cowardly Yankees" for not bursting through the gate, after he had been at so much trouble to give them a reception. It is needless to add that the "Yankees" did not come out.

The Captain was greatly exercised with a fear that the prisoners would escape, and this dread, undoubtedly, caused him many sleepless nights; he seemed to think that every escape detracted so much from his honor, and to that extent, damaged his reputation as an officer. On this account, on one occasion, when the prisoners had crowded close upon the dead-line, to witness the introduction of a new squad of men into the pen, the old rascal ordered a shell fired directly over the heads of the throng. No harm resulted from it, but we felt that it was hazardous remaining in that position, and "changed our base," with a degree of haste and disorder highly unbecoming a body of veteran soldiery; but we did not relish being operated upon by an undrilled militia gun squad, when a slight depression of the piece, in their unpracticed hands, would land a shell in our midst.

Sometime in the early part of August, a violent thunder shower came up; the Heavens seemed to be one sheet of flame, and in an instant the earth was converted into a wide lake. The little creek suddenly assumed the proportions of a large stream, foaming and dashing furiously through the stockade. Becoming dammed up by the gathering weeds and sticks, it finally swept down the walls on both sides, leaving wide gaps, through which escape would have been feasible and easy, had the prisoners known it in season. On discovering the breach in the wall Capt. Wirz fired the signal gun, and the whole prison guard, consisting of some five regiments, was turned out, with the Captain at the head, to prevent accident ; and there they stood, drenched to the skin, the Captain's plumage drooping like a wet chicken's, swearing at the poor Yankees, as being the occasion of his soaked skin. The storm, however, passed away leaving the creek and swamp well cleansed and purified ; and what pleased the Captain most, none of the prisoners escaped.

On Saturday afternoons, some of the fair sex usually paid a visit to the stockade, gratifying, at the same time, their desire to see their husbands, brothers and cousins, and their curiosity to witness an exhibition of live Yankees. These females were generally much pleased with the sight of us, and contrasted our decidedly untidy appearance with the looks of their gentler blooded friends, much to our disadvantage, it is to be feared. An officer's wife, a Northern lady, inquired of one of the Surgeon's clerks about the treatment of the prisoners, and was answered with a general statement of the facts. Capt. Wirz overhearing something that did not please him, called the man to him, and, by dint of much sharp questioning, learned nearly the whole conversation, when he ordered the poor fellow back into the stockade again.

After this, we were prohibited, by an order, from conversation upon the treatment of the prisoners, with any one not connected with the pen.

Some of these little incidents seem out of place; and to laugh at the brutal 'jokes' played off upon us, is like smiling in the face of death. But they exhibit the total unconcern, manifested by our jailors, for our misery, and the ease with which men delight in torturing others in their power, when all their better feelings are absorbed, by the base passions of hatred and revenge.

CHAPTER VII.

Rations—Cook Houses—Escapes—Punishments—Removal of Hospitals—Sick-Call—Hospitals—The Dead—The Burial—Gen. Winder—Capt. Wirz.

On the 26th day of May, I was paroled as a Surgeon's clerk, and removed from the interior of the stockade; from this time, during the day I was at liberty, when off duty, to wander any where within the circuit of a mile, but at night was placed under guard at the hospital. When my duty was done for the day, I generally improved the opportunity to look about me, and to examine, as far as I could, into the practices of the prison authorities. By this means, I became acquainted, not only with the character of the men and their disposition toward us, but also with the manner in which the whole government and supply of the prison was conducted.

The rations consisted of corn-meal, bacon, fresh beef, peas, rice, salt and sorghum molasses. The corn-meal was unbolted, some of it ground with the cob, and often filled with sand and gravel. Much of it had apparently been put up while warm, and had become sour and musty, either during transportation or while in store. The bacon was lean, yellow, very salt, and maggoty; it had been brought to us unpacked, and was covered with dirt and cinders; it was so soft with rust that it could easily be pulled in pieces with the fingers. The beef was slaughtered near the prison, to which it was brought and thrown down in a pile, in the North cook-house, where it lay until it was issued to the prisoners. Here, in the hot climate, it was soon infested with flies and maggots, and rapidly changed into a greenish color, emitting an offensive odor peculiar to decaying flesh; it was very lean, but the heat rendered it quite tender, before it was served up. The article denominated black peas, or cow peas, was brought in sacks, apparently just as it had left the threshing ground of the producer; having never been winnowed or cleansed of the fine pods, and the dirt which naturally mingles with all leguminous plants, while growing in the field; besides, they were filled with bugs, and many of them were so eaten as to leave nothing but the thick, tough skin of the pea, in its natural shape. The rice was sour or musty, and had apparently been put up in a half dried state, where it became heated and wholly unfitted for use.

There were two cook-houses used in connection

with the prison; the first of these was in process of erection when the detachment to which I belonged, entered the pen, and went into operation about the middle of May. It was located on the North side of, and near the swamp, West of the prison, and was subsequently enclosed by the defensive stockades. At the time it was built, it was supposed to be of sufficient capacity to perform all the cooking necessary for the prisoners, and contained three large brick ovens and several kettles, set in brick work, for boiling the meat and peas, or rice; but it being found inadequate to supply the wants of the men, another building was constructed some time in the latter part of August; it was located about a hundred yards North of the defences, on a line with the West wall of the prison. This was designed and used exclusively for boiling the peas and the meat, and contained, perhaps, a dozen large potash kettles, set in brick work; the old cook-house was thereafter used for baking the corn-meal. A strong force of paroled prisoners was appointed to perform the work in these cook-houses; but with constant labor, it was unable to supply our wants, and about one half of the rations were issued raw.

The meal was prepared for baking by first pouring it in quantity into a large trough made for the purpose; a little salt was then added, when water enough was poured in to make it of the proper consistency, and the whole stirred with sticks to mix it thoroughly. The dough was baked in sheet-iron pans, twenty-four by sixteen inches in surface, and two and one half inches deep; the whole was divided into pones containing about a pound, and each of these pones constituted a day's ration of bread for one man. The utmost cleanliness could not be observed in mixing this "stuff;" the meal, as above stated, was partly corn and partly cob, and often contained materials that were neither of these; the water was dipped in quantity from the creek, and no means of cleansing it were furnished, and these, with the haste necessary to be made in preparing the dough, conspired to make the mixture unpalatable and sickening, particularly when cold. The prisoners who had charge of the cook-house, undoubtedly tried to prepare the food as well as they could, but all their efforts were vain, with such limited facilities as they had.

The peas and rice were boiled in the North cook-house; they were turned from the bags as they were brought to the prison, without cleansing or separation from the chaff and dirt, into the large potash kettles containing the water in which the meat had been boiled; the cooks here as in the South cook-house had no means of cleansing the raw material, and had they possessed the facilities, they had no time to devote to the purpose. To winnow, semi-weekly, a sufficient amount of peas for 16,000 rations, allowing a third of a pint to each, requires a long time, even with the aid of the best machines; but for twenty men to pick over, by hand, this vast amount, is simply impossible. Of these cooked rations there were daily issued to each prisoner about a pound of bread, a fourth of a pound of bacon, or four or six ounces of beef (including the bone) in place of the bacon, and a teaspoonful of salt; twice a week, a pint of peas or rice were issued in addition, and occasionally a couple of tablespoonfuls of sorghum molasses. Sometimes, a sort of mush was made to take the place of the pone, but, although it was a change from the monotonous corn bread, it was so unpalatable that the bread was preferred.

About half of the rations were issued raw, because of the vast amount of labor necessary to cook them in bulk at the cook-houses, or rather, because the Confederate authorities were too poor, too indolent, or too brutal, (probably the latter,) to furnish facilities for the purpose; had the prisoners been provided with the means, they would gladly have performed the requisite labor. The manner in which these raw rations were issued, has been already described; it is only necessary to state here that their amount was such as would make the same quantity as the cooked, and that they were issued alternately with the latter, one half the prisoners receiving raw food one day and cooked, the next. I have here given the quantity issued during the early part of the season; but as the hot weather advanced, and the number confined here increased, the daily allowance diminished, until it became but a mere morsel to each man. How we endured such prolonged famine is a mystery; and that ten thousand men were that summer killed, in this most horrible of ways, by Gen. Winder, aided, advised and comforted by Capt. Wirz, is most certain.

From the inauguration of the prison, constant and frequent attempts at escape had been made by the prisoners; and, although in almost all cases, these efforts had proved fruitless, the men were willing to engage in them, at almost any hazard. But the attendant difficulties were numerous, and hard to be overcome, and had no end till the runaway was safe within our own army lines. Not only were the walls of the stockade to be passed, under the scrutiny of of the sharp-sighted guards, who were stationed upon their summit, but there were guards posted at night around the prison pen, with bright fires burning, so as to render it impossible to pass them without being discovered. In addition to these precautions, a pack of fifteen blood-hounds was kept near at hand, which

were every morning led around the stockade, when,
if the track of the fugitive was discovered, it was followed up by the dogs, until he was found, or the
scent was lost; and, as if these were not sufficient,
scouts were picketed upon the principal roads at a
distance of some fifteen miles from Andersonville, to
intercept the fugitives traveling upon the highway.
The nearest point of safety was nearly two hundred
miles distant, and could be reached only by crossing
an enemy's country, where to inquire for food or direction, would be re-capture; yet the fugitive must
seek both these, with the only alternative of starvation or being lost.

But with all these difficulties before him, many a
man attempted to escape from the prison, and although few ever succeeded, their misfortune in no
wise deterred others from making the endeavor; and
many persisted in their efforts, even after several
unsuccessful attempts. There were, of course, many
ways adopted in getting outside of the stockade;
some, though the number was few, scaling the walls
with the aid of a sentinel who had been bought over;
others passing out in the ration wagons; one man
simulated death and was carried out by his comrades
and deposited in the "dead-house," from which he
departed, when it became sufficiently dark; still others feigned sickness, and were taken to the hospital,

whence they fled. A frequent method of escape was to elude the guard, when the prisoners were foraging for wood, in the forest, but this was soon stopped by Capt. Wirz refusing to permit them to go out of the stockade on these foraging expeditions. In fact, every method was so strictly guarded against, by the officials, that the same mode could not easily be tried a second time, without danger of immediate detection.

But the most frequent attempts to escape were by means of tunnels, the nature of the soil being peculiarly favorable to their digging, though but few ever succeeded in getting away by this means. There was no want of labor in excavating them, or of perseverance in carrying them on, and no lack of persistence in beginning new ones after the old had been abandoned and filled up, on account of its being detected. But there were traitors in the camp, who to curry favor with Capt. Wirz, and to gain an extra ration, divulged the work, before its completion, when he would visit the spot and direct the unlucky operators to re-fill the "d—d hole," under penalty of being deprived of rations, until it was done. The only implements the prisoners could obtain, with which to dig the tunnels, were half canteens, and their hands; and the dirt was removed in haversacks, and bags made of coat sleeves, or other cloth which could be picked up, and was thrown into wells, or the swamp. The time for performing the labor was during the darkness of the night, while the tunnel was yet in its infancy; but when it became advanced, one of the joint operators dug during the day, removing the earth to the mouth of the hole, whence it was carried away at night, by his partners. Weary weeks and months were spent in these long tasks; but after continued and patient labor; after, it may be, some who had begun the enterprise, had found freedom through the gates of death; after the work was brought so near its completion, that liberty seemed within their reach, these patient laborers, compelled to abandon the scheme by the cruel and cowardly informers, yet nothing disheartened, formed a new plan, selected a new place and carried on a new tunnel, to end in the same manner as the first. A sergeant of a Minnesota regiment, told the author, at Millen, that he had been engaged in digging thirteen different tunnels, every one of which had proved a failure, through the reports of his fellow prisoners to the authorities; yet, he said, he was as anxious as ever to try again.

At one time, several important tunnels had been for a number of weeks in operation, before being discovered, and a general plan of escape based upon them, was resolved upon. They were to be carried directly beneath several of the sentinel stands, and, when the stockade walls were reached, the earth was to be excavated five or six feet back from the timbers, leaving a shell at the top of sufficient thickness to prevent its falling in, by its own weight; when all was ready, a number of strong men were to hurry rapidly past the dead line, after dark, and push the sentinel stands outward, when an organized force was to be in readiness to rush through the openings, overpower the guards and seize the forts and guns. Desperate as this project seems, it could easily have been effected, if it had not been divulged. In all probability many of the prisoners would have made their escape, for we had men capable of commanding us, and the guard, being raw militia, would have been easily overcome in the surprise and darkness. The leaders in the plan were arrested and put in irons. The scheme did not seem chimerical to Capt. Wirz, for immediately after it was discovered, he caused the stockade to be strengthened by spiking scantling across the logs, so as to prevent their being pushed over.

The fact that tunnels were being dug was easily discoverable, by the color of the dirt thrown up in heaps, around the enclosure. There was one, however, which troubled the military detectives considerably, and which was not discovered, until reported by some of those who were in the secret. It was begun in one of the wells, at a proper depth from the surface; the workmen labored upon it every night, until near daylight, when, concealing their work by placing a board three or four inches from the mouth of the tunnel, and filling the intervening space so as to make it resemble the side of the well, they retired to their burrows for the day. A plan so ingenious, and so faithfully persisted in, deserved better success, but the traitors getting hold of the secret, an extra ration of corn bread overcame their sense of honor. It seemed impossible for a number to escape together; for where there was a combination, there was sure to be a foolish or weak one, to turn informer. It would also seem impracticable to construct a tunnel among so great a number, so secretly that none but those engaged in the work, should know of it; yet such was the case in several instances.

After the fugitive had released himself from the stockade, his next effort was to elude the pursuit of the dogs, but he was generally overtaken by them sooner or later, notwithstanding every precaution he might make. The animals employed at Andersonville, were owned, it was said, by an old negro-hunter, who lived about a mile from the station, and who received fifty dollars from Captain Wirz for every prisoner caught, through their agency. Armed with a pair of navy revolvers, astride of his mule, and accompanied by his dogs, this old man made his appearance every morning, at Captain Wirz's headquarters, and passed around the stockade, his dogs meanwhile snuffing the ground eagerly; when the track was found, the successful animal, set up a fearful yell of announcement, which was answered by the remaining members of the pack, when the man upon the mule's back blew a ferocious blast upon the horn, he carried slung over his shoulder, and all the brutes set off together, with rapid speed, in the pursuit.

When the prisoner had a "good start" of twenty-four hours or more, as was sometimes the case, the chase was long and difficult; but nothing would throw the fierce hounds from the track; they followed on, through swamps and thickets, over hill and ravine, across streams of water, and through the woods, until the unhappy fugitive was overtaken. Two of the dogs, of the pack employed at Andersonville, were trained to attack the man, at a signal from the keeper; and this signal was sure to be given if any resistance was offered. Some of the fugitives were terribly bitten, while offering resistance, and many an one, who had eluded the guards and pickets, had been returned to the prison with legs, neck and ears bitten and torn in a most fearful manner, and nearly dead with loss of blood. Some of the worst cases of gangrene in the stockade, originated in the merciless bite of these savage animals; and no medicine was ever issued to the victims, nor were they allowed to be removed to the hospital. Death by hanging or the bullet was preferable to the slow process of decay caused by the gangrene, which was certain to infect the wounds they had received.

The prisoner upon recapture was subjected to several grades of punishment, the first of which was the " standing stocks." This instrument of torture, equaling in barbarity any thing which history has ascribed to the cunning invention of the Spanish Inquisition, was formed of four upright posts strongly connected together at the top and bottom, so as to make a nearly square frame. Upon the sides of this frame and near the top, were moveable bars, in which holes were cut for the hands; each of the bars was made to separate into two parts, for receiving the arm— the notches fitting closely to the wrist, when the hand had been placed in position. Above these bars, and at right angles with them, in the middle of the frame were two other bars, containing a notch for the neck, which also had a lateral and a perpendicular motion, the latter to enable them to be adjusted to the hight of the culprit. At the bottom were two similar and parallel bars, with notches for the legs. When the victim was "put up," his feet were first fastened, then his arms extended on a line parallel with the shoulders, and also fastened, and finally his neck " shut in," when he was left to his misery, for twenty-four hours. In this painful position, unable to change in the least degree, starving, thirsting, bleeding, with the hot sun of a July or August day pouring floods of liquid fire upon his unprotected head, the sufferer paid the initial penalty of his rash attempt to regain his liberty. After the stocks came the ball and chain. For this punishment two men were usually required; a thirty-two pound cannon ball was fastened to the outside leg of each, with a chain about two feet long, and another ball, weighing sixty-four pounds, chained between them; the chains by which these balls were attached to the legs, were so short that they could be carried only by attaching a string to the thirty-two pounder, and raising it by the hand; the sixty-four pound weight was supported by a stick, when the victims wished to " walk out." The "jewelry" was continued, upon the men for three or four weeks, or during the whim of Capt. Wirz.

There was one refinement upon the ball and chain which deserves special mention; it was devised by Captain Wirz himself, and did great credit to his fiendish nature, and his hellish gust for torment. It was denominated the "chain gang," and was used in only one instance. The "gang" at first contained twelve men; they were first fastened together with short chains, twenty inches to two feet in length, which were attached to iron collars, riveted around their necks, each man being thus chained to the man on his right and left, and the twelve forming a circle; to one leg of each a thirty-two pound ball was chained, while one sixty-four pounder was fastened to every four by the other leg. There was no possible manner in which the men could lie down, sit down or stand erect, with any degree of ease; yet they were kept in this state for four weeks, in the open ground outside the stockade, exposed alike to storm and sun, with no covering but their ragged clothing, and no protection against the cold dews of the night. One of the gang was sick with Chronic Dysentery, but the surgeons' clerks were all forbidden to give him any medicine, and he died under the torture. He was taken out of his irons, after he was dead, and the remaining eleven forced to carry his share of the weight, attached to themselves, until the period of their torture had expired. The crime for which these men were "put up" in this atrocious manner, was an attempted escape; some of them had broken from the hospital, and others had been re-captured once before.

Another form of punishment, but somewhat milder

was adopted for less flagrant offenses, although it was also sometimes employed for attempted escapes; this was the "lying down" stocks. The offender's feet were fastened about twelve inches from the ground, and he was left to lie down or sit up, as pleased him best. It was certainly no easy or desirable position, as the author had occasion to know, but was much preferable to the standing stocks, or the ball and chain.

About the 20th of May, the hospitals of the prison were removed to the outside of the stockade, and located in a piece of timber to the Southeast of the main enclosure, and the two consolidated into one, which included about two acres of land. It was enclosed by a board fence about six feet in hight, was laid out in regular streets, or wards, and supplied with water from a creek that ran through the Southwest corner, and was unadulterated with the filth and garbage, either of the rebel camps or the prison pen. At first the only covering was several pieces of canvass stretched over poles, which formed simply a protection against the sun and rain; but aftewards, wedge tents were provided, and in a few instances, bunks were placed in them, upon which the sick men could be laid. Further than this, there was nothing between the patient and the earth, except his clothing and such a rag of a blanket as he might chance to possess.

There were two classes of paroled men, whose duties connected them with the sick,—the one was known as "Surgeon's Clerks," the other as "hospital attendants," or nurses. It was the duty of the former to attend upon the surgeons at sick-call, write, in a book prepared for the purpose, the name, company, rank, regiment, detachment, division, diagnosis, and prescription, for each man applying at the gate of the "sick-call" enclosure, for medicine or treatment; they were also required to put up and distribute the prescribed remedies, to the sick who were not admitted to the hospital. I was recommended by the men from No. 6 prison in Danville, for the position of surgeon's clerk, (for which act of kind remembrance on their part, I shall ever feel grateful,) and removed from the stockade, as above stated, on the 26th of May. In this position I continued to act until the 8th of September following.

When the hospital was first established outside, only two surgeons were in attendance at the sick-call, but before the summer was past, twelve additional ones, with each a clerk, were required,—so rapidly had disease increased among us. It was the duty of the "Sergeants of Division" within the stockade, to report with the sick, at the South gate every morning, at eight o'clock, or immediately after roll-call. Those of the men who were able to walk,

14

marched to the enclosure, while the disabled were brought upon blankets, old coats, and sometimes, by being supported upon the shoulders of two of their comrades. The enclosure used for the sick-call, was built about the South gate, and contained twelve clerk-stands or booths, which were fitted up with awnings, and boards for writing upon and depositing the medicines.

The principal diseases treated at the sick-call, were scurvy, diarrhea, dysentery, pneumonia, ulcers from vaccination, fevers, gangrene, ophthalmia and erysipelas; a few others were sometimes met with, but they formed but a small part of the great whole of the misery and wretchedness to which the men were exposed. To facilitate the treatment for these diseases, formulas had been prepared, in tabular form, and numbered so as to conform to the name of the disease, or class of diseases, which they were intended to remedy; thirty of these formulas were used at the sick-call. The medicines consisted of Quinine, Mercurial Preparations, Cayenne, Chlorate of Potassa, Acetic and Tartaric Acids, Gum Camphor, Salts, Sulphur, Oil and Fly Blister, a few decoctions of indigenous roots and barks and newly distilled Whisky; but for a great part of the time, no medicines of any kind were in the dispensary. All our prepared medicines came from Macon; Quinine and the more valuable drugs had labels of English manufacture, and had run the blockade at Charleston and Savannah. Bandages were so difficult to be obtained, that the same ones were washed and used, again and again, until worn out; they were made of common, coarse, cotton cloth, and were used without lint or cotton, and from their repeated application, became unfit for use, being liable to infect the wound to which they were applied, with virus from the one from which they had been removed.

The patients examined at the sick-call were of two classes,—those prescribed for at the clerk's stand, and those admitted to the hospital; the former of these two classes, was by far the most numerous, on account of the lack of accommodations for the latter; those who remained behind, were such as did not require special care, and those too far advanced in their disease to be saved by hospital treatment. The number of admissions was limited to the number of vacancies; and these were caused, not by the recovery and discharge of the patients,—not by the enlargement of the hospital,—but by death, which silently and swiftly made way for fresh victims; every man knew full well, when he received his ticket, admitting him to that living house of death, that the grim messenger had removed a comrade, whose place he was to occupy, waiting and watching painfully, till his turn should come, and another be brought in, as he was carried out.

The prisoners who had not recently been vaccinated, were compelled, under severe penalties, to undergo this operation, the surgeons having been requested, it was said, by the United States Government, to do this, as a preventive against the small pox. It seemed strange to us that here, where the instances of that disease were so extremely rare, such an order should be given; but the sequel showed the develish cunning of the authorities at Andersonville. *The virus used was impure*, and if the inoculation with the poison failed, (as it did in many instances,) of carrying off the patient, the wound would not heal, under the influence of the heat, starvation and impure air, and invariably terminated in horrible looking ulcers. I have said that the virus was impure; I judge it to have been so, from its effects, and not from a chemical anslysis of it; but there were cases of inoculation which had been made at Danville, three months previous to our removal to Camp Sumter, that took the same form, as every case assumed, after our incarceration there. The worst cases at Andersonville were caused by the vaccination; the ravages of the scurvy, it is true, were fearful, and it worked in slight scratches and open sores, caused by the bites of insects; but in none of these did it assume the horrible form that characterized the inoculated wounds; and the only inference that can be drawn from this fact, is that our prisoners were deliberately poisoned by vaccination.

The scenes at the sick-call were horrible beyond description, yet I will attempt to paint the dreadful picture as clearly as it is possible with words, for here and at the hospital, can alone be witnessed the true result of the privations and cruelties to which we were subjected. It must be remembered that diseases here are not of the ordinary form, such as may be seen at any hospital in the vicinity of a populous city, nor are they the result of voluntary excesses on the part of the patient; but they are such as were forced upon strong, able-bodied men, with robust health, made more robust by the regimen of long military service in the field, and fortified by the hardships of such a life, against disease in every form; upon men, in whose blood no disease had ever lurked, but who, from childhood until now, had been strong and healthy. And it must also be borne in mind that these diseases did not come suddenly upon us; but that they were the results of a slow process, that crept quietly, but certainly on, beginning with insignificant signs and ending in death, or, what is worse, in permanent and incurable disease, that must follow the victim as long as life lasts,—an unremitting source of pain and misery.

When the surgeons and their clerks have taken their places within the sick-call enclosure, the gate in their rear is closed, and the wicket in the great gate opened for the admission of the patients. My "stand" was situated near this wicket, and one half the sick passed it on their way to their surgeon for examination. Each surgeon had charge of a certain number of detachments, the numbers designating which, were painted upon a board, and hung conspicuously over the clerk's stand; by means of this guide, any man could readily find the surgeon to whom he must apply to be examined; and severe punishment was inflicted upon any clerk who issued medicine to a sick man that had not submitted to this examination. From my position, I could see the men as they came into the enclosure, and trace the line far back into the stockade itself. There on the road running nearly across the area, the wretched invalids had gathered, in a dense crowd; some were standing, or leaning faint, emaciated and weak, upon their stronger comrades; others were lying down upon the bare ground, and over all, there hovered a hideous specter of death, which was reflected in their squalid forms, upon their thin, pale faces, and in their large, hollow eyes, that stared glassily upon us. The earth was black with human beings, a living, writhing mass of famishing, agonizing life. Three thousand men, daily visited the surgeons for remedies, at this place,—besides those to whom medicine was administered without a daily examination. On my own book, there were at one time nine hundred and forty-five names of sick men, under treatment, by one surgeon; taking this as a basis, the fourteen clerks would have in charge, 13,230 patients; and these were exclusive of the men who refused to report at sick-call, and those who were confined in the hospital, the latter numbering about two thousand men. At this time, it is believed that there were not five thousand well men among the thirty-two thousand confined in the stockade. Those who had been longest in the stockade, and those who had come among us in a destitute condition, were the earliest and greatest sufferers. It required time, even in that den of filth and disease, and upon the scanty allowance given us, to break down the strong constitutional health of those men; but time did effect it, though some struggled long and bravely for life.

The detachments were called in regular order, each surgeon beginning with the lowest number on his list, and proceeding to the highest. The surgeon upon whom I attended, had charge of thirteen detachments; this would give him, if each division were full, 3,510 men, over whose health he was called upon to preside; but the divisions were not full, many of them having become reduced more than one half since they first entered the pen. Each applicant was separately presented, his name, &c., entered by the clerk, the date of his examination and the diagnosis of his disease, and the formula or formulas applicable to his case, carefully noted, when he was turned back into the stockade to wait till three o'clock, before his medicine was served out to him.

Let us take the list, as it stands upon my notes, for one day's duty, (and it shall be a fair sample of any day during the months of July and August, and the first eight days of September,) and read the ills that prisoners at Andersonville are heir to. The first man in the file before us, is called, and after being duly enrolled, begins to remove the filthy rags that he has bound around his arm, disclosing a sickening sight. It is a case of vaccination; the impure virus has wrought its terrible design, and here is the result. The incision has become infected with gangrene, and the upper arm is one mass of putrid flesh, which hangs in lumps in the running sore; it is but slightly swollen, and where the flesh is not entirely gone, presents a fiery red appearance; the arm is nearly eaten in two, and unless the progress of the gangrene is stopped at once, the main artery will be severed, and death ensue from loss of blood. A nauseating stench arises as the bandage is taken off, and this the man must carry with him till death closes the scene; for though he is sent at once to the wound-dresser, and his arm is washed with Nitric Acid, the disease is too far advanced to be cured, and only temporary relief can be afforded him. Eighteen similar cases follow, some of them in a less advanced stage, some even worse than this; all the cases of ulcerous vaccination usually report first in the morning.

Next follow the patients afflicted with gangrene; of these there are a great number, for the character of the food, the exposure to rains and sun, with the poisonous air they constantly breathe, render the blood impure, and the slightest abrasion of the skin, soon becomes a putrid sore. A description of one of these cases will answer for all, for few of them ever received any attention until they were so far advanced as to obtain but little benefit from medicine. This is gangrene; the patient hobbles painfully to the stand, supported by a crutch which he has in some way procured, removes the foul shreds of woolen cloth that are bound around his left foot, and discovers the wound. The corrupted flesh has fallen from the bones, and the worms are crawling and tumbling riotously among the naked cords and ligaments, wantonly holding a premature feast upon their unburied food. Terrible as this may appear,—it may be called impossible—it is the truth, and a hundred cases equally awful, were to be witnessed daily at the sick-call and in the hospital. This man had become so weakened in his intellect by exposure and starvation, that he was unable to take proper care of himself; to protect his naked feet from the blistering sun and the insects, he had torn off the sleeve of his coat and wrapped it around them; gangrene had found a scratch, and this was the result. The gangrene was a most fearful enemy, searching every pore of the skin for a wound, however slight or insignificant, where it fastened itself remorselessly and clung with a tenacity whose grasp could not be loosened. Sometimes where the incision in which the vaccine had been placed, had apparently healed, it would break out afresh, and the gangrene would find it out and commence its revels; sometimes, kernels under the arm, would swell and require the use of the lancet; a wound was thus made, in which the monster poison reveled, till death cut short its career. And these infected men were turned back into the crowded prison, to communicate their infection to others, until nearly all the wretched inmates were decaying, rotting, dropping piecemeal, into the grave.

The scurvy is another and most frequent disease, and like the gangrene, can receive only temporary relief here. It generally makes its first appearance in the mouth, the gums becoming spongy, frequently bleeding, and the teeth loosened; the breath becomes fetid; the patient is pale and languid, and the flesh swollen and livid in spots. It is caused by confinement to a limited range of food for a long time, and usually terminates in a dropsy, when the cords are drawn up, and the limbs become contorted and useless; the body swells to twice its natural size, the skin puffing out, as if distended with air; the flesh loses its elasticity, and being pressed upon by the finger, retains the indentation for a long time. Sometimes the skin bursts open, when a wound is formed and gangrene, with its auxiliary worms, and tormenting vermin and insects, brings a horrible aid, and they, working in conjunction, soon destroy the victim. Nearly one half the number of patients examined daily, were afflicted with this fearful scourge, very few of whom recovered, some of them lingering for weeks before the fatal termination of the disease. The patients exhibit a hideous spectacle, with their long, matted hair, their glaring eyes, in whose hollow depths the unappeasable craving for food is unmistakably read; their faces and hands, and naked feet covered with dirt and filth; their foul rags hanging in tatters over their limbs and their bodies, and swarming with vermin; yet this spectacle was daily witnessed at the sick-call, was fully known and understood by the prison authorities, and nothing was done for our relief, no additional care bestowed upon us, no look of pity or sympathy from them ever met our eyes.

But these were not the only diseases to which we were exposed; Death busily plied his relentless work, in other, and if possible, more painful forms. Diarrhea and dysentery, gaunt and grim, attacked the destined victim, and in a few days his strength waned, till the strong man was weak as childhood; his skin became livid, and clung tightly to the bones from which the flesh had wasted away; his eyes sank back deep beneath his forehead, and were dull and expressionless; and his thin lips were blue and trembling as if with cold. Eighty-seven names of men afflicted with these diseases, are on my list, for this day's work. Yet what can be done for these men here? They cannot be admitted to the hospital, for there is no room, and if there were room, it would be useless to send them there, as we shall presently see; we have no medicines that can counteract the influence of their scanty food, mixed, as it is, with dirt, and decayed till a dog would refuse to eat it; and in this climate, with its hot days and cool, damp nights, the naked earth to sleep upon, and the poisoned air to breathe, are swift auxiliaries to these diseases. The patients must inevitably die; some of them may live a few weeks longer; but in ten days at farthest, eighty of those eighty-seven men, will lie beneath the turf in yonder Golgotha, beyond the reach of the atrocious tortures that have made their last days a hell.

In the month of June, there were twenty-two days of rain, and the sky was not clear of clouds for one moment, during all that dreary period. At times, the Heavens opened and poured floods of water down upon us; then the sun forced its way through a rift of clouds and for a few minutes, scorched us with his flames, when his fire was extinguished by another torrent. The men were drenched in their open pen during the day, and at night they lay down still drenched, to sleep upon beds of sand which were saturated with water. When the long rain ceased at last, the hot sun burst out upon them, raising deadly vapors from the swamps, which they breathed, and scorching and parching them with fire; the thermometer stood at 104° in the shade, and in the open ground the heat was terrific. In consequence of this storm, malignant fevers broke out among the prisoners, and for a long time after, they raged with fearful violence. Pneumonia prevailed to a very great extent, and hundreds fell victims to its ravages. These cases continued for many weeks, and we find their diagnosis upon every clerk's list, during the months of July and August. Erysipelas also appeared, but its career was soon run, for the unhappy patient died in a few days, unless the little wash of Iodine, which was applied to the infected spot, succeeded in checking it at once. The glaring sun had smitten men with blindness, and they groped their way darkly, among their comrades. Yet in all this misery, squalor and filth, there was not a ray of hope; the men must suffer on without succor, and without help; the weary days seemed months, and the weeks an eternity, till it was as if we had been removed to a land of fiends, which the omnipresence of God could not reach, and a Demon more merciless, more relentless than the Prince of Hell, ruled over us.

From eight o'clock till two, the work of examining the sick continued. Day after day, for weeks and months, those surgeons labored, breathing the unwholesome air, and in constant contact with those horrible diseases; but they were patient, faithful, men, and their sympathy with the victims often benefitted them, as much as the medicines they prescribed. But they acted under the orders of Gen. Winder, and Capt. Wirz, and could do little beyond secretly expressing their abhorrence of the barbarity, with which we were treated, and their wish to alleviate our sufferings. I gladly record the little acts of kindness performed by them, for they were verdant spots in that vast Sahara at misery. Drs. Watkins, Rowzie, Thornburn, Reeves, Williams, James, Thompson, Pilott and Sanders deserve, and will receive, the lasting gratitude of the prisoners who received medical treatment at their hands, during that memorable summer, at Andersonville. These, with five others, whose names need not be mentioned, were connected with the sick-call, and are to be distinguished from the hospital surgeons, the latter being exclusively engaged within the hospital enclosure.

After the examination at the sick-call, the clerks repaired to the dispensary, which was under the control of Chief Surgeon, R. H. White, to put up the prescriptions, made by the surgeons; this process required about an hour's time, and when it was completed, they returned to the sick-call stand, with the remedies, to distribute them to those for whom they were prescribed. The medicines were issued both in powder and in liquid form; the former were enclosed in papers, but the latter,—the dispensary furnishing no bottles—were poured into tin and wooden cups, or whatever else the invalid possessed. It often happened that strong sulphuric or nitric acid, was the medicine prescribed, and this was received in the same utensil as was employed in cooking their food. It is left to the reader to judge what the result might well be. Their work done, the clerks were at liberty, till six o'clock, at which time, they were required to report at the hospital, where they remained under guard, till the following morning. Much of the time the dispensary was without medicines, and very often only a few of the remedies prescribed were to be had there. Yet the farce of examination was frequently gone through with and prescriptions made, even when it was known beforehand, that there was nothing in the dispensary, with which to put them up. Whether the fault lies at the door of the Chief Surgeon, or Capt. Wirz, or of the Confederate surgeons at Richmond, is not known. Probably Capt. Wirz is not to be blamed in this matter, for he could not increase his gains by keeping back the medicines. There were many times, also, when there was no sick-call, for several days in succession; and sometimes after the examinations had commenced, the Captain came down from his headquarters, ordered surgeons and clerks away, and sent the sick men back into the stockade. The reasons for these interruptions, were various; sometimes a new lot of victims had arrived, and were to be admitted to the prison;—a thing easily done to be sure without disturbing us, by opening the North gate; but the Captain in such a case would have failed to exhibit his martial bearing, at the head of his Georgia Militia, and the whole prison must be collected to witness the warlike spectacle; sometimes rumors of an extensive outbreak had exercised his mind, and he must get his men in line of battle, a long tedious undertaking, (there being no fences against which they could be dressed) in performing which the doughty warrior expended much patience and many oaths; sometimes, again, the pen must be searched for tunnels or for missing men; and on all occasions of like public character, the sick must be neglected; perhaps the villain feared the Confederate medicines might be of benefit to the Yankees, if regularly administered, a consummation most undesirable, both to Winder and Wirz.

The number of men admitted to the hospital by each surgeon, never exceeded eight at one time, but the usual number was three. On one occasion, however, soon after the enlargement of the hospital, Capt. Wirz issued an order that all sick men, who were brought to the sick-call, upon blankets, should be admitted; acting under this order (the surgeon whom I attended being absent) I issued eighty tickets of admission—by far the largest number ever issued in one day. The Captain was exceedingly angry with me for doing this, and cursed me roundly for it; but I pointed him to the order and continued about my business; none of the men were sent back into the stockade, but the order was speedily revoked.

15

Every person to gain admittance to the hospital grounds, was provided with a ticket, signed by the surgeon who examined him. This ticket contained the name, rank, company and regiment, of the patient together with the name of his disease, and was necessary in order that in case the man died, as frequently happened, before reaching the hospital, his name might be properly registered in a book kept for that purpose. When he reached the hospital he was laid upon the ground, near the gate, and inside the enclosure, where he remained till the hospital attendants had sufficient unoccupied time, to place him beneath the shelter of a tent; sometimes he was compelled to lie in the open air till sundown, and sometimes he was not moved till the next morning; many died at the gate while waiting to be placed in the tent. If he survived long enough, he was taken up by the nurses, carried to a vacant spot in the hospital, and deposited upon the bare ground, to remain until death should make his place also, vacant.

The hospital enclosure was laid out in streets, (see engraving) and the tents were pitched in rows or blocks, to facilitate communication with the patients; the tents were of the wedge form, arranged so as to face due North, and were open at both ends; the center pole was about five feet high, and the canvass sloped quite to the earth, forming the sides of the shelter; five men were usually placed in each tent. There were, besides the "regular" tents, a few coverings made of canvass, stretched over poles; these were more open than the "wedges" and were larger and more convenient; a few wall tents were also to be found, but they were mostly used for storing the medicines. There was nothing on the ground for the sick to lie upon, and their feverish forms, with no covering except the wretched rags they chanced to wear, were deposited upon the naked earth. About 2,000 sick were constantly in the hospital; some of the patients remained there for a long time, but the majority were speedily released by death.

The diseases treated at the hospital, were similar to those already described, while we were speaking of the sick-call, the only difference being that they were generally at a more advanced stage, and that there were a great number collected in a small area. For convenience in visiting the sick, the surgeons had divided the hospital into wards; in each of which was a ward-master, with a company of nurses. The internal regulations for performing duty, were similar to those of the United States Military Hospitals. Each of the surgeons had charge of two or more of the wards, which they visited daily, passing around among the men and hurrying through with their disagreeable duty, as rapidly as possible. There were generally six, and sometimes seven physicians in attendance, and dividing the sick equally among them, would give nearly 300 to each. With so many to visit daily, and with so few conveniences for supplying their demands, these men could do very little good. The invalids did not want the surgeon's skill; food was the only medicine that could afford any relief, and the surgeons could not furnish that.

The rations for the hospital were prepared by paroled prisoners, and did not differ materially, either in kind, quantity or mode of cooking, from those issued to the prisoners in the stockade. Occasionally, however, a few vegetables found their way to Andersonville, but their quantity was too small to effect much good; these, together with the liquor, in which the meat had been boiled, were made into a soup,—a kind of food which the men afflicted with bowel complaints, could not eat with safety, and such as no well man would taste at home.

The sick who were afflicted with gangrene were generally separated from the others, and filled two wards of the hospital. These wards presented a most horrible spectacle. I have passed through them in the cool of the morning, and in the heat of the day, when the purer air of the one had caused an abatement of the corroding distemper, and when the sultriness of the other had spurred it into a swifter career; and I have seen living men lying there, upon the bare ground, uncovered by anything except the filthiest rags, which were saturated with purulent matter, and green with mould, rotting silently away, though tortured with intense pain, the dead flesh dropping from their bones, on the sand upon which they were lying; while hideous worms, too greedy to wait till life was extinct, before commencing their ravenous feast, tumbled and reveled and rioted in the putrid mass. I have visited the field of battle, and walked among the dead, many days after the conflict, and witnessed the unburied bodies of men, thrown together in heaps by a bursting shell, slowly decaying in the hot sun, but the stench arising from them, and their horrid appearance, were less sickening and less repulsive than this. I have seen men in this hospital suffer amputation again and again, in a fruitless effort to stay the ravages of this fearful disease; and under the knife, and while lying upon the ground, blistering and burning, the ceaseless gnawing within forced from their otherwise silent lips, the low, moaning, pleading cry for food; and I have listened to this heart-rending call, and looked upon those emaciated limbs, till my blood boiled with helpless rage against the worse than brutal villains who planned these atrocious crimes, and the coward who delighted in carrying out their details.

No language can describe this bed of rottenness; since the tongue of man first learned to syllable his thoughts, such cruelties were never before devised and practised,—and words are wanting to depict them. The surgeons made their reports, in which were represented the true condition of these dying men, and begged for reform, for food, for covering; but they might as well have sought mercy from death,—better have done so, for death is merciful, sometimes, but our tormentors, never.

The gangrene wards were the worst in the hospital, but the others were shocking. Famine! famine is everywhere. Pass among the fevers; hear the dying moans of the victims of diarrhea, of dysentery; listen to the hollow cough of the pneumoniac; look upon the trembling limbs and pallid faces of all these men, and the burden of every cry, as it goes out into the solitudes around us, is food! a morsel of food! And we hear that fearful cry, growing fainter and fainter, as the famished victim sinks down into the darkness; and the feeble echo vanishes, as the turbid waves of death close over him, forever.

There was among the surgeons who attended in the hospital, a Dr. Burrows, who belonged to a Massachusetts regiment; he had been captured and sent here, early in the season, and was paroled to act in the capacity of surgeon. He was a kind-hearted and skillful physician, and devoted his time to the sick under his care, with tireless industry and patience. Yet he could do little to alleviate their sufferings, in the condition in which they were placed. He attempted to procure men from the stockade, to go with him, under guard, to cut timber in the adjacent woods, with which to build cabins for the hospital, pledging himself for their return; but Captain Wirz denied him the request, and the cabins were never built; could he have succeeded in his attempt to erect these huts, he would have vastly reduced the suffering and wretchedness of the inmates of the hospital. His well-meant endeavors were fully appreciated by the sufferers, and the survivors will hold him in lasting gratitude.

The men were deeply grateful for the smallest favors shown them, and their thanks to those who did even the slightest thing in their behalf, were such as would draw tears even from the eyes of a stoic. On one occasion, I saw a man lying upon his back, almost in the last agony; his eyes were rolling fearfully in his head, and he seemed utterly unconscious. Going to the steward, I procured a little whisky and gave him; it seemed to bring him back from the grave, and he feebly took my hand and poured out his thanks so profusely and so fervently, that (I must confess to a woman's weakness), tears came to my eyes.

Cheerful conversation upon every subject, but more especially upon exchange, had an almost wonderful effect upon the men; the poor fellows would sometimes catch a gleam of hope from them, which would brighten them for days. But there was little opportunity for the nurses in the hospital to engage in conversation with them, and they were left to their own thoughts mostly, which were of a gloomy, hopeless cast.

A Catholic Priest visited the hospital almost daily, and ministered freely and faithfully to the wants of the dying. I am sorry to be unable to state his name, for he was the only clergyman, as far as I remember, that ever visited us. He was a noble man, a hero,— for by coming here, he exposed himself to great danger of infection with the diseases. He seemed actuated by the holiest motives, kneeling down by the side of the decaying bodies of living men, in the stench and filth of the gangrene wards, and interceding with Heaven for that mercy to the sufferers, which they could not obtain on earth. Many and many a time have I seen him thus praying with the dying, consoling alike the Protestant and the believers in his own peculiar faith. His services were more than welcome to many, and were sought by all; for in his kind and sympathizing looks, his meek, but

earnest appearance, the despairing prisoners read
that all humanity had not forsaken mankind.

A number of small boys had been captured by the
rebels at various places and brought to Andersonville; some of them had been drummer boys in the
army, but many were mere hangers-on of camp.
Among them was a little bright-eyed fellow, who went
by the name of "Mike;" he was the Johnny Clem of
Andersonville, and performed many exploits that
would render a much older person famous. Being
very active, shrewd and self-possessed, he soon became the pet of the men at the hospital, where he,
with the other little boys, was allowed to remain;
the prisoners sewed a Sergeant's chevron upon his
little blouse, and Capt. Wirz told him that he was
henceforth to be considered responsible for the good
conduct and faithful "attendance" of the boys in the
hospital. When the blackberries were ripe, Mike,
having gained permission of the Chief Surgeon, marshaled his squad of boys into the fields, to gather
them for the sick. He was generally quite successful, and the cool, luscious fruit was more highly prized
by the grateful men, for the hand that gave it to
them. One night Mike did not return to the hospital, and being sought for, was found at the butchers'
quarters; for which act of disobedience to orders,
Capt. Wirz commanded him to be returned to the

stockade. He had not remained there long, however, before Capt. Wirz allowed him his liberty again. He belonged to the 2nd New Jersey Cavalry; what disposition was subsequently made of him, I never learned.

Among the prisoners at the hospital, was a crazy soldier named Jones. This man had become insane through long exposure to the sun, aided by famine, and was at times a source of great annoyance to the sick. His insanity took an immoral form, and he was constantly stealing articles of food or apparel. One of his tricks was to pilfer the wood which the surgeons' clerks had gathered for cooking, and to make a bonfire of it, warming himself with the greatest enjoyment, even when the day was excessively hot. He had, also, a decided "proclivity" for washing himself and his clothes, performing the operation at all hours of the day and night. So great was his *penchant* for washing, that he frequently picked up old worn-out coats and pieces of pants, and carrying them to the little creek, cleansed them with as much perseverance and gusto, as a professional laundress. He considered his comrades as an inferior class of beings, whose habits and tastes led them to remain in their filth, while he being a gentleman, must keep clean or lose his rightful superiority and dignity. To this end, he often took off his coat and washed it thoroughly, putting it on while still dripping, and strutting around among the prisoners with his head erect, like a Broadway dandy. He would sometimes beat the weak prisoners unmercifully, for which offence, the Chief of Police tied his hands behind him, Jones, meanwhile, grating his teeth and cursing fearfully. His pranks were generally of a harmless character, and the volubility with which he talked of his importance as a member of society, and the fearful retribution in store for the rebels, through his means, served to amuse the sick and to divert their thoughts from a contemplation of their own misery; and in this manner the poor fellow unwittingly did much good. He died, however, some time in the early part of August.

The guard posted about the hospital, either acting under orders, or from some other motive, were very reckless in the performance of their duty. They frequently discharged their muskets into the hospital ground, and performed other acts of violence, wholly uncalled for. One night, a sick man, feeling chilly upon his cold, earthy bed, arose and crawled to a fire which was burning in the enclosure. A sentinel saw him sitting before it, drew up his piece and discharged it. The ball passed through a crevice between the boards of the fence and hit the man, breaking his arm and splintering the bone of his leg. Dr.

Burrows immediately came out of his quarters, and dressed the wounds, but the unfortunate victim never recovered. There was not the slightest occasion for this murder; the invalid was on the ground assigned to all the inmates of the hospital, he was quietly sitting by the fire which it was customery to light every evening, with no thought of wrong in doing so; the sentinel could see him only by looking between the boards of the fence, which was six feet high; he gave no word of warning, but after the victim had seated himself, fired upon him in cold blood, as if he had been a dog. It was murder, as much so, as if the man had been sleeping peacefully in his bed; yet the assassin was never called to account for it, although Capt. Wirz knew the full particulars of the affair, and by virtue of his office, could, and should have punished him severely, as an example to others.

The dead-house was located in the Southwest corner of the hospital enclosure; it was formed by setting four posts in the ground, upon which boards were nailed to the hight of six feet. A piece of canvass was stretched over it, for a roof, and an opening left on the west side, which served the purpose of an entrance. To this contrivance all the dead were removed during the day, both from the hospital and the stockade. The manner in which these remains were treated, under the direction of Captain Wirz, will illustrate the value placed upon the life of a Yankee prisoner, by him; for the respect in which the living are held, even among savage nations, is oftenest known by the treatment of their remains, after the spark of life has been extinguished.

In the early morning, the dead of the preceding day and night, were gathered up, under the directions of the sergeants of divisions, and deposited in irregular lines, on the road leading from the South gate, and near the dead line. When the gate was opened, (which was at eight o'clock) they were taken up, one by one, placed upon a hand-stretcher and carried out to the dead-house. At these times there was always a large crowd of men gathered around the dead, eagerly and clamorously asserting their right to carry the bodies out. Those admitted to this ghastly privilege, were allowed, on their return, to collect a few sticks of wood, which lay upon the ground between the stockade and the hospital. The wood was almost priceless to them, for a small handful, such as they could pick up, readily sold for five dollars, and with this money they could purchase fifteen Andersonville rations, paying even the exhorbitant prices demanded for food. Sometimes the poor men, in their anxiety to get outside the stockade in this manner, quarreled and fought, claiming priority of right, in performance of the melancholy office.

In the latter part of August or the early part of September, the number of the dead increased so rapidly, that it was found impracticable to take the bodies from the stockade to the dead-house; and they were placed in rows, under an awning of pine boughs, just outside the defences and near the road to the cemetery; here they remained in the hot sun, or the storms, until their turn came for burial.

The men who died in the hospital, were carried out by the nurses of the ward to which they belonged, and placed in the street in front of the tents, whenever, at any time of the day or night, they were found, whether in the melting heat or the drenching rain. Here the bodies remained until the two men who were appointed for the purpose, came around with a hand-stretcher and carried them to the dead-house.

In the stockade, the dead were found in a great variety of places; sometimes they were lying beneath their rude tents, with their comrades, the time of their depature being unknown, even to him by whose side they were lying; sometimes they had crawled into a hole in the earth, which had been excavated for shelter, and where they remained unknown, till the stench arising from their decay, or the search at the roll-call revealed them; sometimes they had dragged themselves to the swamp, to quench, by a draught of water, the burning thirst that consumed them, and died with the effort; sometimes unable longer to endure their misery and pain, they threw themselves beyond the dead-line and were shot by the guard. In the hospital the dead and the living lay side by side until the nurse discovered them; and it was not infrequent that hours passed, before the living and the dead were separated. I have known three men in the same tent to bid each other good night; and the morrow's sun to waken the third to find his comrades upon his right and left, sleeping forever. The prisoners at Andersonville died without a struggle, and apparently without pain; they expired so quietly, that one standing beside and watching them, could not distinguish when the last breath was drawn; they were so wasted by disease and famine, that the spirit parted from its earthly tenement, as quietly as the flame expires among the embers.

The dead-house had been constructed of insufficient dimensions to contain the bodies of all that died; sometimes forty, often thirty, were placed upon the ground outside its limits, where they lay in the open air, with some vain attempt at familiarity in their arrangement. Within and around this place, the final results of our treatment were to be seen; here, indeed were the fruits of the "natural agencies," which were to do *the work* "faster than the bullet."—I have said that the attempt to place the bodies in regular lines, was vain; it became so, because of the contorted forms of the deceased, particularly of those who died from the effects of scurvy. In these the cords had became affected, and by their contraction had drawn up the limbs, into every hideous shape; the flesh was livid and swollen, even to bursting, in many places; large open sores—pools of corruption—were upon their bodies and the vermin swarmed in the rags that covered them. The victims of gangrene presented a sickening sight; the flesh was eaten from their cheeks, exposing the teeth and bones, and upon their faces sat a skeleton grin, horrible to behold. There was also the meager frame-work of men wasted away by diarrhea and fever, and the pallid lips of the consumptive. And the dead lay there upon the bare ground, clad in the filthy rags in which they died, covered with filth and dirt and parasites, their sallow faces upturned to heaven, their lustreless eyes fixed, large, staring and hollow, and their jaws dropped wide apart; their naked feet pinched with leanness, and dark with smoke and grime, and their fingers, fleshless and bony and black beneath the nails, lightly clenched as they had faintly struggled in the last agony. Pinned upon the breast of each was a white label which contained the number of the deceased.

Nor were the numbers of the dead few and occasional; during the month of August 2,990 bodies were deposited in the dead-house previous to burial,—an average of more than 96 per day,—exceeding by 1,000 the largest brigade engaged in the battle of Stone River, and being nearly seven-eighths as many as the entire Division of Brig. Gen. Van Cleve, in that famous engagement. But during the latter part of the month, the mortality was much greater than at the first, the number of dead being 100, 110, 120, 125, 140 per day.

In the early morning the dead-cart came for the bodies; this was an army wagon, without covering, drawn by four mules, and driven by a slave. The bodies were tossed into the cart without regard to regularity or decency, being thrown upon one another, as logs or sticks are packed in a pile. In this manner, with their arms and legs hanging over the sides, and their heads jostling and beating against each other, as the sable driver, whistling a merry strain, hauled them to the grave, hurrying rapidly over roots and stumps, the Federal prisoners were carried out to the burial.

The cemetery was located Northwest of the stockade and nearly a mile from the hospital, upon a beautiful open spot, surrounded by the forest of pines, and slightly sloping toward the Northeast. The dead were buried by a squad of paroled prisoners, selected for this purpose; a trench, running due North and South, was dug about four feet in depth, six feet wide, and of sufficient length to contain the bodies for the day. In this, the bodies were placed side by side with their faces to the East, and the earth thrown in upon them. A little mound, a foot in hight, was raised over each body; a stake, branded with the number on the label, placed at the head of each, and without a prayer said over the dead, without a tear from the strangers that performed the last rite, the ceremony was ended. The number upon the stake referred to a register, kept in the office of the Chief Surgeon, by a Mr. — Atwater, a paroled prisoner, in which were the number, name, rank, company, regiment, (when these were known,) date of death, and name of disease. This register was kept with great care, and if it is still in existence, will correctly refer the inquiring friend to the spot where the loved one lies. But some of those who died in the stockade, expired without revealing their name; of such only the number is recorded, and the little word, "unknown," comprises all that is left of many a brave man's history.

There were three men at Andersonville, in authority over the prisoners, upon whom the major part of the crimes committed there must rest; these were

Sergeant Smith, Gen. Winder and Capt. Wirz; and however much infamy belongs to Jefferson Davis and Gen. Lee, for permitting atrocities, of which they must have been fully cognizant, and which were done by their sanction, if not by their direction, since a word from either would have prevented their being practiced; to these men, and especially to Capt. Wirz, who devised and carried out the details of the brutal crimes, history will attach an odium and a disgrace that will last forever.

Of Smith little need be said; he was to Capt. Wirz what Sikes was to Fagan, the Jew,—a tool that could please his master best by the meanest actions; who delighted in nothing so much as in putting irons upon brave men in his power, and in mocking their tortures by his horrid oaths and ribaldry. It is not worth while to attempt to elevate him to an infamy of fame;—he was a puerile instrument in the hands of an unscrupulous villain, and in his corruption let him wallow, without farther notice.

Gen. Winder was connected with Andersonville in the capacity of Commissary General of Prisons. To him belongs the guilt of permitting the prisoners to starve and rot in filthy dens, under his own eye, and with his sanction, not only at Andersonville, where his headquarters were established, but at twelve other places, where the captives were confined. His character was that of a ruffian, viewed in whatever light it is placed; he witnessed and understood the infernal practices of the men who had the prison interiors in charge, and it was in his power to prevent them; he knew the paucity and the quality of the rations, and he could have increased and improved them; he had cognisance of the fact that the guard fired recklessly upon the prisoners, killing and maiming them unnecessarily, and he praised them for their prowess. If the Confederate Government was too poor to permit him to purchase medicines for the sick, he could have allowed the healthy men to protect themselves against the climate, by building huts within the enclosure, whereby more than fifty per cent. of the sickness would have been prevented. In short, he had supreme and absolute control of the prison, and if his subordinates failed to practice the ordinary traits of humanity, of their own accord, it was in his power to compel them to do it. But such was evidently not his desire; his whole career at Andersonville indicated that the results before him were such as he had planned, and he seemed to pride himself that he alone and unaided, was successful in exterminating the enemies he hated with his whole soul and strength, with greater rapidity than the Generals who had command of large armies at the front. By his directions, the wounded captured from

Sherman's army, were brought to this place, where he knew infection and death were sure to follow. The positions of Quartermaster and Sutler were held by members of his family; the spoils taken from prisoners were appropriated by them and Capt. Wirz. Gold and silver watches, jewelry, treasury notes, every thing of value, which the men possessed, and which, if they could have retained, or drawn upon them through the sutler, would have saved many lives, were distributed among his friends, or stored up for future use. His only hope of ending the war seemed to be in slaying and disabling his enemies, and in this respect he met with what, to him, seemed most gratifying results. Like the Tartar Emperor, he gloried in seating himself upon a pyramid formed by the skulls of his foes; but unlike him, he lacked the mercy to slay them outright with the sword, and preferred to witness their agony, to hear their groans, as they slowly wasted into the grave, by famine and disease.

Captain Wirz was of an exceedingly tyrannical disposition, and naturally a coward, coarse, brutal, intolerant, and vain. Such a man, without sympathies with the woes of humanity, and with a positive love for the exhibition of torture, when he could be placed beyond the reach of retaliation for his cruelties, was the most appropriate selection the Confedcrate authorities could have made for the fell purpose they had in view. He was unscrupulous in the exercise of his authority, which seemed to be unlimited, excessively cruel in the punishment of light offences, indifferent to the horrors by which he was surrounded, and apparently happiest when the misery of the prisoners was greatest. He was by nature fitted to become distinguished only in the infliction of suffering, and during the entire time he was in charge of Andersonville Stockade, was never known to relent, or manifest the smallest symptom of pity or commiseration for the helpless men consigned to his care. He was profane, obscene, mean-spirited and ferocious. In history he must rank with Nero for cruelty, with Robespierre for wanton butchery, with the Spanish inquisitor for fiendish cunning in the invention of new torments; without, however, the genius which threw a cloak of respectability over the infamy of those scourges of mankind. In consequence of the lack of the ordinary traits of humanity, this human blood-hound resembled more the blood-thirsty savage, than any character in modern history. If he still lives, no remorse of conscience will affect him, no upbraidings of his fellow men, disturb him; nothing, in short, will ever touch his heart save the lash he so brutally inflicted upon the helpless men in his power, or the severer punishments he caused them to suffer.

Certain orders and forms were necessary to preserve quiet and order among thirty thousand prisoners; but in most instances, ordinary police regulations would have been sufficient for this purpose. Had the prisoners at Andersonville been treated like human beings, been properly fed and protected against the climate, they would have conducted themselves in such manner as to avoid the necessity of punishment. For the lack of rations and protection against exposure, Capt. Wirz was not responsible; but in his position, with almost absolute authority, he could have done much to alleviate suffering, if he could not remove it entirely. Had he been a man of spirit, of humanity, of honor, he would have resigned his commission, rather than have remained an instrument of torture in that den of wretchedness. In whatever light his conduct is viewed, it has no palliating circumstance. Judging his motives by his actions, the candid inquirer will ever reach the same general conclusion:—that he was a moral monster— a hideous abortion of nature, devoid alike of humanity and honor, and lustful of blood;—a beast, whose instincts led it to revel in horrors, whose ear was charmed with the groans of famishing men, whose insatiable appetite craved misery and wretchedness, as its natural aliment, and turned yet hungry away from the abundant supply here afforded it.

CHAPTER VIII.

Atlanta taken by Sherman—Order of Gen. Winder that 20,000 Prisoners are to be Exchanged—Escape of the Author with two Comrades—Avoiding the Dogs—Encounter Hood's Scouts—Hair Breadth Escapes—In the midst of Hood's Army—Surrounded and Re-captured.

Daily Macon and Atlanta papers were received at the Surgeon's headquarters, containing extended accounts of the successes of the rebels, in resisting the march of the veteran army of Sherman into the interior of Georgia. They all advocated the policy of allowing Sherman to advance far from his base of supplies, without opposition, even to the taking of Atlanta, if necessary; when by a combined attack upon his rear, his communications could be cut, and his gallant army forced to retreat through the enemy's country. The rebel Generals, however, rejected the advice of the stragetic editors, and in a few days we heard of a glorious victory in front of the city, in which 4,000 Yankees were taken prisoners; and a short time after came the news that Sherman was so crippled that the Confederate forces, (out of pity, it is presumed,) had fallen back upon the Chattahoochie, leaving all their mounted guns as a present to the vanquished foe; and that orders from Sherman had been found, commanding that, owing to the *temporary* scarcity of provisions, only half rations should be issued to his men. Scarcely had the cheers which greeted these tidings of great joy to the Georgia militia, on duty at Andersonville, died away, before a negro reported to the clerks, that Gen. Winder had just received a dispatch, announcing that Sherman's whole army had occupied Atlanta, Johnston barely escaping capture, with all his command. Atlanta, the heroic city, whose inhabitants to a man, had sworn (to take the charge of perjury from their souls, let us hope, with a mental reservation,) to die before surrendering their town to the plundering Yankees, Atlanta, the great, the powerful and—the gasconading, had fallen, and its citizens were not all sacrificed. Indeed, in a few days the Macon papers were so far convinced, that it would be useless to resist the victorious arms of Gen. Sherman, that they advised the citizens of that city to remain quietly at their homes, and offer no opposition to the conqueror.

Two weeks had elapsed, since the last medicines in the dispensary had been issued, and the sufferings of the prisoners had increased with frightful rapidity.

It was evident that something had occurred to disturb the regular supply of rations, as well as of medicines, and our faithful negro soon informed us, that it was believed at Winder's headquarters that the objective point of Sherman's advance was Andersonville, and that our security was seriously threatened. We were not surprised to receive, after dark on the 6th of September, an order from Gen. Winder, that there was to be an immediate exchange of 20,000 men, and that Savannah and Charleston were the points, at which the exchange was to be effected. This news was at once conveyed to the prisoners within the stockade, (who at this time were ignorant of the capture of Atlanta,) with orders to be ready to start next morning, in detachments. The inteligence was greeted with cheer upon cheer, by the famished men, and the air was rent with the noisy expressions of joy at their speedy deliverance. The clerks, who had better sources of information than the prisoners in the stockade, did not, however, credit the proposed exchange, but saw in it only a *ruse* to induce the men to submit quietly to a removal to some place of greater security. On the morning of the 7th a train load started, followed by another at noon of the same day, and two more, on the next. The clerks reported as usual at the sick-call, but had nothing to do, for lack of medicines. In passing back to my quarters near the dispensary, I sat down as the long file of wretched prisoners limped slowly on, toward the Railroad station; and the misery here seen, presented forcibly to my mind the gloomy fate in store for us. As before stated, I did not believe this to be a movement for exchange, and the forebodings of another terrible winter in some desolate field, or filthy warehouse, added tenfold intensity to the dreary prospect. While reflecting upon the probable fortune of these men, a clerk came up to me with the inteligence that all the clerks must go on the noon train (on the 8th) or return to the prison. I came to an immediate decision as to the line of conduct I should pursue,—I had considered for the last two months a plan of escape, which I had confided to three only, of the fourteen that constituted our mess.—With two of these, Hudson of a Maryland regiment, and Beach of the 21st Wisconsin, I had conversed quite freely, and with them the plan, or rather the chance of success, had been fully discussed. Some time previous to this we had decided to escape, unless relief came to our aid, but had deferred the attempt from time to time in the hope of exchange. Hastening to them I urged that now, while the excitement attendant upon the removal lasted, was the most favorable opportunity for our project; every day we waited lessened our chances of "living upon

the country," without visiting the houses on our
route. We had to consider that we were breaking
our parole; that disappointment had attended most
of those who had made the attempt; that if it were
suspected we had tried to escape, the terrible dogs
would be set upon our track and would surely over-
take us. We were not skilled in casuistry, but it
seemed to us that it was right to adopt any means,
in our power to escape the tortures of another winter
in the hells in which we were kept, even though they
involved the breaking of our paroles. It was simply
a case of self-preservation, and we certainly felt no
compunctions in acting upon this, the first law of
nature. The only consequences we dreaded, were
those sure to follow upon recapture, and we knew
full well what these would be. As we must risk our
lives equally, if we remained or ran away, we came
to the conclusion to avail ourselves of the present
opportunity, and accordingly made our few preparations, without a moment's delay. Sometime previous
I had accidently found a small piece of a map of the
States of Georgia, Alabama and Tennessee; it was
less than five inches square, but gave the location
of the rivers, railroads and towns, from Nashville to
Chattanooga and Atlanta, cutting off half the last
name; thence it was burned in a sort of semicircle,
below Andersonville to Americus, Am being all of

that word left, thence it was torn across the State of Alabama to Corinth, Miss., and round to Nashville again. It had been in the possession of one of the guard who had thrown it into the fire, and I had picked it up from among the ashes. It seemed as if Providence had preserved it for our party. Mr. Hudson, while on duty had seen a compass upon the desk in the Chief Surgeon's office; it was about three inches in diameter, and was enclosed in a strong box. This he had secured, and, with my help, secreted beyond the reach of discovery. We expected that it would be missed and of course that the clerks would be suspected of stealing it; but by good fortune its loss was either unnoticed, or it was considered of too little consequence to be sought for. The compass and map were now invaluable accessories in our scheme.

We determined to start directly after dinner, and with that view arranged our little affairs with one of our friends, I. P. Tedrow, a sergeant of the 89th O. V. I., that in case we were never heard from, our friends at home would know that we had made one effort to regain our freedom. Our usual dinner of black peas was already over the fire, but when cooked, we were too much excited to eat. The fearful hazard we were about to make, created a feeling of uneasiness, which we could with difficulty conceal.

It was now our great object to procure as much corn bread as we could conveniently bestow in our haversacks, and convey it into the swamp, without exciting the suspicion of our own "boys," of the surgeons, and the military detectives, that were constantly on the alert for such cases. By closely watching our opportunities, we succeeded, one by one, in conveying our things, wrapped in old shirts, into a place of safety. To provide against the pursuit of the dogs, we had agreed with one of our friends, that in case any inquiry was made for us, he should report us, as having gone on the train to Charleston, in accordance with Gen. Winder's order. Unless some one escaped from the stockade, in all probability the hounds would not be let loose, and we hoped to avoid them altogether.

The day before we started, I held a conversation with a man who had formerly been the cook for our mess. He had taken great pains to gain, from the guards and from private, personal explorations, a considerable knowledge of the nature of the country round about, and had even passed beyond the picket lines, in a suit of gray cloth, which he had in some way procured. From this man, I obtained some valuable information of the nature of the swamp, and the best route across it, together with a correct notion of the situation of the scouts and pickets without the prison. Our map had been very carefully studied until we were familiar with all the points of importance in our undertaking, their location and general direction, as well as an approximation to their real distances from each other. I was perfectly familiar with the most approved methods of finding the North star, even in partially cloudy nights, and had practised running lines with the compass several years before, while at school. The knowledge then acquired, was still fresh in my memory, and we felt sure that if we were once fairly on our route, we should reach our lines successfully.

At the time appointed we bade farewell to the hospital and dispensary, and pushed into the swamp, feeling our way carefully from bog to bog, until we were quite out of sight of the building. It was the first time we had attempted to cross the swamp, and we found the undertaking much more difficult than we had anticipated, sinking sometimes to the waist in the quagmires that secretly lay in wait for us. By dint of much struggling and pulling, we succeeded after a time in reaching solid land. We came out on a steep bank, where the small pox hospital had been located, and keeping as near the earth as we could and make any progress, we moved forward through the underbrush, briers and thickets, until we reached a high, rolling piece of ground, partly cleared. Our route had thus far been in a Southeasterly direction, and as we looked back towards the Northwest, the sight of the stockade and its swarming inmates, caused a deep shudder to thrill our frames. We were bidding, as we hoped, an eternal farewell to its horrors, but a sense of commiseration for the sufferers left behind, excited a strong desire for vengeance against the villainous perpetrators of so many crimes against humanity; and we there solemnly vowed, if we ever reached our homes in safety, to do all in our power to spread a knowledge of the terrible scenes here enacted, over the whole land, and arouse, if possible, our Government to take measures of retaliation upon a barbarous enemy that could carry on such a system of cruelty.

No time was to be lost, however, for it was necessary to put as many miles between us and the stockade, before sunset, as it was possible, in case the dogs should follow us. Changing our course due South, and traveling in the woods, to avoid observation, we passed on till we came to a large field of corn. This obstruction caused us to bend to the right, keeping well in the bushes, when we were startled by the sound of human voices. Peering cautiously through the leaves, we discovered a dwelling house not more than a hundred yards distant, from which the voices that had alarmed us, proceeded. It was a man and his

17

children at play; fortunately they had not seen us, but the timely discovery made us draw back hastily into a deeper thicket, and consider the "situation." This obstacle directly in our front compelled a retreat, which was effected in good order, when we flanked the house upon the left, proceeding with great caution, lest our blue uniforms should betray us. Exerting our powers of locomotion to the utmost, we were soon beyond the reach of this danger, only to expose ourselves to still another; for scarcely had we passed out of sight of the house, before we were confronted by a large plantation of corn-fields and open land. This was a greater impediment than the other; the negro huts and the dwelling of the master were in plain sight, a half a mile or so to our left; we could cross these fields only with great risk, in the daylight, and to remain where we were, involved an equal hazard. It seemed imperative that we should continue to advance, and so we scaled the rail fence and crossed the field as rapidly as we could, keeping near the ground to avoid observation, and anticipating that at least a dozen men were on every row of the cornfield, watching all our movements with keen eyes; and though every alternate row was planted with peanuts, which grow in this climate in great abundance, we did not stop to examine or gather the tempting fruit, but hastened on with all our speed, towards the timber, which we gained in safety. The heat was terrific, and when we reached the shade of the pine forest, our clothes were completely saturated with perspiration; but we esteemed this as light, when compared with another winter in a rebel prison, and we hurried forwards through the woods, till we arrived at what appeared to us a lower open country, when we changed our course by the compass to the Southwest, leaving a planter's house and hundreds of acres of corn in plain view.

In passing over a hill covered with shrub oak, we crossed numerous well-traveled paths, in whose sand we found many human foot prints, looking fresh, as if they had just been made. We were careful to leave no trace of our feet, and concealed ourselves as much as possible from sight, by taking advantage of every bush, and scrutinizing every open spot, before passing over it. The woods were very open—which, characteristic of all Southern timber lands through which we passed, was undoubtedly of advantage to teams, for purposes of transit, but it seemed superfluous to us, in our "business." Plantation roads now began to appear, traversing the woods in various directions, before crossing which we made careful reconnoisance, listening attentively to any sounds that we might hear. Growing bolder as we advanced, we pressed on through fields and orchards, pastures and meadow lands, until we came to a piece of timber, through which a deep, dry ravine led in the direction we wished to follow; pursuing this, we were almost shrouded in darkness, though in the open spaces without, the sun was still shining. At last, emerging from the woods there appeared, directly in front of us, what seemed to be a sheet of water. Bearing off to the left we found ourselves in the midst of another swamp. This was a piece of good fortune, for while we were in the swamps, we felt sure that our track could not be followed by the dogs—a fallacy as we afterwards learned—and here also, we were less liable to be discovered, as few persons, unless driven hither for purposes of concealment, would venture into it. A sluggish stream ran through the swamp, but the water was so low that many fallen logs bridged it, though they were yet covered with mud and slime. Breaking some large sticks from the shrubs that grew here, we felt our way with them, over the logs and bits of timber, for what appeared to us the distance of a mile or more. About sundown we heard the terrible yelp of the hounds; we started as if the fiends of hell were upon our track; in an instant the awful punishments we had seen inflicted upon "runaways," flashed upon our remembrance, and we imagined ourselves bitten and torn by these ferocious beasts, returned to Andersonville,

standing in the stocks and exposed to the gibes and
leering mockery of Captain Wirz, as he laughed in
glee over the unsuccessful termination of our adventure. Back into the swamp we hurried, to conceal
in its bogs and fens, the scent of our footsteps, seeking that sympathy with the filthy reptiles that inhabit
those horrid sloughs, which civilized man denied us.
Here we waited, anxiously listening to the howling
of the dogs, till it died away in the distance, when we
knew that either they were not on our track, or that
they had lost it. Just as the sun was setting, we
emerged from our hiding place, and advancing rapidly to make up the time we had lost, we found ourselves on the edge of another swamp, by the side of
which was a field of sorghum, in which there was
some one moving about. Peering in among the
stalks, we saw several negroes still at labor, and the
plantation dogs were running and barking about the
field. Fearing immediate discovery, we beat a hasty
retreat to the swamp, and plunged through it, with
all the speed we could, stumbling over bogs and decaying wood, sometimes sinking to our waists in the
soft mud, and sometimes falling headlong over prostrate logs, or getting entangled among the tall, coarse
grass which grew in various places around us. Leg
weary, and faint from our long and difficult journey,
and footsore and hungry, we finally reached dry land

again, near an extensive field of corn, through which we skulked rapidly to a piece of woods directly in our course. Supposing ourselves completely out of danger for the night, we hurried forward through the thickets, when we discovered but a few rods ahead of us, some twenty negro huts, completely surrounded by the woods. The voices of the negroes came distinctly to our ears, as we stood watching them at their work. Flanking this place by a circuit of a mile or more, we came upon a small village on the Railroad that leads South from Andersonville, and we supposed that we were near Americus. The Railroad at this point ran through a deep cut, just in the edge of a piece of timber; the excavated earth had been thrown up on the side towards us, forming a sort of high breast-work, up which we crawled, to reconnoitre the position. Just across the Railroad was a plantation, or rather a large cleared field, over which a white man was driving some cattle. We were secure from observation, from him at least, but if he had seen us, he would no doubt have been much alarmed, for the people of this part of Georgia have a great dread of the " infernal Yanks," whether armed or unarmed.

We had now reached a place where it was necessary to halt, until after dark, for it would be impossible to cross the open space before us in daylight;

so we crawled carefully back into the thicket and waited patiently for night's curtain to fall. While remaining here, the locomotive whistle sounded, and presently the cars came thundering past, showing us that we were much nearer Andersonville than we had hoped. Soon after the train passed us, although it was not dark enough for absolute safety, we ventured on again. Finding an easy place to cross the deep cut, we clambered down to the track, where Hudson discovered a mile post, which told us, much to our disappointment, that we were just four and a half miles South of Andersonville station. We had thus traveled in a circuit of some twelve or fifteen miles, and had made an absolute distance of four and a half. But one thing we felt quite sure of, namely : if we were pursued by the dogs, they would be obliged to follow us over every rod of ground we had traversed, and we were at least twelve miles ahead of them, even if we had come out at Andersonville station itself.

Before crossing the Railroad we had determined upon the course we would take, and had now a long night before us. We should have no more doubling back upon our course to avoid houses and the human face, which was more to be dreaded than wild beasts; henceforth, our line of march was straight forwards for by traveling all this night we could place so great a distance between ourselves and Andersonville, as to preclude the possibility of pursuit by the dogs,— another fallacy learned by experience. The plan we had marked out was to travel due West, cross the Chattahoochie and proceed beyond it some twenty-five miles; then, making a right angle, to turn due North, until beyond Columbus and West Point,— both places some seventy-five or a hundred miles Northwest of Andersonville; being safely past those points, to take a Northeasterly direction and strike the Railroad some where in the vicinity of Marietta, which we knew to be then in our possession. We concluded that Sherman would follow up his recent success, using Atlanta as a new base, threaten Columbus and West Point with his right, Macon with his center, and Augusta with his left; and that in all probability there would be a considerable Confederate force both at West Point and Columbus, which it would be convenient and proper for us to avoid, if possible. Hence, we deemed it the best policy to steer clear of those two points, and, although it would involve a great deal of traveling, to make our way up through Alabama. So with compass in hand, we took a course due Westward, striking into a beautiful woodland, where the ground was clear of sticks and logs. It was smooth and covered with a thick carpet of grass, which rendered the walking both pleasant and easy, while here and there the roads leading to the interior plantations passed beneath a vault of green foliage, and looked very alluring to us; but we knew they must be avoided for the sake of our safety.

This pleasant scene soon ended, and, judging from the appearance of the region ahead of us, that it was another of those low swampy tracts, which abound in this part of Georgia, we determined to bear a few degrees to the Northwest, to avoid it. Picking our ground, as we thought to the best advantage, we stumbled into the edge of a black alder swamp, so thick that we could with the greatest difficulty force ourselves through it. Patiently pushing on, after incredible exertion, we reached a piece of timber, and presently came to a ravine which was followed some distance; but when it turned from our course, we abandoned it, ascended its steep sides, and found ourselves on the summit of a hill, from which as well as we could discern in the darkness, a tract of cleared land reached for considerable distance. We mounted a "stake and rider" fence with the intention of crossing this space, when our ears were beset with a fearful yell, which shook us from head to foot. It seemed to proceed out of the earth at our feet and echoed and re-echoed from the forest we had just left behind. We thought for a moment we had reached the far-famed "jumping off" place, and had jumped; and here were the ushers to announce the arrival of &c., to his Majesty, the patron saint of—Andersonville. Interpreting his "by your leave," in our own way, we scaled the high fence in a twinkling, and waited the result. We had been so long away from the army that we no longer recognized the once familiar bray of the mule. Fearful that there might be a herd of these indocile animals in the pasture, and that they might charge our lines to our disadvantage, if we again invaded their territory, we concluded to pass around their dominions and leave them to the undisturbed enjoyment of their vocal entertainment. Making all haste in our power, we soon came to a plantation road, upon which a cart, driven by an old negro, was hurrying along with a furious noise, accompanied by a dog baying loudly. The buildings of the plantation soon hove in sight, which, from the sounds issuing from them, we concluded were occupied by negroes, cows, hogs, dogs, cats and mules. The effect of this strange medley upon us was, for a moment, to silence our fears, and we forgot that we were fugitives from an oppression, worse than that which held these chattels, human and otherwise, in bondage. The old thought that we were not yet free men, soon came back to us, and with stout hearts we again took up our line of march.

During the early part of the evening, our way led through the darkness and solitude of the woods, where we were exposed to the attacks of brush, sharp-pointed sticks and twigs, which constantly "punched" us in the side, face and eyes. This was a serious annoyance, but we pushed on with little attention to it, knowing well that our journey was no pleasure trip. After the "shades of night" had sufficiently deepened, to bring out the light of the moon, we had the pleasure of its company. It being the early part of the month, we had calculated upon its aid in our night wanderings, and were not deceived. Its rays aided us materially in avoiding the natural obstructions in our path. At about one o'clock we came upon a road, which by the compass, seemed to run in the direction we wished to take. Following this, we found we could more than double the distance in the same time, besides resting ourselves from the intolerable annoyance of the limbs and twigs of the timber. Upon all roads, we marched at intervals of about eight rods from each other; in order, in case of alarm, that sufficient notice might be given to enable the two in the rear at least, to escape. We had followed this road for a short distance when the man in front discovered a bright light directly before us, which we supposed to be the camp fire of "scouts," who were stationed on all the principal roads at the distance of some fifteen miles from Andersonville, to intercept such adventurers as ourselves. We moved cautiously up in the shade of the fence, until within ear shot of the light, and listened. A series of loud groans reached our ears, and we concluded that some one had incautiously approached too near, and been fired upon and wounded by the picket. Satisfying ourselves that the sounds proceeded from a fork of the roads, one of which ran North from that point, we carefully retraced our steps, and when at a sufficient distance to avoid observation from any who might be stationed near the light, we leaped the fence into a large cornfield, and proceeded rapidly and noiselessly in a Northwest direction, so as to strike the imagined North and South road. Passing out of the cornfield, into a large patch of sweet potatoes and sugar cane, yet unripe and unfit for eating, (the season seemed to have been very backward, here,) we reached the road, as we expected, and proceeded Northward upon it. Several dwellings, with the lights still burning, were passed, and large, savage dogs flew out at us with loud yells, as if with the intention of devouring us on the spot.

This road was leading us too far North for our purpose, and we accordingly abandoned it, after proceeding a short distance. Striking off into the woods in a Westerly course, we came to one of the numerous plantation roads, which in this part of the South lead in various directions to the "inland" plantations, and followed it for some distance, it being in our course; but conceiving that we were going too far West, we once more left the beaten track and plunged rapidly through the woods, receiving the usual salutations in our faces and eyes from the low brush, until we again struck a road, this time a main avenue of travel, leading Northwest. It was sandy and dry, and we continued upon it for a long distance, walking in the ruts, in our usual file.

Light soon began to break; the crowing of the cocks announced that it was time to cast about for some place of security and rest for the ensuing day. Traveling as late as we dared without risk of being seen, we filed off into a large body of timber, lying West of the road, where we established our headquarters beneath a group of thick shrub oak. We had been upon the road about eighteen hours, with no rest, no halt, except for a few minutes before sunset, when we had reached the railroad near Andersonville, and were weary, faint and hungry. Our entire commissary contained only a pint of salt and four pounds of corn bread, we having found nothing but raw corn, in the way of edibles, upon our route. Having made a light breakfast upon a part of the bread, we subdued our longing for more as best we could. We had determined before setting out, in no case to approach a house, as nearly every man who had been fortunate enough to get beyond the scouts and pickets, had been decoyed and retaken while stopping for the purpose of obtaining food; we therefore knew that there was nothing more for us to eat until we found it upon our next night's march. We slept lightly till ten o'clock in the morning, catching every rustle of the leaves, and breaking of the twigs, and starting up, with our imaginations full of sudden capture and fierce bloodhounds. We found on waking, that we were quite near the road, much nearer than we considered compatible with safety, and moved to what seemed a more secure spot, farther back in the woods, where we soon discovered much to our disappointment, that we were in close proximity to a large house and another highway; and that the road must be crossed in plain view of the house. We skulked across quickly, and took up a new position beneath the friendly shade of a clump of shrub oak. We had remained here but a very short time, before we heard a man pounding, as if splitting shingles or staves, not more than thirty yards distant from us. This was new cause of uneasiness, and we were compelled to retire still farther back into the woods, where we lay undisturbed until sunset. We congratulated ourselves upon our success thus far; we had taken every precaution against all the difficulties we could foresee, and had in many instances had cause to test the usefulness of our little sagacity. But we were especially satisfied with our escape from the bloodhounds, for we felt sure that they could not track us to this point. Our travels in the swamps would tend to throw them off the scent; besides this, we had walked in the rut in the main road, in order that the wheels of the first vehicles, which might pass in that direction, would obliterate the scent of our footsteps. We were now at least, twenty-five miles from the prison, and if the dogs had not been started, we had full thirty hours the advance, with another long night to march in.

In our last night's expedition, through swamps, rivers and briers, we had obtained sufficient experience to give us an idea of the magnitude of the undertaking before us. We determined, therefore, to shape our course for the future in such a direction that, while we were secure from the enemy, (we considered no one our friend) we should also save all the distance possible. To follow out our original plan and pass due West, twenty-five miles beyond the Chattahoochie, would require many a weary mile of unnecessary traveling. During the afternoon the map was re-examined, when it was found that by taking a Northwestern course, until within twenty-five or thirty miles of Columbus; thence North, across the Fort Valley Railroad to Newnan, a small town forty miles from Atlanta, on the West Point and Atlanta Railroad, we should save about a hundred miles,—a matter of no small consideration in our then condition,—and we determined to modify our original design, so as to adapt it to this new route. We thus definitely settled upon our next two weeks' campaign, and trusted to its successful execution, to develope the proper course to be followed afterwards.

The locust, which abound in great numbers in this region, set up their shrill piping, just about sunset, making the whole woods ring with their notes; and the commencement of their song was agreed upon as our signal for moving forward; the exact course by the compass was laid out, from which we never departed, materially, lest in the darkness we should lose our latitude and longitude. Crawling from our hiding place, and having carefully reconnoitered our position, to be sure we were not noticed by any one, we commenced our long weary nights' march. A miles walk brought us out of the woods, past a large plantation, to a stream meandering through a field of corn, where we slaked our thirst (we had been without water all day) and partook of some refreshment, in the way of cold corn bread. Having finished our repast, and bathed our hands and faces, we pushed on with all possible speed over the broken-down cornstalks, and the ridges of the field into a piece of timber, through which we marched hastily, emerging at length point blank upon a large mansion, situated just out of the woods. Making a short *detour* around the building, we reached the road, but had scarcely reached it, when we heard the light gallop of a horse just around a bend, and concealed from us by the bushes, but apparently coming with great speed upon us. We scarcely touched the high rail fence in leaping over it, and hardly dared to breathe until we were secreted in a friendly cane field, and the horse and his rider had passed quite out of hearing. Fortune had favored us by this alarm, for thinking it unsafe to return to the road, we continued on in the cane field, and had proceeded but a short distance when we discovered a melon patch, in which a few melons had been left ungathered. We made no scruple in helping ourselves to such of them as suited our purpose, and sat down upon the ground to enjoy the luscious fruit. But our enjoyment was soon interrupted; a fleet horseman passed up the road, apparently on the search for us, trying, as we thought, to head off our course; when in a few minutes after he had gone, a little to our right, and in the direction in which he had come, a long blast upon a horn was

18

heard calling together a pack of dogs, which immediately set up that familiar, but none the less horrible yell, that had filled our imaginations with so much dread, for the last day and night. Our blood seemed to curdle in our veins, as we lay flat upon the ground listening to those fearful sounds; expecting momentarily to be seized and returned to our prison. But fortune again favored us; the sounds of the galloping horse grew fainter and fainter, and the deep bay of the dogs died away in the distance.

Drawing a long breath of relief, we rose to our feet, and went forward. Presently we came to a rice field,—the first we had met with—and as we waded through the tall, dense growth, wet with the heavy dew, our clothing was saturated, higher than our waists. We then crossed an extensive corn-field dragging ourselves wearily over the high ridges, while the heavy growth of the stalks, constantly thrust itself in our faces. The air was filled with the shrill tones of the locusts and the merry voices of the negroes, who had just returned from labor, and were relieving themselves after their toil, by singing, dancing, and lively chattering; until nine o'clock, we could easily locate the plantation buildings by the noise these negroes made; after that time, silence, unbroken except by the barking of the dreadful blood-hounds, prevailed. We came out into a large pasture, in which at the foot of a hill stood a house, when we were again beset by a ferocious hound, that obliged us to turn off into a pine forest, so dense that the moon could not penetrate it with its rays. Forward through ravines, reeking with moisture and poisonous vapors; over hills, where the loose stones rolled back as we trod upon them, and tripped us bruised to the ground; through pine forests, where the thick darkness became visible, and the silence so profound that the faintest rustle of the leaves was painfully loud; forward, scratched and torn by the pointed sticks, with bleeding hands and limbs, into the long fields of corn, stretching far away in the distance and looking in the silvery light of the moon like vast lakes; forward, many miles of weary marching on the furrowed ground, with nothing to break the settled monotony, except an occasional fence over which we clambered in haste, lest some keen-eyed watcher might observe us, and send us back to the tortures we had left, until it seemed as if the earth had become one vast granary, and we were lost in it. Still forward, out at last upon the broad highway, wandering among its deflections, now right, now left, over bridged streams and through marshes; stopping where the warp and woof in this intricate net of roads crossed each other, to examine the direction of each by the compass, and select our proper course; forward, past the costly mansions of the masters, the hovels of the slaves, protected alike in their slumbers by the "deep-mouthed hound;" through villages, where countless curs followed us with vulgar cries strangely contrasted with the louder tones of their royal brothers; forward, cringing and cowering, like criminals, whom justice, yet unappeased, pursues with tireless feet, glancing anxiously around, our hearts startled into a more rapid beating, by the shadows upon the doors, and the moaning of the wind through the pines near by on either side. In a shed by the roadside, a man with a lantern was seeking something, what we did not stop to learn. He turned the full blaze of his lamp upon us, as we passed lightly by, but he did not see us, and we sped on. Two men were heard talking in the road just before us, approaching nearer and nearer, as we knew by their tones. Bounding noiselessly over the fence, we lay with bated breath in a friendly corner, until their voices were lost in the distance, when we resumed our monotonous tramp. Tramp tramp, with weary feet, forward for liberty, skulking over fences to avoid the noisy rebuffs of the dogs, and back again when we had reached a safe distance beyond them; into orchards, in vain pursuit of the fruits that had long been gathered; through more corn fields, where we plucked the large, yellow spikes and ground them with our teeth, to silence the hunger within us; confronted by other dogs that chased us in double quick, from the vicinity of dwellings, which had been unrevealed or too late discovered for safety, but for them. Tramp tramp, now leaving the highway, because the light began to break in the far-off East, admonishing us that we must seek a hiding place for the day; where the unfriendly eyes of man would not find us; in the woods, over logs and through thickets, more and more scratched and torn and bleeding, yet still forward. We traced a little stream to a spring, its source, hoping to find security near the living waters; but too many footpaths converged here for perfect concealment, and we hastened off, far into the dense forest, where the disturbing foot of man would be less likely to come. And here we threw ourselves upon the bosom of our common mother, and sought rest. Remaining until noon, one of our number set out in search of water; making discovery of a swamp a short distance in our rear, he returned to conduct us to it. Bending low upon our faces, we slaked our burning thirst from the bogs, and lying down again, slept.

When we awoke, the rain was pouring down in torrents; but it soon cleared off, leaving us, strange as it may seem, greatly refreshed. We made a hasty meal of raw corn, moistened by water from the swamp, and marked out our course for the coming night. The locusts commenced their evening concert, announcing that it was time for us to begin our journey. Our path was due North, and led us through woods and fields, through swamps, and over ridges. The high rolling lands seemed to lay in beds, with a ravine upon one side, and a swamp upon the other. On these rich lands we usually found several melon patches, upon which enough of the fruit was left ungathered, to satisfy our wants, and we did not hesitate in appropriating it. Traveling on in this manner, without incident or adventure, save being drenched with crossing through six swamps, and as many intervening fields, covered with high grass and weeds, and wet with the recent rain, we came to a region that seemed to be low and level and to stretch far away in front and on our right. The night fog had settled heavily down upon it, giving it the appearance of a fertile tract, such as frequently occurs in the lower valley of the Mississippi. Having rested a few moments, to take observations of our position, we pushed forward, and immediately encountered the tall, stubborn weeds of the low lands, through which we forced our way with extreme difficulty, they being strong, wet and high above our heads. These overcome, after a painful and protracted struggle, we reached clear ground again, or rather another of those almost interminable cornfields. Field after field of the tall, white stalks, upon which the grain was still unpicked, succeeded each other for miles, in one continuous line, interrupted only by an occasional swamp or ravine. Tired at length of the mud, we left the plowed ground and struck upon a pine ridge which promised better traveling. But we were disappointed in the change, for scarcely had we entered the pines when we began to descend a declivity, down which we handed ourselves, as it were, by hanging to the bushes. It seemed as if we were going down into the mouth of some bottomless pit, so profound was the darkness, and so steep the descent. At the bottom we found another swamp. We were each armed with heavy oak sticks, both to defend ourselves in case of sudden attack, and to feel our way, when, as in the present case, the path was rough and uncertain. It was my turn to lead the advance, which I did, using my "stick" to probe the foundation at every step. At first the mud and water were shallow, but as we advanced, they became deeper and deeper; the prickly vines crossed and re-crossed each other, in every conceivable shape, forming a complete net-work, through which, in the darkness, we found the utmost difficulty in forcing a passage; to this, were added tall cane brakes and a species of palm, whose broad leaf closely resembled those used at the North for fans, and what with mud and water, vines, brakes and palm, we found our enterprise anything but a pleasure excursion.

By the feeble moonlight, the tall decayed trees could be faintly traced upon the lighter back ground of the sky, standing farther and farther off in our front, and indicating that the morass continued in their direction as far as the eye could reach. Probing the foundation, we found our walking sticks could be buried vertically in the yielding mud. We had now struggled with all our might for an hour, and had made a distance of ten rods, since entering the swamp. It was impossible to go on any further in that direction, for at every step forward, the ground grew more and more unfavorable. We already stood in the mire up to our knees, with every prospect of sinking still deeper if we attempted to advance. There was no alternative but to retrace our steps as rapidly as possible, and to change our line of advance in some other direction. Turning back accordingly, we took a course along the left border of the swamp, which led us in a Westerly direction, and pursued it for the small matter of twelve miles. It is not probable that the swamp extended that distance in a direct line; whether it did or did not, or even much further, we never knew;—for to us, as we followed its outline in the darkness, it seemed like a monster star in form, with rays situated something like a mile apart; and, in our progress, we, for want of a knowledge of its true position, were obliged to trace each ray separately, so as to keep near the main body and not lose our course.

We had encountered the swamp at about ten o'clock, and it was now two; we had thus far made no actual progress, and, halting for a few minutes to recover our breath, we prepared for another assault, at a point which seemed to be easily carried. We successfully beat down the tall reeds which were placed as a close body of skirmishers upon the front, and sharply attacked the main works. But we were here met with a strong line of briers, so firmly interwoven that we were forced to retreat, after each of us had been severely wounded. Satisfied that a close engagement was no longer practicable, we returned to our old tactics and proceeded to flank the enemy, which we did triumphantly just as morning began to dawn. We had traveled twenty miles, in the swamp and out, since ten o'clock. It is needless to add that we were completely jaded; it was the hardest night's work upon our trip, for the bushes were wet with the heavy shower that fell in the early part of the evening, and when we struck a field, the mud adhered closely to our shoes, compelling us to carry a mass of earth, in addition to our own weight, that made it very tiresome, to say the least. We had not seen a road for the last twenty miles; and we began to feel apprehensive that we had become lost in a wilderness of morass and cornfields.

We sought the friendly shelter of a piece of timber which was situated upon a slight rise of ground, and from it we could overlook the monster swamp which had proved so inimical to our progress; when the consoling fact was revealed that, if we had turned a short distance to the right, on our first encountering it, instead of taking the left, we could easily have crossed without going much out of our course. In fact, we had struck it near its northern limit, and had passed almost around it in the darkness. So we betook ourselves to the wet leaves and waited patiently for the sun to rise and dry our clothes and our bed. Our larder contained the remains of the corn bread we had brought with us from the prison, but it was wet and sour; we made the most of it, however, rather than to fast, and rested as best we might. During the day, we were visited by a member of the porcine tribe, that grunted his " good morning " to us, and after a short inspection, departed with a satisfactory " all right." The voices of the blacks informed us that we were but a short distance from a dwelling, and soon we heard one of them praying a little distance off. These sounds admonished us that we must remain very quiet in our hiding place; which we did until night.

As usual, we had marked out our course for the night's march, and when darkness came, we set out again, much refreshed from our fatigue, but nearly famished. The route lay through interminable cornfields, on each alternate row of which peas were growing. The growth of these was remarkable, nothing in the North that we had ever seen, equalled their luxuriance. It was impossible to believe that our scant rations of these two articles was caused by a scarcity, as we had been so often told at Andersonville; every plat of arable land, whether large or small, was carefully planted with these kinds of food. In all the lowlands through which we passed, we found a system of drainage. These drains, as nearly as we could judge in the darkness, were from ten to twelve feet in width, and from eight to ten in depth; where the land was very low, there would often be three or four of these drains in the distance of half a mile, running parallel with each other. In many of them, the water was six feet in depth, while in others, it was not more than eighteen or twenty inches. On either bank was a heavy growth of blackberry vines, forming a perfect hedge, sometimes growing over the ditch, so as nearly to meet in the center. As our route lay in a direct line, we often found great difficulty in crossing these; the briers had to be pulled apart and trampled upon; the steep side of the ditch to be clambered down; the water to be waded through or swam over; and when the opposite side was reached, it could be climbed up only by pulling upon the vines growing there; while the darkness added greatly to the difficulties of the passage. The briers tore our clothing badly, and scratched our hands and faces, leaving wounds that did not heal for weeks. We had traveled but a short distance through the fields, before we came to a well-trodden road, the first we had seen for nearly two days, which from its appearance of being much used, and having an East and West course, we concluded must lead to Columbus; we thought it best, for this reason, to avoid it as much as possible, and therefore, crossed over into the adjacent fields where we found a patch of ripe sweet potatoes, to which we helped ourselves with the freedom of proprietors, and went on.

It was now eleven o'clock by the stars, and we had traveled thus far undisturbed. To vary the stillness of the tramp, three of those terrible blood-hounds suddenly set up a fearful howling, a few rods ahead of us, in the road, by the side of which we were walking. We sprang off to the left, to give them a wider berth, but the farther we advanced, the louder they barked; when quite near them we found ourselves in the vicinity of a large pond, which stretched quite out of sight both to the right and left. Following along its edge to the left for a couple of miles and finding no place to cross, we retraced our steps to the point where we met the dogs. Though they were still baying, they had passed back a half a mile or more, and we ventured to cross the water upon the long bridge which spanned it at this point. We carefully scrutinized each turn and bend, each corner and shadow, lest some lurking foe might intercept and seize us, for we anticipated that rebel pickets might be stationed here, to apprehend runaways from their own lines. Nothing, however, occurred to disturb us, either while crossing the bridge, or while passing through the silent village that stood at the farther end of it.

The remainder of this night was passed much in the usual way; the dogs did not alarm us again, (they had already cost us four good miles of extra travel) and we hurried on, over the accustomed number of hills, fields, ravines and drains. Late in the night we were fortunate in finding an apple orchard, where we filled the space in our pockets and haversacks, left by the sweet potatoes and sugar cane, which we had likewise picked up in our route. We sought shelter for the day on a rocky hill which rose high above the surrounding eminences, and had the appearance of being seldom visited. Its summit was covered with loose chestnut leaves which were lying upon the ground to the depth of several inches, affording a fine and warm place for rest; and from it we had an excellent view of the surrounding country for a great distance on either hand. We spent the long day very agreeably, dividing our time between munching our raw potatoes, apples and sugar cane, discussing the prospect before us and the difficulties we had already overcome, and taking a needful amount of rest. Our map was carefully examined, and our locality ascertained as nearly as might be; we had kept a full and correct record of our course from the start, and estimated the distance we had traveled as accurately as we could; we judged ourselves to be in the vicinity of the railroad running from Columbus to Fort Valley, and made, in our calculations for the night's march, all preparations for crossing it.

Our journey was again through fields and timber land. We passed the residences of many wealthy planters, whose surroundings were pervaded by an air of opulence and luxury. Large groves of various species of trees, were spread out in their front, affording a grateful shade, in the fierce heat of the climate. The "servant's quarters," were usually arranged in lines around the main building; and on many plantations were various kinds of shops, a gristmill, and a church, the whole resembling a small village. In passing these houses we were invariably assailed by the dogs, which we tried to avoid by making a circuit of greater or less extent. Sometimes, however, we drew near together and pushed boldly past them, being careful to do nothing to irritate them against us. About midnight we entered a forest of pine, in which we continued until morning. We chose our resting place for the day beneath a giant pine, where we remained till night undisturbed except by a flock of quails that visited us.

At the usual signal, we resumed our march. The greater part of the night was spent in getting clear of the forest, and though we occasionally crossed a wagon track, we saw no signs of cultivated land. It was a matter of much wonder to us, that we did not find the railroad, for if our distances had been correctly estimated, we must be very near it. Towards morning we heard the loud roar of a heavy body of water, and turning in the direction from which it seemed to proceed, we soon came to a high mill dam, over which a torrent of water was rushing, and crossed the stream on a foot bridge of hewn timbers. We had scarcely reached the opposite side when the welcome sound of the locomotive whistle, assured us that we were traveling in the right direction, and were near our journey's end. With light spirits we bounded forward, and after walking about two miles we discovered the track, at a point which we judged to be near a station, because of the numerous forsaken, dilapidated shanties, which we found there. We now desired to discover a mile-post, to learn how far we were from Columbus, as that would give us our exact latitude and longitude, and enable us to perfect our plans for the remainder of our flight. We accordingly continued upon the track for the distance of two miles or more, searching for the post, but without success; for as we afterwards learned, the mile posts upon this road, (an exception to the general rule, upon Southern railroads) were placed away from the track, and near the fence. Daylight again appearing admonished us that we must abandon the open country and seek security in some more retired spot. We found a favorable locality in a patch of "hog brakes" and low bushes, and passed the long day without food.

We had been so long in reaching the railroad, that we thought our course hitherto had been too far West; so when the hour for starting came, we took a line due North. Our first experience was in a piece of thick woods, in which the darkness of a dungeon reigned; no sooner were these passed than we entered a hedge of cane brakes, growing so compactly and so interlaced together, like a strong net work, that we could penetrate it only by exerting all our strength; these overcome, we next encountered a river which was easily forded, then another hedge, then low timber land. The night was exceedingly dark and we were in danger of losing our way, because we could not consult the compass; but we caught a couple of lightning bugs, (being without matches) and these being confined in the box, and touched up as occasion required, afforded sufficient light to disclose the needle. It was necessary to refer to the compass at nearly every step, while we were in the woods, or any other dark passage, lest we should change our course; many times, five minutes after having entered the darkness, in an exactly North direction, on consulting our guide, we have found ourselves going exactly South. The same result will follow, if one attempts to walk blindfold to a distant object. In fact, the compass was our sole reliance upon our entire journey; for without it we must have inquired our way or have been lost, either of which events would surely have occasioned our recapture.

The river made several short turns at this point, of which fact we were of course unaware, at the time, and following the compass in a straight line, we were compelled to cross it three times in as many miles. The second passage was effected upon a log lying about a foot under the water which was fortunately found to extend nearly to the farther side of the stream. The third, however, presented a greater difficulty. The stream was too deep to be forded, and too wide for any but experts to attempt to cross by swimming. Luckily a grape vine which had grown up into a tree, on the opposite side of the river, was within reach; this we seized and cut off, so that it would swing clear of the water. It being about three-fourths of an inch in thickness, was easily climbed, hand over hand like a rope. I was the leader of the party, for that night, and it devolved upon me to make the first trial of our novel suspension bridge. Ascending it rapidly until my feet would be above the water, as I passed over it, I commenced oscillating like a pendulum, until I had gained sufficient momentum to carry me over, to the tree, when clenching its trunk with my legs, I slid down safely to the ground. I then threw the grape vine back to my companions, who each followed successfully. This was our "bad place;" and after resting a few minutes, to recover our breath, we resumed our journey with no farther adventures for that night.

The next night's march was much like the others,

and being accomplished, we sought concealment. We had hardly awakened from our first brief nap, when the noise of some one splitting timber and the rumbling of wagons, announced that we were very insecure. We kept our place till afternoon, when Hudson and myself lay down to sleep. Scarcely had I become unconscious, when I was aroused by a twitch of my blouse by Mr. Beach, who was standing sentinel, and springing suddenly to my feet, I saw two small boys, accompanied by a large, fierce looking dog, passing on a little foot path, directly in front of us. The dog attracted by the scent, made toward the spot where we were crouching, barking furiously. The situation was dubious, for a moment; for the bristling mane of the beast and his savage growl evinced hostile intentions. We did not, on the whole, so much fear his bite as his bark; for we could defend ourselves against the one, with our stout oak cudgels, but if the other attracted the boy's attention to us, they would alarm others, and we should be discovered. Fortunatly, as we raised our clubs to ward off any attack, he might be disposed to make, the boys whistled to him, when, dropping his tail as if he was aware that he had made a mistake and was ashamed of himself, he ran away. It was an exceedingly narrow escape, for if the boys had advanced a half a dozen yards towards us, we must have been discovered. As soon as they were out of sight, we proceeded to change our base with great rapidity. We heard them return a few hours afterwards, but escaped their observation.

It was now Thursday, and we had been on our route just one week; our success thus far had been all we had reason to expect, while our prospects of ultimately reaching our lines in safety, were bright and promising. With cheerful hearts we pursued our way, as soon as the gathering darkness afforded protection. Our course during the early part of the evening, was through ravines, over steep, rocky ridges, where we were in constant danger of tumbles and bruises, from stepping upon the loose cobble stones that abounded, and through forests and fields. Coming suddenly to the terminus of one of these long ridges, on the top of which we had traveled for the matter of ten miles or more, we saw a broad belt, like silver, stretching far away in our front, and winding gracefully around the base of the ridge, to the right. No river had been set down at this point in our calculations, and it was, therefore, a matter of no little surmise, what stream it could be. Descending the hill, and examining the river, we found that its course was Southeasterly; while from its size we judged it to be the Flint, which we supposed was far to the East of us. Our first thought was to follow it up, until we came to a ford, but in the attempt, we discovered that we should be obliged to cross so many tributaries, if we continued, that it would be better to effect a passage of the one stream, and have done with it, than to be compelled to wade through so many. We accordingly made search for a shallow place through which we could safely wade; but finding none, we abandoned that plan also, and turning back from the river, struck off to the Northwest farther inland, in the direction, as nearly as we could make out, of Newnan, on the Atlanta and Montgomery Railroad. No new adventure worthy of narration, occurred to us, during the night, and we passed the following day upon a high ridge, overlooking the country for miles on either hand; from which, also, we caught sight of the steeples and chimneys of Greenville.

The sun being out of sight, we proceeded, in the usual order, on the left of the road,—which we had abandoned late the night before, on account of a furious assault of the dogs,—with the view of flanking the dwelling, which they protected; which piece of strategy being victoriously effected, after spending an hour in attempting to ford a stream that was not fordable, and to get over a swamp that could not be got over, and in coming back to our original base,— we reached the road. Scarcely had we settled into a walk, when two men were discovered a few rods ahead, approaching us. We bounded over the fence and waited until they passed by; returning again, we were startled by the baying of a hound in pursuit of something, cheered on by its master with his horn. This circumstance, together with the fact that the road was beaten with much travel, warned us that the better policy was to abandon the highway entirely. Acting upon this hint, we struck off into the fields, traveling over the accustomed variety of ground. Rain commencing to fall about midnight, rather than continue exposed to it, we turned into an old log building, that had been used for storing cotton, where we remained until daylight, changing our quarters at that time, lest they might be visited during the day. Striking into a thicket on one side of us, a chestnut tree was discovered, upon which was a grape vine, whose clusters of rich, ripe fruit, tempted us to halt. Gathering our hats full of the grapes, we hurried through the thicket to avoid some boys that were playing in the cotton field we had just left, and finally stopped upon the bank of a beautiful stream of clear water. Here Beach and Hudson threw themselves upon the ground and were soon lost in sleep, while I stood sentry over them. The boys were approaching nearer and nearer to us, in their play in the cotton field, and had already passed over the ground we had occupied but a few minutes before. I was intently watching their motions, fearful that they would make their appearance on our side of the thicket and discover us, when I suddenly heard the crackling of twigs behind me. Turning quickly round and seeing nothing, I supposed it to be a pig making his way to the brook for water, and returned to my observation of the boys. Presently the crackling in the thicket grew louder, and upon looking again, I saw to my great terror, an old negro coming directly towards us. My first impulse was to rouse my companions and flee; but as the intruder was not more than a hundred yards from us, and would certainly discover us if we moved, I determined to wait till he came up, and throw myself upon his good nature. With a feeling of horrible curiosity, I watched his approach, speculating upon how near he would come before discovering us; whether he would be frightened when he saw us; whether he would run back and report his discovery, at the plantation, or whether he would not be so intent upon his pursuit (he was angling) as to pass us without observation. I even counted the number of steps he took forward, and calculated with eager curiosity, how many more he would have to make, before reaching us; and it seemed hours that I stood there with my gaze fixed upon him. He came within fifteen yards, before he saw me, and when he raised his eyes and I knew that I stood revealed before him, all my fear was gone, and in its place was as strong a feeling to conciliate him and make him our friend. This I proceeded at once to do, and found it an easier matter than I had hoped. I gave him as vivid an account of our treatment at Andersonville as I was able, and then rapidly sketched the perils of our escape. His sympathies were strongly enlisted in our behalf, and he volunteered us all the aid in his power to render. Feeling sure that he might be of service to us, I then aroused my comrades, when we learned from him the situation of affairs in our front, which, as it afterwards proved, was entirely accurate.

Three days before, there was a force of one thousand men encamped a mile and a half from where we were resting, which had since moved East; Hood's whole army was, at that time, stationed near Griffin, East of the Flint river, and was probably there still; we were on the direct road to Atlanta, by way of Newnan, to which latter place it was nineteen miles; our best and shortest route to Atlanta, was the one we were then upon. After giving these particulars, the negro told us that his master, formerly a Colonel in the rebel service, had been killed in the battle of Kenesaw mountain, and that his mistress was destitute of nearly all kinds of provisions, for which reason he could not answer our urgent appeal for food. Having wished us success, and promising to reveal our presence to no one, he passed on down the stream; as soon as he was fairly out of sight, we moved three miles farther back into the woods, as a precaution against being informed against, where we remained unmolested until night.

We pushed forward after sunset, calculating to reach Newnan in two nights, if the difficulties of the journey were not greater than usual. Coming suddenly upon a stream in the midst of a piece of timber land, we were forced to strip ourselves and ford it; narrowly escaping drowning, for the water was over our heads, we finally reached the opposite side in safety, only to encounter new difficulties and dangers. The late rains had swollen the streams, which had laid the surrounding country under water, or converted it into one vast slough; the mud and water were "awful," in the strongest sense of that term, and with the darkness, made the scene absolutely appalling. There was, however, but one way out of it, and that was straight forward. Plunging on then in our course, we floundered through the mud, scrambling about in the darkness, with the compass and lightning bugs as our only guides, for several hours, until by dint of hard labor, we reached a highway, pointed out to us by our colored friend. This gained, our progress for the remainder of the night was as rapid as it had formerly been slow, and when day dawned, we sought our usual refuge in the woods, where we remained secure till dark.

Striking out at the accustomed hour, we reached the road we had abandoned in the morning, and pursued our journey in safety upon it for a long distance. We came at length to a point where a second road crossed the one we were pursuing in an oblique direction, and we were extremely puzzled which of them to follow up. Selecting the one which appeared the most eligible, we advanced upon it, and were led directly into the grounds of a wealthy planter, where the track abruptly terminated. There was no other solution of the difficulty, we now found ourselves in, than to retrace our steps to the highway we had left, which we proceeded to do. With this little delay, we pushed on rapidly for the railroad, which runs from Atlanta to Montgomery, and reached it at one o'clock the next morning. Passing up the road a short distance, we found a mile post, by which we learned that we were forty-one miles from Atlanta and forty-five from West Point. Our feelings on making this discovery can be better imagined than described; two nights more—and we should be safely lodged with our friends; our trials and labors would be over; the liberty we had sought, through so many hardships and dangers, would be gained. But, as it proved, our perils were not yet over.

We marched on with light hearts and firm tread, Hudson in the van, Beach in the center, while I brought up the rear. It was agreed that whenever the leader came to a switch, he should halt and wait till we all came up; when, as the switch was pretty sure evidence of a station near by, we were to flank the place, either to the right or left as circumstances might indicate for the best. We saw many of the effects of McCook's recent cavalry raid upon the railroad, and inferred from the fresh earth in the fills, and the number of new ties, that he had damaged the rebels considerably. Two long side tracks were soon met with, but Hudson, either not noticing them, or led by a spirit of recklessness, passed on rapidly; we dared not shout to him to call him back, and followed on with great caution. As soon as we reached the station, a dog flew out at Hudson, barking furiously, and while we were yet abreast the platform, a man, aroused by the barking of the dog, jumped to his feet. We kept on as fast as we could, concluding that we had fallen upon a difficulty, that could best be solved by putting on a bold face and resolutely proceeding. When I reached the platform, the dog sprang for me, but, as I raised my club to smite him, the man on the platform called him off. Scarcely was this danger passed, when we came upon a fresh one, in the form of a rebel soldier, who was sitting on one of the rails of the track, with two canteens swung from his shoulder. He saluted Hudson and asked him, "where we all's gwain"; to which the reply was, that we were going a short distance up to see our friends, before Sherman advanced. When I came up he propounded the same question to me, to which I replied like Hudson. Thanks to his bibulatory taste, he did not prosecute his inquiries further; and as we did not incline to make an intimate acquaintance with him, we hurried on, with increased faith in army whiskey. It was evident that no trains ran on this road, for the reason that the track between the rails was filled with thick mud, washed upon it by the heavy rains, and there were no marks such as would have been made by the flanges, if the car wheels had passed over it; from which we also drew the inference that no considerable army could be stationed further up on the road, because, if such had been the case, it would have been employed to transport supplies.

Hudson's blundering through the place, in the manner he did, although it led to no disaster, rendered us somewhat timid of his leadership; and by common consent I took the van, as I thought I could see objects which neither of the others noticed. Every mile was now bringing us nearer Atlanta, and it is safe to assert that the "grass did not grow under our feet." Some three or four miles from Newnan, in the direction of Atlanta, where we encountered the "inebriated soldier," there is a deep cut, curving round to the left, nearly three-fourths of a mile in length, with banks so high and steep that it is next to impossible to ascend them. It occured to me, on entering this cut, that it would be a bad place to be caught in, and I took every precaution against that event. When nearly through the pass, I imagined that I saw picket fires, a little on one side of the track, reflected upon the clouds; at the same instant I caught sight of what appeared to be some object moving directly toward us. Not wishing to give a false alarm, or turn back a half a mile or more, without a certainty of the necessity for doing so, I lay down by the track, in such a position as to get the object between me and the light, when the figure of a man was plainly to be perceived, approaching us. I turned back as quickly as possible, and whispered my discovery to my companions, when we retreated upon a double-quick out of the cut. As soon as we were fairly out, we sprang over the railroad fence, and waited further developments. Nothing more occurring, we marched on in the fields by the side of the railroad, until Hudson, becoming disgusted with the tall, wet grass and weeds, which made the walking disagreeable enough, and complaining of our childish fears, we finally told him to lead on, and we would follow him. He did so, making direct for the railroad again; we came in sight of it, after struggling through swamp, briers and thicket, at a point where there was a heavy fill. Following Hudson through the last patch of briers, I looked up towards the railroad, where I saw two soldiers, with fixed bayonets, walking rapidly in the direction of Atlanta; we had been recognized as we passed through Newnan, and they were in pursuit of us, fortunately missing us on account of our having been frightened from the railroad by the supposed picket fire. I whispered Hudson, who had not then seen them, but could not make him hear me, when I sprang forward, and, touching him with my cane, pointed them out to him. He was perfectly satisfied that it was no longer safe to travel upon the railroad that night, and consented to leave it for the present, keeping well to the left of the track, though near enough to it to hear a train if one chanced to pass. We soon struck into a body of woods, when, as it was near morning, we concluded to stop and await the coming night. The negroes in the adjacent fields kept up a continual chattering during the entire day; and the crowing of the cocks, which seemed like notes of triamph and omens of success, cheered us in our solitude.

The day was dark and rainy, and about three o'clock in the afternoon we ventured to move forward under the shelter of the woods, in a line parallel with the railroad. For some distance we continued in this manner, but the woods gradually becoming thinner, we could remain in them no longer, except by crossing the railroad. Carefully reconnoitering the road, and finding it quite clear of anything human, we skulked across it, into the woods beyond; here we came upon a highway, and were about to hurry over it, when we heard a swift galloping, as of a large body of horse, rapidly increasing in loudness as the troop neared us. We lost no time in retreating under the bushes, where we watched the animals' legs until the whole number had passed, when we crossed the road and continued forward until we came to an open field, where, for prudential reasons, we halted until darkness should render a further advance secure. It was now the 20th of September, and the moon did not rise till near eleven o'clock; if it should continue cloudy and misty as it now was, the darkness would be so great as to render traveling in the early part of the evening, until the moon rose, almost impossible. We were in the midst, or at least in the immediate vicinity of, a body of soldiers, but whether they were our friends, or our enemies, we could not determine. When it finally became dark, we again set out, keeping close together, to avoid being separated in the darkness, and near to the railroad fence, to avoid losing our course. The difficulties and dangers seemed to increase at every step, while, with incredible labor, we were making almost no progress. We therefore lay by under a pine tree and slept, until the moon should rise. Fortunately, we awoke just as it was coming up, so that no time was lost, and started at once. We were successful in very soon finding a road, which had the same general direction as the railroad, crossing and re-crossing it at many points; this we followed for a considerable distance, when, becoming satisfied that by keeping straight on upon the railroad we should be quite as secure, and at the same time save much needless walking, we took the track, and learned from a mile post that by rail it was 26 miles to Atlanta. Before leaving the highway, however, the signs of the presence of an army had continued to increase. Before the door of one farm house, past which we traveled, a carriage and horses were drawn up, and the building was brilliantly lighted, as if some important personage were present; in the corners of the fences were found half eaten corn cobs and bits of sugar cane, evincing that cavalry scouts had been there but a short time before.

These things made us watchful, and we proceeded with the utmost caution, inspecting every suspicious object, and listening to every sound. Scarcely had we reached the railroad, when the leader discovered a man upon the track, approaching us; we sprang out of the slight cut we were in at the time, leaped over the fence, and crouching upon the ground in a corner, awaited the result. The man came to where we left the track, halted and looked carefully around him; it was a moment of terrible suspense, for he had certainly had an indistinct vision of us, and we lay in perfect silence, even holding our breath, determined that we would not be recaptured, unless overpowered by numbers. Thinking he had been deceived he passed on, much to our relief; but we had seen enough of him to know that he was a rebel infantry soldier, and that if there were cavalry still in our neighborhood, they must belong to the rebels, also. We presently had an opportunity to test the accuracy of this opinion; for scarcely had the soldier passed us, when the clattering of horses feet announced that a cavalry force was upon us. Hugging the ground still closer, we saw at once, as they hurried by, that it was genuine secesh, being mounted partly on mules and partly on horses, and armed with carbines, shot guns and pistols. The rear man said to the others as he passed us, "the Yanks will soon be along," and we fervently hoped that he spoke the truth. Hudson, thinking they all had gone by, commenced climbing over the fence, when we whose ears were sharper than his, whispered to him to wait a moment, as we thought we heard another horse coming, but he did not heed us and had scarcely reached the ground when the last horse came thundering by. Luckily he crawled into the dark fence corner and escaped observation. We were now more fully satisfied that traveling longer in the road was unsafe, as it rendered us liable at any moment to be discovered and recaptured; it was evident to us that the men we had seen were scouts, watching Sherman's advance, and that they were picketed upon every road. We tramped on again, across the fields, past a cotton gin and through a drove of cattle feeding in a field of corn. Ascending a hill scarcely a mile from the railroad, a long row of camp fires, stretching far off to the front and right, met our astonished eyes. Keeping on to the left to avoid them, we saw in the red light, wedge tents with men standing before them, and picket fires with others walking around among them. It was so near day, that the teamsters were beginning to search for their mules, which had been turned loose to pick up their rations for the night. Finding no convenient place of concealment at hand, we continued walking much longer than we intended, and finally took up our day's lodgings in the leafy top of a tall oak tree, which was lying prostrate upon the ground. The air was filled with a cold mist all day, and our position was one of great discomfort, but we solaced ourselves with the thought that we were but a few miles from Atlanta and freedom, and that with so great a boon so nearly within our grasp, we could afford even greater inconveniences for the present. We were so near our lines that with ordinary success, we could reach them in another night, or at any rate, we should be so far on our way, that we could travel the next day, without fear of being apprehended. So we clung to the protecting limbs of our old friend, without repining.

A number of infantry and cavalry marched directly past our hiding place, and musketry firing was heard at irregular intervals, during the entire day;—perhaps for the purpose of frightening any stragglers, who might be skulking in the thickets, to evade duty. The bullets whizzed past us, as we lay concealed, but did not frighten us particularly, as we had frequently heard them before. We were, however, obliged to keep unusually quiet, and were not molested. At night we crept out from our position and proceeded on our way, keeping well to our left; at about eight o'clock, we struck into a large body of woods, in which we kept for a long time. We traveled swiftly, stopping occasionally to listen to the snorting of the horses, that were passing upon the road, a short distance from us; when we came suddenly upon an open spot, in the timber, where the low shrubs and small trees had been cleared away. Here we were alarmed by the sound of horses, eating corn in the ear. It was about ten o'clock; the darkness was almost blinding; we could see nothing definitely, but the objects picketed in irregular lines revealed themselves by being darker than the open sky beyond; and by the noise of their eating we knew what they were. We traveled a long distance along that line, to find a passage through, and it seemed as if a whole corps of cavalry were encamped in that place. At last, after much patient search, we found a path, which, being well trodden, looked in the surrounding blackness, like a strip of white cloth stretched upon the ground; and walking on tiptoe upon it, we passed successfully through the line, without waiting to satisfy our curiosity, as to whether the riders of the horses were on the ground or not; neither did we consider it safe to stop and inquire, whether the force belonged to C. S. A. or U. S., although for all that we knew, they were Unionists. A short distance from us, on the road, were heavily loaded wagons, truckling along in either direction; striking rapidly across the road into an open field, we found where a train had been parked the night before. With all these indications of the presence of an army in our neighborhood, we could do nothing but proceed slowly, with every faculty strained to its utmost to detect any movement, hostile to our enterprise.

We soon came upon a creek, whose waters, upon examination, we found to flow West; this was the first instance of a Westerly course we had discovered, in any stream, and we were rejoiced to find ourselves so near the Chattahoochie, into which the creek must empty. Crossing it, we came into a patch of sweet potatoes, with which we made haste to fill our haversacks, in the expectation that the next time they were filled, it would be at the expense of our worthy Uncle. Passing on, we entered another body of woods, having traveled some three miles since passing through the cavalry force; here, about twelve o'clock, we ran into the infantry picket line; as soon as we discovered the picket walking his beat, we carefully crept back, thinking by keeping well to the right, we could flank the force. Moving, therefore, a considerable distance in our new direction, we again sought a passage through; but the same line of pickets confronted us again. Judging by this time that we had struck their left wing, we retreated to our original line of march, determined to advance far enough to go completely around them. In pursuance of this change of plan, we struck a due West course, and traveled until daylight, when we again turned our faces towards Atlanta. But at every point at which we approached the picket line we found a heavy force of infantry. It had now became light, and it was necessary to seek concealment. While we were looking for it, we came in sight of the Headquarters and the teamsters were hunting for their teams. A Lieutenant and a private passed so near us that we were compelled to skulk back into the woods, to avoid their observation. We returned a considerable distance before we found a retreat sufficiently secure, for we felt sure that we were completely surrounded by our enemies, and that all hope of final escape, lay in our avoiding discovery for one day more. We chose a thicket for our hiding place, and to make it the more secure, cut small shoots and brush, which we stuck into the ground around it. At ten o'clock an unarmed man passed within half a dozen rods of us, but fortunately we remained unnoticed. It then occurred to me that we were not safe here, for any one passing in that direction, either in search of swine or on any other errand was quite likely to visit the spot. I thereupon proposed to my comrades to climb a tree, which stood near us, among whose thick leaves we should be less exposed. Beach coincided with me at once; but Hudson, who was tired of his last night's experience in a tree top, refused to go with us, and remained in the old position, while we hastily clambered up the tree. A couple of hours passed in silence, when we saw two men coming through the woods, the one armed with a musket, the other with his walking stick. From our elevated position we could distinctly overhear their conversation; they were searching the woods for stray pigs, and we scarcely breathed while they remained in sight, fearful of making the lightest sound, to invite their attention toward us; nor was our anxiety at all relieved when we saw them separate, the unarmed man going directly towards the thicket in which Hudson lay.

Hope died in our bosoms as we saw him thrust his cane among the limbs we had so carefully arranged, and we felt that we were already captured. But a few moments elapsed before we saw Hudson coming out of his hiding place, when a long conversation ensued, during which Hudson claimed to belong to the 45th Georgia Reserve, and to be making an effort to get home, in this manner, because he could not get a furlough. To the question how he came to be dressed in blue uniform, he replied, that he had been stationed at Andersonville, during the summer, and had exchanged his old clothes, with a Yankee prisoner, for a full suit of new ones, giving a few vegetables " to boot." The man continued to question him for some time, hoping that some one would come along to arrest him; but no one coming, he finally went away, when Hudson came to the tree in which we were concealed, informed us of what had passed, and told us that he would seek a new hiding place, wherever he could find a suitable spot. This man told Hudson that the whole rebel army was in line of battle, not two hundred yards from the woods in which we lay. The bands at the Head Quarters and along the whole line, had been playing Dixie during the entire morning; we therefore knew into whose hands we should fall if we were captured at that place, and we were not surprised to see a file of men armed with muskets, approach the spot where our comrade had been discovered but a few minutes before. Not finding him, they naturally instituted a search among the tree tops, well knowing he could have escaped in no other direction. We were not sufficiently concealed to avoid detection, and it required but a brief search to espy us. They called upon us to surrender, and we saw at once the propriety of doing so; clambering down as quickly as we could, we gave ourselves up without any explanation to the guard, and were immediately taken to the Brigade Head Quarters, to be disposed of as seemed best to the powers at that place.

CHAPTER IX.

Rebel Headquarters—Opelika, Columbus and Fort Valley—Plan of Escape Detected—Andersonville Again—Savannah—Special Exchange of 10,000 Sick—Removed to Millen—The Prison Pen—Recruiting among the Prisoners—Free.

Our feelings, upon being re-captured, can be better imagined than described. We had been out just fourteen days and nights; had traveled 175 miles, through ditches, rivers, swamps and briers; had performed incredible labor, and met with many hair-breadth escapes; had been exposed to storm, cold and hunger; had overcome all these, and arrived within sight of the goal, only to be delivered up to our enemies, through the imprudence and obstinacy of one of our own number. Had we fallen into toils that had been set for us; had we been captured through a combination of circumstances, which ordinary prudence and sagacity could not have controlled; we should have accepted the situation, as a stroke of evil fortune which we could not evade. Repining, however, would effect no good in our behalf, and we put the best possible face upon the matter, feeling that if we were conquered, we were not subdued, and resolved to embrace the first opportunity for escape that presented itself.

We were first taken to the Headquarters of Brig. Gen. Gibson, and sharply questioned as to our object in being where we were found, how we came there, and where we were going. We had agreed, before setting out, that, if we should be captured, we would each tell the same story of our escape, so that, in case we were examined separately, our accounts would agree. I therefore told the General, in reply to his first inquiry, that we made our escape, while on the cars from Andersonville to Charleston. This view of the matter, though a flight of imagination, seemed best to us, even at the sacrifice of truth, for if we should be remanded to Andersonville, we should be less exposed to the vengeance of Capt. Wirz, who esteemed his honor (in his sense of that term,) in a high degree compromised, if a prisoner escaped from him; while he considered the offence by many degrees less criminal, if made from any one else. To the question why we wished to escape, we replied, that the sufferings, caused by starvation, sickness and exposure, which we had been forced to undergo for more than a year, had impelled us to make an attempt to regain our freedom and preserve our lives. The General then inquired about our treatment, and we explained it to him plainly and firmly. He did not relish the statement, as we made it, and, it is to be presumed, believed no more of it than he pleased; but we "cleared our conscience," in improving the only probable opportunity we should ever have of setting the matter right before him, and felt a degree of relief in the performance of the duty. He replied that he owed the Yankee nation no favors, not even that of his good will, and if he could have his own way in the matter, he would raise the black flag and take no prisoners at all; which specimen of conceited bluster and braggadocio, so inseparable from modern "chivalry," we had heard so often, that it did not produce the effect of frightening us, as he intended, but on the contrary, made us still more obstinately firm; when he informed us that we were prisoners of war, and entitled to treatment as such. We were then sent to Gen. Clayton, a Division commander, and from him to Gen. S. D. Lee, who commanded a Corps. They said very little to us, except that it was rather hard, after we had made so desperate an effort to escape, to be sent back to Andersonville—a view remarkably consonant with our own—but that it was their duty to remand us. They further comforted us, by the intelligence that we were only six miles from Sherman's pickets, and that, if we had succeeded in getting two hundred yards further, we should have been outside of their lines. We were soon sent to the Provost Marshal's Office, near Hood's headquarters, where we passed the night. One of the guard as he walked by our side quietly informed us that their army was essentially beaten,—"licked all ter pieces," was his expression, and that every private, as well as officer, knew it perfectly well, and that it was of no use to fight any longer. He stated, moreover, that he should desert as soon as a favorable opportunity for getting North should offer,—with much more to the same effect. The same sentiments were generally expressed by the sentries who guarded us here; whether for effect, or because they really felt as they said they did, we had no means of determining.

While at this place, two new prisoners were brought in, one of whom was an orderly on Gen. Kilpatrick's staff, from whom we gathered the latest news from Sherman's army. Hudson was also brought in, in a short time after our arrival; the man who discovered him had reported at once to Gen. Gibson, who immediately ordered out a regiment to skirmish through the woods, till he was found. At three o'clock on Friday afternoon, the prisoners were marched to Palmetto Station, where, as it proved, we had been forced to leave the railroad, by discovering a soldier upon the track; here we took the cars, which that day ran up from Newnan for the first time since McCook's raid. The depot and all the principal buildings had been burned by that gallant raider, only a few weeks before, and the blackened ruins lay scattered around on every hand. Here, too, the whole of Hood's transportation train was parked, in readiness to march;—in fact, every thing seemed to indicate that a movement in force was on foot, and we surmised that it was Hood's intention to move North, and, cutting Sherman's line of communication, force him to retreat. At five o'clock we started for West Point, eighty-four miles from Atlanta, where we arrived at an early hour next morning. Halting but a short time for wood and water, we pursued our journey to Opeliki, Ala., and waited some four hours for the train to Columbus. This place showed the ravages of war, having received a flying visit from the Union cavalry, from the effect of which it had not recovered. All the public buildings had been destroyed, and charred remains and tall chimneys marked the sites where they had stood. While halting here, we improved the time in manufacturing various kinds of dishes from the tin that had been used for roofing the depot. A large crowd of citizens gathered around us, partly to talk with us, and partly to witness the dexterity of the "mud-sills" in changing a sheet of tin into a plate or a cup, with no other tools than a stick of wood and a cobble stone. Our handicraft surprised them, and their credulity was so great, that there is no doubt, if we could have donned a grey suit, used profane language and boasted loudly, we should have made fortunes—in Confederate scrip—by converting those roofing materials into table ware.

They manifested the greatest anxiety about the ensuing Presidential election; and when we told them that Abraham Lincoln would probably be elected, they expressed great satisfaction, because they believed under his administration their leaders would be unable to buy a peace, which would amount to no more than an armistice at best. They wanted independence; if they could not get that, then subjugation was the next best thing; for then the questions which divided the two sections, would be settled, in a manner, from which there could be no appeal; while if a compromise was made, the war would have been a failure, because they could have compromised before it commenced, and because such a termination would be but a cessation of hostilities, to re-commence whenever the parties might differ, in the interpretation of the compact. This view was taken by the "last ditch" men, who were spoiling to be subjugated, and they talked loudly and long in their boasting way. We did not wish to enter upon any discussion with them, but their braggadocio forced us to reply, after we had endured it as long as we could. We told them, after their own style, that we should subjugate them; that if, as they boasted, every man of them would die, before that event was accomplished, they had better take leave of their friends as soon as possible; for as sure as another September came, they would all be in —— a climate more intensely tropical than any they had yet experienced. We had millions of tons of iron and lead in our unworked mines, and thousands of thousands of men, women and children to work the ore into guns and bullets; while powder actually grew upon the Western prairies, without cultivation. Our Government was running the armories and iron works day and night, without cessation, and thus far had utterly failed to supply guns and ammunition for the forces as fast as they wanted to come into the field; there were five millions of men, who would join the army, if they could only obtain the arms they needed. The Yankee throve best under difficulties, and the philanthropists of the North had declared that war was their natural state, and advocated the policy of provoking a contest with England and France, as soon as the South was used up, that the Yankees might have room to grow; for they were sure to wither away, unless they could fight. The only way to stop the "effusion of blood " was to withdraw their armies from the field, surrender the forts, arsenals and other property they had stolen from us, go quietly home and obey the laws, like good citizens.

Another class who conversed with us, whose first question was " What are all you 'uns fighting we 'uns for?" whose education had not reached the point of acquiring correct use of their vernacular, but who nevertheless would be required to dig the ' last ditch ' for those who coveted it so much, and stand a living wall in front of it for their protection, while in the article of death; was much more reasonable. They had realized what war meant, and were quite willing to submit to the old regime, if their rights could be guaranteed to them, as they enjoyed them before the war. They seemed most to fear negro equality, and ridiculed the idea of fighting side by side with the darkey. Our most obvious reply to this thrust was, that it was much better to fight with him than run from him; with which terrible sarcasm, the crowd abandoned the contest, and retreated. We were here joined by four prisoners who had made their escape from Andersonville the same day we did, and were recaptured near West Point. There were now ten prisoners, in all, and we had six men to guard us.

We were placed on board a passenger train and

moved forward for Columbus, where we arrived at sundown. This village is situated on the East bank of the Chattahoochie, at the head of navigation; it contained several large cotton factories, and the dwellings of the operators were arranged in regular streets, upon the West side of the stream; they were built exactly alike, and presented a fine appearance. Arriving at the depot we were delayed long enough to exchange our comfortable passenger coach for a box car, and halted for the night. While we were on the side track, Jeff. Davis and Gen. Beauregard passed us on a special train, the President being on a stumping excursion. He had just exhorted the "fellow citizens" of Macon and Columbus to rise and drive the invader from their soil, or the cause was lost; if they but took heart, (together with guns in sufficient numbers,) they would soon compel Sherman to beat a retreat, more disastrous than that from Moscow, and the "plundering hordes" would be forever expelled from their borders;—and much more of the same sort. It was amusing to us, in our intercourse with Southern Chivalry, to hear the constant recurrence of the words "plundering foes," "thieving enemies," "pillaging hordes;" their theory of the war being, that it was carried on by two independent nations and that private property, such as stores of bacon, flour, corn, oats, &c., which were only in their owners hand, awaiting the appraisal of the Confederate Quartermasters, was to be sacredly protected against capture by us; while on the other hand, in virtue of superior intelligence and purer blood, on their part, they were entitled to appropriate anything belonging to us, without returning any equivalant therefor, except the precious privilege of being robbed by a "chivalrous" highwayman; from which view of the case we, as prisoners of war, considered ourselves at liberty to dissent, and also to levy upon them whenever an opportunity presented itself, and were therefore denominated "plundering hordes."

On Sunday morning, our train left for Fort Valley, a point sixty-five miles from Columbus, and thirty-five from Andersonville. Arriving here at two o'clock P. M., we were transferred to a negro pen to await the train, which did not move till morning, to convey us back to the old prison. The pen was a small building with two little windows opposite each other, about twelve inches square, and grated with heavy iron bars. As we entered the building the door was shut and locked; this was the first time since our recapture that we had been locked in, and we felt it incumbent upon us to effect our escape, if we could. We decided to get through the floor by cutting away a board with our pocket knives, and then to creep out under the building. To ascertain whether we could get out without digging, if we once reached the ground, three or four of the boys obtained permission to go out to procure drinking water, and reconnoitred the position. It was found perfectly practicable, and upon their report, we immediately set to work cutting through the floor. It was matched pitch pine boards, twelve inches wide by one and a half thick, as hard as oak; but we cut away as fast as we could, blistering our hands, and getting very warm, until a length of board sufficient for our purpose was cut at one end and near the wall of the room. The boys then commenced dancing, shouting and rattling some chains that were found on the floor, making such a din that I could not be heard while I was prying up the board. We had completed our arrangements before dark, and to prevent attention being called to our project, I spread an old blanket which I had purchased of the guard, over the loose board, and lay down upon it.

We had received no rations since leaving Opeliki at which place were stationed some soldiers, who had been recently exchanged, and who had given us some hard bread. At seven o'clock, the guard came into the pen with corn bread, which had been sent to us through the liberality of the surgeons of a Confederate hospital located at that place; a short time afterwards, the guards revisited us, with a request that we sweep the floor. To sweep the spot upon which I was lying would at once reveal the "fraud," and under a plea of sickness, I was permitted to lie still, inasmuch as I had already made my bed for the night. In the rubbish which was swept out, they found a case knife, belonging to Hudson, which had been hacked like a saw; this excited suspicion against us, and they immediately came in and demanded our pocket knives. Thinking it would pacify them, we surrendered the knives peaceably, upon the promise that they should be returned to us next morning,—and they left us. But they were not yet satisfied, and came in again about eight o'clock, and wanted to inspect the floor. I was obliged to get up and take up my blanket, when, of course, the severed board was discovered. In another hour we should have all been free, and as we had agreed to take different directions in our escape, it would have been impossible to retake all of us, with our experience in nocturnal travels.

We had now no hope of a better fate than another trial of Andersonville, and the treatment of re-captured prisoners, in the merciless power of Capt. Wirz, presented itself to us, in all its terrible colors. We did not have much time then to think of it, for the guard kept firing a volley of oaths at us, for even attempting to escape from them. They threatened to shoot the first man that moved, and to put us all in irons, unless we would divulge the name of the one who cut the board away. They questioned each man separately upon this point, unsuccessfully, however, for there were no traitors among us. Coming to me last, I acknowledged that I knew who did it, but did not consider it my duty to inform them; and that if they wanted to put irons on me for it, they had the power to do so, but that it would add no jot or tittle to their wisdom. They suspected Hudson and a man named Crandall, of being the guilty parties, and next morning put irons upon their wrists, which were not taken off till we reached Andersonville. This feat accomplished, there came a lull in the shower of profanity, for a few minutes, when one fellow, with a more vivid imagination than the others, began to depict their consternation, if they had opened the door in the morning, and found the cage empty and the birds flown; this was a new view of the case, and as the thought flashed upon them, their expiring anger seemed to receive a sudden and fresh stimulus from the contemplation, and they discharged another and fiercer storm of curses upon us.

The next morning we were placed in a box car and forwarded to Andersonville. The car contained a large quantity of salt, to which we freely helped ourselves, filling our haversacks. We arrived at the station at noon, and immediately marched to the stockade. A great change had taken place here, since our departure, nearly all the prisoners having been sent away; those that remained had a much improved appearance, as if they had been better fed. We were sent directly to headquarters, where, as good luck would have it, Capt. Wirz was sick, (we earnestly hoped he would never recover,) and Sergeant Smith received us. Four of the men who came with us, including Crandall, had been paroled to dig trenches for the dead, and were employed in this duty when they made their escape. Crandall had been on this duty for some time, before escaping, and when the prisoners were sent to Savannah and Charleston, he had asked permission to go with them, which Capt. Wirz had refused. He made his escape on the following day. These four men were at once ordered into the "lying down stocks," and the next day loaded with the ball and chain. Our party escaped punishment, until night, probably because it was supposed that we had jumped off the cars, after we were beyond Capt. Wirz's jurisdiction; but after sunset we were also put into the stocks, and passed the night in them. It was by no means a comfortable position to lie, with our feet twelve inches from the ground, but we thought ourselves fortunate in escaping the standing stocks, and did not murmur. In the morning we were released, and accompanied by the guard to the cook house, where good rations of bread, peas and beef were issued to us; they were given us, however, by the prisoners in charge, and we took care to say nothing to implicate them, for we knew the punishment to which we should expose them, if their sympathy with us were known. After breakfast the four boys were ordered into the stocks again; we expected the same attention would be paid to us, but fortunately were overlooked. A train load of prisoners was to be transferred to Savannah immediately, and we were ordered to fall in and go with it. The order was very readily obeyed, for we were satisfied that any change could not but be for the better, and our second experience of Andersonville was very brief.

Our trip to Savannah was in some respects pleasant, the distance from Andersonville being 236 miles by rail. We reached that place at sundown, on the 28th September, but were not allowed to get off the cars until dark, for what reason, it was unexplained. We were then marched to the prison south of the old jail, which had been built by the British; there were many of the prisoners that were unable to walk, who were carried by the able bodied. The pen into which we were presently inducted, was constructed of planks nailed upon posts twelve feet in hight, set firmly in the ground; it was surrounded with a deep ditch, which had been dug after the prison was inaugurated, on account of several of the first prisoners having escaped by tunneling, the first night they were confined. As at Andersonville, no shelters of any kind had been provided here, and we found ourselves exposed to sun, wind and rain, without any protection. The water, which was supplied from the city water works, was pure, and in sufficient quantity for our needs.

At the time of our arrival, there were four or five thousand prisoners confined here, the greater portion of whom were from Andersonville. The change of locality had not benefited them; in fact, except in the matter of water, our situation was the same as it had been at that place. The "camp" was under the command of Lieut. Davis—a man of doubtful valor, who was afterwards captured on the cars in Ohio, while he was carrying despatches to Canada, and sent to Fort Delaware. He was in command at Andersonville, during the sickness of Capt. Wirz, some time in the summer, and treated the men, at that time, with as much humanity as his orders would allow him to do; but at Savannah he endeavored to imitate Capt. Wirz in manner, perhaps because he could see promotion in no other way.

Our rations were issued by the commissary to the

police—a body of prisoners organized to keep order in the camp—who delivered them to the sergeants of divisions, by whom they were divided among the men. They consisted of corn meal, rice, sorghum molasses and fresh beef, in quantities too small to satisfy our needs. It was evident, upon the day of our arrival, that the commissary department at Savannah was no more generous than it was at other places where we had been confined.

Hudson, Beach and myself, had been unfortunate in not being able to find the sergeants, with whom we had deposited our blankets when we had made our escape, and we were now utterly destitute of any protection against the beating storms and the scorching sun. Our clothing, some of which had been worn since our capture, more than twelve months before, was very thin, even where any of it remained; and in many places was completely gone. A hat, unlike any thing ever before known by that name, covered our heads in places, and our feet made vain attempts at concealment, in the almost soleless shoes we had not removed for weeks. Death seemed inevitable, and, indeed, would have been preferable, to a long continuance of the present treatment. To add to our discomfort, the police had rendered themselves particularly obnoxious to their fellow prisoners, by appropriating their rations, in the division of them;

they began by abusing us with profane taunts, with unnecessary orders about little matters, and, in many instances, ended by spurning us with their feet or with a blow from their cudgels. Physical chastisement, however, was confined to the helpless,—those who were unable to give blow for blow; but it was none the less aggravating to the able bodied. We had no means of protection against these scoundrels, for, upon the first appearance of resistance, we were called to a strict account by the authorities.

Though in the heart of a populous city, we were as much shut out from a knowledge of the scenes enacted in the busy world, as if we had been in the midst of the Pacific Ocean. We could distinctly hear the tumult of business in the neighboring streets, the rumbling of the cars as they passed to and fro, and the roar of cannon, but a short distance down the river, where our friends were leisurely bombarding something, near Fort Pulaski. If we could only escape.—One of the prisoners made the attempt, but was re-captured by the dogs, brought back and suspended by his thumbs, as a warning to the rest. The punishment for running away was of small consequence to us, but we feared the dogs,—those ferocious blood-hounds, by which we were sure to be overtaken and torn in pieces, and against which we had no protection. The enterprise of the prisoners at this place took the same direction as at Andersonville, and a brisk trade was carried on in taffy, (made from sorghum,) in beer, and the exchange of one kind of ration for another. This served to relieve the terrible monotony that was killing us, by furnishing something to think about and by stimulating our mental energies into something like action.

Day after day passed in this manner, without change, until the 13th of October, when a Savannah paper found its way into the pen; in which it was stated that Maj. Mulford had just left Fortress Monroe for Savannah, with 10,000 rebel sick and wounded, to exchange for a like number of Federals. This news was cheering to every one, both the well and the invalid, for it was horrible for the strong man to be confined side by side with the sick, especially when, as here, the morning sun would often waken him and reveal the comrade whom he had bidden "good night" but a few hours before, stretched cold and lifeless beside him. Lieut. Davis issued an order the same morning for several detachments to prepare to leave the pen on the following evening, but for what point, was mere matter of conjecture, some of the prisoners thinking Charleston, others Millen, to be their destination. All the sailors had previously been sent to Charleston for exchange, and it had been several times reported that that place had been agreed upon as the exchange point. At night the train was filled and started.

The next morning another train load was ordered to be in readiness, this time we were informed, for Millen. The detachments were taken out in the order of their entering, and, as we were among the very latest of the arrivals, our detachment was not included in the order. Notwithstanding which, Beach and myself, desirous of seeing as much of the Confederacy as possible, by a little strategy, succeeded in joining the departing column, just as it reached the gates, and though Lieut. Davis discovered the trick, he confined his wrath to a "terrible cussin," for which he ought to be made famous, for he manifested more original genius in that line than even Capt. Wirz himself ever displayed. We were marched through some of the finest streets in Savannah, and escape from the column was easy and tempting; but the swamps around the town, were a more formidable guard than bayonets, and no one made the attempt. Reaching the railroad, which runs for some distance into the city, we were placed on board a train of cattle cars, and with sixty men in each car we started, bidding farewell to the quiet city of Savannah, of whose hospitality we had partaken at the public expense, although it had been marred somewhat by the constraint which had been put upon our free movements about the town; and to Lieut. Davis, who signalized his last moments of authority over us, by riding down upon some helpless sick men, who were trying to get aboard, in his anxiety to see us safely on our journey.

Starting from Savannah before sunrise, we reached Millen at five P. M. Although as usual upon setting out, we had been regaled with a direct promise of exchange, that ingenious bit of pleasantry on the part of the Confederate government had lost much of its merit by constant repetition;—indeed it seemed as if the C. S. A. had exhausted its entire stock of wit in inventing that joke, for we never heard any other from it,—and we fully appreciated its staleness. This plum intended to insure our quiet removal from the prison at Savannah to the prison at Millen, failed in its designed office, for many of the boys jumped from the train while it was in motion, and although fired at by the guard, succeeded in getting away for a time. Most of them, however, were retaken by means of the blood-hounds and brought back. It was undoubtedly a piece of reckless daring to jump from a railroad car while in motion, especially under fire of a dozen or more guards, in a strange country, with no knowledge of its geography, and with no means of obtaining it, except by inquiry of residents, which would have been sure to lead to detection; but when life is the stake to be played for, there are few obstacles which men will not encounter to win it. Indeed death by any other method than suicide would have been preferable to another winter's imprisonment in the Confederacy, and but for the hope of ultimate release, either by exchange or escape in a less desperate manner, the prisoners who were able to run would have overpowered the guard, seized the train and rushed upon death at once.

We left the railroad some five miles beyond Millen junction, on the Augusta R. R., and took up our line of march for the prison, situated about a mile distant in a Southwest direction. The pen was an open enclosure like that at Andersonville, being built of unhewn timbers, set vertically in the ground; it contained about forty acres in area, in a nearly square form, and through it ran a stream of clear water, whose source was a beautiful spring just outside the walls. A battery of eight guns was planted in a large fort near the Southeast corner of the pen, arranged to rake the enclosure diagonally in case of insurrection among the prisoners. The stockade was located in the midst of a pine forest, but all the timbers within it, except a narrow strip of small trees near the stream, as well as those for half a mile beyond the walls on either hand, had been cut down. At the time of the arrival of our party, which formed the second train load, after the pen was "inaugurated," a large quantity of timber was lying upon the ground, as it had been felled. The bodies of the trees had been cut into two or three pieces, and such of the logs as were fit for lumber, hauled away; the remainder being left for the use of the prisoners. We lost no time in gathering the wood and carrying it to our quarters, and in three days the camp was pretty well cleared off; logs too heavy to be carried were rolled, and our wood piles assumed very respectable proportions. Those who could procure axes, split some of these logs into slabs, and erected quite comfortable huts, which, though not models of excellence in architecture or neatness, were nevertheless a protection against the inclemency of the weather. It is to be remembered that the majority of the prisoners had been in the hands of the rebels more than a year, and that, in all that time, no new clothes had been given them, except what were issued at Danville and Richmond, ten months previous. It was now October; the fall rains had set in; the ground upon which we were compelled to lie, was saturated with water, often becoming a mere mud puddle; and when the weather was pleasant for a few days, the night air was charged with moisture, and the heavy dews completely soaked through our scanty apparel. But few of the men had provided themselves with huts, for the reason that axes could be procured only with the greatest difficulty, the prison authorities furnishing none. Many dug holes in the ground, into which they crawled, burrowing in them, as at Andersonville.

Our rations were two-thirds of a pint of cornmeal, three table spoonfuls of rice, four ounces of fresh beef, including bone, and a tea spoonful of salt. In lieu of rice, black peas, or sorghum molasses, were sometimes issued. A certain number of barrels of sorghum were allowed per week to the camp. In many of them, the molasses had crystalized and adhered to the sides and bottom of the barrel, to the depth of three or four inches; this formed the most valuable part of the article; but Quartermaster Humes* would not allow the prisoners this part of their ration, so that our supply was often cut off one-third from the little the Confederate government designed for us. The peas were filled with bugs, and at least one-half the amount allowed was utterly unfit

---

* As nothing good can be said of this fellow, no mention was made of him in the account of the Andersonville prison, although he held the post of Quartermaster at that place. He was a Baltimorean, and, like all deserters, was naturally predisposed to little acts of meanness, of which the above is an example. He made himself particularly obnoxious to the prisoners by first gaining the confidence of the unsuspecting, and placing them in the stocks, in return. He had all the natural villainy of Capt. Wirz, without sufficient intellectual vigor to carry it out; hence he confined himself to petty annoyances and little tricks.

for use; refining somewhat upon our cookery at Andersonville, we placed our ration of peas in water, before boiling it, when those that were worm-eaten, rising to the surface, were skimmed off and thrown away.

As at camp Sumter, the hucksters soon made their appearance among us. Taffy, made from sorghum, sweet potatoes, tobacco, red pepper, thread, &c., purchased from the guards, formed the chief articles of sale; a thriving business was also done in soup, and in corn and pea bread. As many of the prisoners had no cooking utensils or wood for fires, the more enterprising often realized a double ration, by exchanging the manufactured article for the raw material. Brick ovens had been built, and two kettles for each 1,000 men set in arches; but they were never used for cooking, because a supply of wood for the purpose was never provided by the Quartermaster; and as the small amount obtained by the men was procured by private enterprise, none were willing to put their individual shares into a general fund, for cooking the rations in a mass, to which, if such a course had been adopted, the contributions must have been very unequal.

A month's experience at "Camp Lawton," proved to us that our condition had been in no wise improved by the transfer from Andersonville. The exposure was rapidly thinning our numbers; our rations were not sufficient to support life for any extended period of time, under the most favorable circumstances; and here, where no artificial heat could be obtained, the blood of the strong man became torpid and refused to do its office. A hospital for receiving the sick was established in the southwest corner of the area; but no shelter was provided, no blankets given those who occupied it, and medicines were not issued there. The only advantage to the sick man, in this arrangement, was that he would be certain to be found by the surgeons, who were examining with reference to the special exchange. From this hospital, those who were deemed unfit to stay in the stockade were transferred to a hospital outside the pen, where they remained, until forwarded to the exchange point. Those who were not taken to the outer hospital, were left to roam at will through the enclosure, without medicine, and with no other treatment than that afforded to the other prisoners. They died at an average rate of nine per cent. per month. It was horrible to pass around the area at sunrise, and see the dead men who had expired the night before. Some of them had fallen upon the open space, and been unable to rise; others crawled wearily to the side of a stump, as if to be near some object, however inanimate, when the last agony came upon them; some sought the borders of the stream, perchance that its soft ripple might soothe the parting spirit, with gentle music, as it quitted the poor tenement which had been its home; others forced themselves into the empty ovens and beneath the unused kettles; while still others burrowed themselves more deeply into the ground, digging their own graves as they nestled down into the bosom of Earth, for its genial warmth to shelter their freezing limbs from the beating storms; and when they were gathered up and removed for burial, their clenched hands still clung to the friendly breast that had cherished them, refusing to release their hold, and carrying the torn fragments with them to the tomb. And yet the dead, turning their glassy eyes upon us, as we passed, were not more horrible than the living, with their pinched faces, blue with cold, trembling as they hugged their almost naked forms with their bony arms, in a vain attempt to retain the heat which was not there; or collecting in groups to gather warmth from numbers, ever and anon changing places, that the outer circle might be relieved from the pinching cold, while those within assumed their places, to come back in turn. So these pale, haggard wretches starved and froze, day by day unnoticed, and were buried like brutes.

Hope of exchange had died within us; not a ray of light penetrated the thick gloom of the prospect before us. The only thought of the strong and healthy was by stout resistance to put off the evil day a little longer; but we felt that it must come soon to all of us, when the brief struggle would be over.

Confederate officers came daily into the pen to solicit recruits for their service. A few hundreds joined them; but their motives were well understood. They intended only to relieve their own personal sufferings, and if ever put in action, at the front, to desert. Though their services in the Confederate army boded no good for the rebel cause, the conduct of these men can hardly be justified. They had already passed many months in prison, had nearly "finished their course;" perhaps, true courage would have refused the offer, and met death rather than disgrace. But what will not a man give for his life? Let us not judge them too harshly, remembering how sorely they were tempted.

On the day of the Presidential election, a ballot box was opened, and some three thousand votes cast for Mr. Lincoln, and nearly a thousand for McClellan. The election passed off very much as elections usually do; the police were principally "dimocrats," and exercised petty tyranny over the sick and helpless, who preferred Lincoln to "Little Mike," by knocking them down and beating them with their clubs. I make mention of these outrages only to show the character of the men who were willing to serve the Confederate cause. The police were a privileged class, serving their masters well. They were in league with those artisans who deserted their colors to labor in Confederate workshops, and all true Irishmen will spurn them, when they hear of the shame they have brought upon the name of a brave, generous and noble race.

The rebel authorities had large handbills struck, offering tempting terms to mechanics, if they would come over to their side. These were posted upon the walls outside the pen; had they been placed within it, they would have been torn down as insults. But few were drawn from their allegiance by this artifice; taking all who were released as mechanics, and those who enlisted, they would not number 300 men. The recruiting officers had honor enough to feel ashamed of their business, though they tried to hide it behind faces of brass.

I had offered my services, which had been accepted, early in November, to assist the surgeon in collecting the sick, and taking their names, &c., for the special exchange; and when the work was finished, one of the doctors had volunteered to use his influence to have me exchanged, with the rest, as a hospital attendant. On the 14th, while I was wandering about the camp, a friend ran hastily to me, announcing that I was desired to report immediately at the gate, for exchange. Thinking that the doctor's promised efforts for my exchange had been crowned with success, and without stopping to look after my luggage, which consisted of an old haversack, several cooking utensils, which I had made while waiting for the train at Opeliki, and a small quantity of rations, ready to be "made up" for next morning's "trade," I rushed for the gate. I passed it "all right" and hurried up to headquarters under guard. Here I found several comrades, among them my old friend Beach, through whose kind offices, my name had been brought to the commander's notice, and reporting myself, waited further orders. When the Captain, who commanded at the post, had allowed us to wait long enough to satisfy his dignity, he approached us and administered the parole of honor, not to escape while on duty. This done, we were informed that on account of so many prisoners being exchanged, the prison post was in want of men to work in the slaughter house, and that we could take our choice between going there and working, or going back into the prison. Although this did not look favorable towards an immediate release, we were not long in choosing, and were soon installed in business. I remained here four days. The business was not new to me, and in it I found something to relieve the terrible monotony of prison life. We slaughtered thirty-five head of cattle per day; the animals were small and very lean, averaging about 350 pounds each; this, after deducting rations for the officers and guards, left about one-fourth of a pound per man, per diem, including the bone, which in lean cattle, bears a large proportion to the meat.

Sunday morning the 20th of November, the Captain sent down an orderly commanding us to report at once at headquarters. A rumor had been put in circulation by the quidnuncs to the effect that those whose term of service had expired, and none others, were to be immediately exchanged, and that all who applied for exchange must take an oath to that effect. Acting upon this rumor, Beach would not go to headquarters, but the rest of us went. When we reached the office, the Captain said, "Now boys, there are twenty-five of you, twelve of whom can go on this exchange, this afternoon. I want to be fair and honorable, in deciding who shall stay." He then put twenty-five ballots, upon twelve of which was written the word "go,"—the remainder being blanks,—into a hat; these being well shaken, we advanced as our names were called, and drew our fate. It was a curious, as well as impressive scene, to watch the shifting shades upon the swarthy faces of those ragged, dirty men, as each advanced with trembling hand and bated breath, and to see the eagerness with which each watched the other as he called the magic word with exulting heart, or crept hopelessly back to his place with the fearful blank in his hand. Every fortunate ticket was counted as it was drawn, and the diminished or increased odds more carefully noted than ever mortal watched the fatal wheel of fortune; for life itself was now at stake. Home, friends, plenty, existence; prison, neglect starvation, death; these were the alternatives; upon those bits of paper, not an inch in surface, hung all our future. The strong men who had faced death upon twenty fields, had marched with scornful pride to the cannon's mouth, had met unflinching, the stern charge, and hurled back the recoiling foe; men who had famished for fourteen weary months, exposed to storms without shelter, to pestilence without the means of warding it off, or escaping from it, and never murmured,—wept like children over the bit of white paper that lay in their hands. Nerves strong as steel, strained to their utmost tension by the hope of release, suddenly relaxed as the new born hope expired, and became soft and weak as those of a babe. My name was the last upon the list, and all the world's goods would not tempt me again to undergo the agony of suspense, with which I watched the drawing of those ballots. The revulsion of feeling I experienced when the little paper being opened, revealed the word "go," overpowered me, and I stood entranced, unable to move, as one in a fearful nightmare, till a desperate effort forced a loud shout from my lips, and I was free. The gloomy prison, with its train of hideous experiences, its spectres of woe, wretchedness and death, vanished. The very air seemed laden with vivifying fragrance bearing health, life, upon its wings. A new world was opened to my eyes, a beautiful world, where every bough dropped healing balm and every hill seemed a paradise.

CHAPTER X.

Paroled—Rebel Truce Boats—On board Ship—Homeward bound—Northern Soil—Furloughed—Views of the Prisoners—Tables—Conclusion.

In the afternoon of the same day, we were paroled while this was going on, a citizen came in with the news that Gen. Kilpatrick's cavalry, forming the right of Sherman's advance, was near Macon, tearing up the railroad and devastating the surrounding country. This news, together with our new "situation," made us jubilant, and three cheers, long and loud, rent the air. We left Millen, and about 8,000 prisoners, just as twilight was deepening into night, reaching Savannah at daylight the next morning. A rain storm had set in about midnight, and heavy clouds still hung about the sky, dropping their chilling burden upon our unprotected persons, as we disembarked from the train into the streets of the city. Many of the prisoners still doubted the sincerity of the exchange, and believed that we were again being removed from Millen to a more secure pen; but to the better informed, the nature of the parole, which was the same as that given to those who had been sent through our lines at the front, just after a battle, was sufficient evidence of its verity.

The first train load of prisoners, which had passed through Savannah for the fleet, had been so well treated by the citizens, who had distributed many comforts and little luxuries among the half starved men, that, upon our arrival, guards of infantry and cavalry had been stationed on both sides of the street, and indeed marched by our sides to the levee, to prevent any little outbursts of tender-hearted sympathy which might be exhibited in our behalf. Whether the Confederate authorities feared kindness would, from its novelty, have an injurious effect upon the prisoners, or that the exercise of charity would quench the far-famed fire which had been so often kindled in the Southern heart, did not transpire; bayonets and cavalry swords effectually repressed every attempt at making the experiment, to prove which of the two hypotheses was correct. Reaching the levee, near the city gas-works, the column halted for an hour, in the cold mist that had settled down upon the river, waiting the transports, that were to convey us to Venus Point, where our fleet lay at anchor. But the storm, and the cold and the hunger, were all forgotten, or unnoticed, in the exulting feelings which animated our breasts. The hour seemed an age to our impatient spirits. I have read of philosophers, who have remained calm and collected, and coolly observant of "things," amid the sudden and unlooked for transitions of fortune, manifesting no emotion of joy or grief by so much as a change of muscle or a sparkle of the eye; but, however desirable such control of nerves, or such stolidity, which ever it is, that can wear an air of indifference on all occasions, it was an accomplishment far below par with us at that time, and I am inclined to the belief that those same Stoics would be completely cured of their insensibility, and that a return to liberty, after a year spent in Southern military prisons, would scatter the dusty proverbs of their philosophical theories to the winds. And if any devotee of indifference doubts the practicability of this view, let him try it; the experiment would be a complete test.

Two small river boats were moored to the levee where we halted, with steam up, waiting for the signal to take us on board and move forward. Dignity and red tape being at last satisfied, the flag of truce boat "Beauregard" steamed past, with the white flag at the mast-head. Instantly we were ordered to embark, and in a few minutes were in motion, following our leader in line down the stream. We rapidly passed the rib work of a new iron-clad, which forcibly reminded us of our own skeleton appearance, and saw the numerous torpedoes lying in wait to blow the Yankee gun-boats into—the surrounding country, upon the shortest notice, if they should dare to pass up the stream. The presence of these formidable machines was revealed by sharp pointed timbers attached to them, and inclining down the stream. Three of these "sharp sticks" were observed close together, in one locality. There was a large fort and extensive earth-works on the right bank, near the "obstructions," bristling with cannon, so trained as to crush any hostile fleet that attempted to pass them. I counted thirty-six heavy seige guns, as we passed through the obstructions alone. In addition to these shore batteries, two heavy iron-clads, like twin Cerberi, guarded the passage through the obstructions. It seemed to us, though we were landsmen, to be sure, that it would be utterly impossible for our fleet to ascend the river past these batteries, and that the attempt to do so, would insure the almost instantaneous destruction of every vessel that made it.

We reached our fleet, which was anchored at Venus Point, at two P. M.; and were kept in waiting two hours before all the preliminaries were settled, when we were transferred to the steamer "Star of the South." The rebel transports, having discharged their burden, turned about and steamed up the river, the cloud of black smoke growing smaller and smaller, finally disappearing in the distance. It was not until these vessels had disappeared around the bend of the stream that we felt ourselves free; and the loved flag, which floated so proudly over our heads, assured us that this indeed was no error. I had been under the guard of rebel bayonets just four hundred and twenty-six days; had passed over more than three thousand miles of railroad; had been confined in five different prisons; it is no wonder, therefore, that, as I turned my eyes from those filthy rebels and their dirty vessels to the neat uniforms and clean deck of the stately ship on board of which we then stood, and noted the contrast, that I felt as if I had discovered a new race of beings, a higher order of existence, than I had ever known before; and I doubt if Columbus and his crew were more joyful, when they landed upon the new Hemisphere, than we were in embarking upon a United States vessel. The next morning we were placed on board the screw steamer "Gen. Sedgwick," and at five P. M. moved down the river, past Fort Pulaski, and onward into the open sea. The wind had blown all day from the ocean, and was increasing in force as we passed out of sight of land into the darkness. Our "rocking in the cradle of the deep" that night, will never be forgotten by the "land lubbers" that were taking free passage to the North. Our acrobatics certainly possessed a high order of merit. Summersaults were so frequent that the beholders lost all interest in them, while constant standing upon our heads would have certainly produced vertigo, if there had not been as constant a change to an upright position.

The next morning found the good ship tossing and tumbling about on the billows, and the wind seemed to us to have increased to a hurricane. The sailors, however, lounged about with such unconcern, as to convey the idea to us that it was but a zephyr; and if we had had any fears of going to the bottom, their *sang froid* would have put them to flight. The storm subsided during the day, and it continued fair for the remainder of the voyage. As we passed the straits and entered Chesapeake Bay, we saw the fleet preparing for the expedition against Fort Fisher. When opposite Point Lookout, we could plainly descry the high wall of a military prison, where the captured rebels were held, and the cloud of smoke that hovered over the spot indicated that they had no lack of fuel, whatever other articles of necessity they might be deprived of.

Reaching the harbor at Annapolis about midnight, we cast anchor, and waited for daylight before proceeding to the dock. Here we were received by a band of music, playing the "Star Spangled Banner";

the sick were placed in ambulances, while the well men marched to the barracks within the city limits. Here facilities were furnished for bathing, a process with which we had been long unacquainted; new clothing was issued, in exchange for the filthy rags we had so long worn. As soon as the necessary acts of cleanliness were performed, the boys, having procured stationery and ink, were soon busy inditing letters to their friends, announcing their arrival in a land of civilization and christianity. And many a loving heart was made glad by the tidings that the dear one, mourned as lost, was once more near.

From the Barracks we were removed the next day to parole Camp, some two miles beyond the city limits, on the Baltimore and Annapolis Railroad. Here the same kind attention was paid us as we had received from the moment we stepped on board the steamer near Fort Pulaski. The officers and attendants of the camp seemed to vie with each other in their efforts to minister to our wants. Anxious friends came seeking for loved ones, but many, very many, turned away sad and disappointed from a fruitless search. The U. S. Sanitary and Christian Commissions deserve a lasting praise for their generous and welcome aid, in furnishing us with stationery, clothing, and a great variety of necessary articles, which the government could not give. After two or three days stay at this camp, the Secretary of War issued an order that we be furloughed for thirty days. Two months pay was given us, and the necessary papers for the commutation of rations. On the 8th of December I received my furlough and immediately started for home, where I arrived on the 11th. Here surrounded by friends and plenty, I rested after my fourteen months experience in Rebel Prisons.

Although my narrative, were it exclusively a personal one, would properly end here, my task would be incomplete without a somewhat more particular account of the feelings and opinions of the prisoners themselves, in regard to the course pursued by our own Government, in the matter of exchange. Four years of war have raised a strong prejudice, as I am aware, against the views and statements of the private soldier. It could not well be otherwise, in the necessary discrimination between an officer and a private; credence being accorded to the former in military circles, upon the theory that he would not dishonor himself by speaking an untruth, or by giving a false gloss to the truth itself; while the mere statement of the latter, unaccompanied by proof, was of no consequence, or at most, was taken with so many "grains of allowance" that scarcely any thing was left to be believed. The government crediting the representation of officers as to their treatment by the enemy, adopted a system of retaliation upon a portion of the rebel officers whom they had captured; while at the same time that these retaliatory measures were taken, there were thousands of private Federal prisoners, whose treatment by the rebels was tenfold worse than that of our officers, but whose cry for relief fell upon deaf ears. It was believed that this discrimination was made because our Government credited the story of cruelty in the one case, and disbelieved it in the other; because a sword and sash conferred upon the wearer a higher character for truth, than a bayonet and body belt. Without attempting any argument to show whether this feeling was just or unjust, I am free to state that it existed generally among the prisoners; and with what seemed to them at least, good reason. For they knew that there was no less occasion for retaliation upon rebel privates, than upon rebel officers, if the Government had been informed of the atrocities daily practiced upon us. That it was informed of them, we believed, because several prisoners had made good their escape, and reached their homes, and their accounts were published in the papers of the time. Petitions had been drawn up giving partial accounts of our sufferings, and asking for relief; they had been signed by large numbers of the prisoners, sent through the lines by men who were appointed for the purpose, and who could give full details of our treatment, and presented to the Government. It is no wonder that these wretched men should consider themselves the victims of neglect on the part of the country they had periled their lives to protect, and should curse the rulers who were so remiss in their duty to them.

It was understood why the exchange was dropped in the first instance, but it was believed that the policy which caused the old cartel to be abrogated, was wrong from the beginning. We admitted that the negro soldier was entitled to the same protection as the white man, and should have received it; but to insure this to him, it was not necessary to insist upon no exchange at all. A system of retaliation could have been devised, by which a body of rebels equal in number to the negro prisoners, could have been subjected to the same treatment as the blacks received, and there would have been still enough to exchange man for man for the white Federals; for after the exchange was abandoned, there was at all times a surplus of prisoners in the hands of the Federal Government. If this system had been proffered by Mr. Stanton and declined by the Rebels, even in that case, it would have removed from our minds the impression that we were left to bear our tortures unpitied and uncared for, and nerved us to greater endurance. But we seemed to be forgotten. When the rebel lines closed around us on the field of conflict, we appeared to enter a horrible abyss, and no thought from those whom we left behind, followed us. We found an earthly hell, and oblivion rolled between us and those we had been separated from.

But it was more galling to our spirits than this seeming neglect, than the superhuman sufferings we endured, to feel that while we starved, our enemies fattened under the government which had abandoned us; for we well knew that no motives of humanity would induce those placed over us to mitigate our condition, that no sympathy from them would alleviate our wretchedness one iota; nothing, in short, would induce them to treat us like human beings, but actual fear of experiencing the same torments which they inflicted upon us. It was understood among us that our enemies when captured, were treated as prisoners of war are treated among civilized nations, and so long as this was continued, there was no hope for us. We felt that they had a fell purpose in view which they would persist in carrying out, until they were *compelled* by retaliation to abandon it. The declaration made by the officers at Danville, that " we *now have them where, with the severity of the climate and harsh treatment, nature will do its work faster than the bullet,*" followed by the continued acts of barbarity which were inflicted upon Federal prisoners, subsequent to that declaration, were sufficient evidence to us that our fate was the result of design on the part of the Confederate Government. For by this means alone, during the year from October 1863, to October 1864, at least, 50,000 men were rendered incapable of ever bearing arms; if the contest could be prolonged for a number of years, at this rate of destruction, nature would indeed do the work, and there would be no need of the bullet.

But the system of retaliation, as adopted by the Government, failed, it was said, of lessening the misery of the officers, the severity of whose treatment it was intended to mitigate. This was in a measure true, but the reason of the failure lies in the manner of the retaliation, and not in the principle advocated; for while the United States deprived certain rebel officers of a portion of regulation supplies, it permitted them to obtain many necessaries and even luxuries, through their friends at the North. The only way in which retaliation could be hoped to be successful, was by reducing all the rebel officers from the highest in rank to the lowest, to the minimum quantity, and the poorest quality of rations, issued to us; by depriving them of their clothing, as we were deprived; by confining them in an open enclosure as we were, with no other means of protecting themselves than was permitted us; and by thus slaughtering them in hundreds and thousands, as we were slaughtered. Had this course been adopted and rigidly adhered to, such a cry would have gone out, from the influential men at the South, from among whom nearly all rebel officers came, as would have forced the Confederate Government to treat its prisoners with more humanity. And it would have been just, for thousands of lives would have been saved thereby; and besides, it would have brought the results of their own policy directly home to them, thus employing their own weapons against them.

It was rumored among us that Mr. Stanton had reported, as one reason why the exchange was not re-opened, that to give a strong, healthy rebel, ready to be put into the field the moment he had passed our lines, for a naked, half-starved skeleton, covered with disease, and incapable of ever again serving in the army, was not an equal exchange. This logic seemed hard to us, for we believed the rumor to be true. If the prisoners, held at the North, had been the only means in the command of the rebels for filling the ranks of their now depleted armies, we should have submitted to our wretched condition, without a murmur, thinking we were still serving our country. Or if, on the other hand, the prisoners in the power of the rebels, had been necessary to keep our armies full to the maximum, we should have considered the reputed statement of the Secretary of War, as being less oppressive. But even if an able-bodied rebel had been exchanged for a loyal "skeleton," and the latter discharged from further service, there was an able-bodied Northern man to take his place; so that even in this view, the "statement" was without good and sufficient reason, to support it. We did not believe it to be just, that we, who had stood, like a wall of fire, upon our borders, that those whom we protected might live in the midst of plenty, enjoying a prosperity almost without a parallel in the history of the country, should suffer death inch by inch, because we had become so reduced in health and strength as to be incapable of further military service; neither did we consider those left behind, engaged in the peaceful pursuits of civil life, to be under less obligation than ourselves, to defend a government as much their own as ours. Surely, if they were not willing to make the sacrifice, if there were not men enough at home with sufficient patriotism to offset the balance which might be made against us by exchanges, while the population of the North was so much greater than that of the South, the Republic was a failure and not worth preserving.

It was urged by some of the prisoners, that it would have been wrong for the United States to adopt retaliatory measures, because the prisoners in its hands were innocent men, in no way accountable for the cruelties we were made to suffer. So were we innocent men, said the other side, personally innocent of any crime against the Confederate States. Yet we were held to suffer for the act of our government in carrying on war; why should they not suffer in the same manner? Besides, as has been said before, retaliation was made upon officers; why not upon privates also? Were not the latter entitled to protection equally with the former? Were they not, indeed, entitled to the greater protection, by as much as they were, by their position, the more helpless?

Every tree is known by its fruit; and, judging the policy of the system of non-exchange by this standard, we see its complete failure. I mean to pass no strictures upon the administration. It is easier to point out errors after, than before, trial, and all the prisoners, whose opinions were entitled to consideration, believed our Government to be animated with a desire to do what was for the best in the premises. But at the same time they did not fail to criticise its acts, while they admitted the purity of its motives. The experiment of non-exchange and non-retaliation, cost the lives of 50,000 as good and true men as ever faced a hostile cannon, more than the half of whom might have been saved and returned to duty.

It is useless to urge that the rebels had no supplies with which to feed and clothe us, in palliation of their barbarity; for food, if not cloth, existed in abundance. There was no reason for their stripping us of our clothing, when we were captured, or of *stealing* the supplies sent us at Danville. They might have provided shelter against the storms and the heat, and wood for fuel. They might have imprisoned us in other places than swamps, reeking with malaria and pestilence; they might have placed us in charge of men, in whose nature the brute was not superior to the human, and by whom our sufferings might have been greatly alleviated. And if they were unable to treat us as civilized beings, they could have set us free. They professed to be fighting for the principles of liberty; but that principle which requires the sacrifice of whole hecatombs of helpless enemies, by the slow torture of starvation, is sprung of fiends and not of liberty.

IN SOUTHERN PRISONS.

Below are tabular statements, showing the relative amounts of rations and clothing issued to prisoners of war by the two governments:

One ration issued by the U. S. Government per day, to Rebel Prisoners of War:	One ration issued by C. S. A. Government per day, to Federal Prisoners of War:
Hard Bread........14 oz., or	
Soft " ....18 " or	
Corn Meal..........18 "	Corn Meal, unbolted..9 oz.
Beef..............14 " or	Beef.............4 " or
Bacon or Pork.....10 "	Bacon.............4 "
White Beans........1-16 qt.,	Peas.............1-16 qt.
Hominy or Rice....1 7-25 oz.	Rice............. 1 oz.
Sugar..............2 1-4 "	
Rio Coffee........1 1-8 "	
Tea..............2 3-4 dr.	
Hard Soap........2-3 "	Soft Soap..........1-32 dr.
Candles, Adam'tine.1-20 or	
" Tallow....1-16 "	
Salt..............1-50 qt.	Salt.............1-100 qt
Molasses..........1-100 "	Molasses..........1-300 "
Potatoes..........3-10 lb.	
Vinegar..........32-100 gi.	

Clothing issued by U. S. to Rebel Prisoners at Fort Delaware from Sept. 1st, 1863, to May 1st, 1864:	Clothing issued by C. S. A. to Federal Prisoners in all places, firom Sept. 1863, to Nov. 1864:
Overcoats..............2,680	None.
Jackets and Coats.......1,094	"
Flannel Shirts..........6,260	"
Pants.................1,310	"
Drawers................7,175	"
Pairs Woolen Socks.....8,807	"
" Bootees..........3,840	"
Woolen Blankets.......4,387	"

I have taken great pains to ascertain the exact

amount and kinds of rations issued at Camps Douglas and Chase, and at other places, where large numbers of rebel prisoners have been confined during the war; I have received statements from several reliable persons, in reply to letters soliciting information upon the subject, and believe what is set down in the above tables, to be true. As regards the allowance afforded by the rebels, I am able to vouch for it myself, having many times weighed and measured what I so often divided among twenty-five men; and there are thousands of living witnesses, in the various parts of the United States, who will corroborate my statement.

Not only was no clothing issued to us, but even a portion of that we had when we were captured, was taken from us. The supplies sent through the lines, while we were at Danville, were in part kept back, and of those who received a portion, the majority exchanged it for eatables with rebel sutlers, in the anticipation of a speedy exchange,—an anticipation excited by rumors set afloat by rebel agencies. It was well known that half-starved men would part with anything they possessed in return for food, particularly when they believed that a few days, at most, would put them into a situation to obtain a new supply; hence the frequent rumors of exchange until all our clothing was in rebel hands.

The following extracts from a report submitted by Brig. Gen. Barnes, in command of Prisoners camp, at Point Lookout, are presented without comment:

"OFFICE OF A. C. S. OF PRISONERS OF WAR,
"POINT LOOKOUT, MD., *April* 15, 1865.

"Prisoners of War, in accordance with General order No. 1, of Brigadier General H. W. Wessels, Commissary General of Prisoners, dated Washington January 13th, 1865, are now allowed the following rations, viz: Pork or bacon ten ounces, (in lieu of beef:) salt or fresh beef fourteen ounces; flour or soft bread, sixteen ounces; hard bread ten ounces, (in lieu of flour or soft bread;) corn meal, sixteen ounces (in lieu of flour or bread.)

To 100 rations; beans or peas, twelve and one half pounds; or rice or hominy eight pounds; soap two pounds; vinegar two quarts; salt two pounds; which rations are of the same quality as those issued to the United States troops, and are drawn by the Assistant Commissary of subsistance of prison camp, from Post Commissary, on requisition for the number of prisoners in camp, and re-issued to each mess-house in bulk, there to be cooked in large boilers made for the purpose, and served out to the prisoners thus: Each cook-house, of which there are seven, originally intended to feed one thousand men per diem, being able to accommodate five hundred at a time, is now made to furnish food for two thousand and upwards, is under the charge of two sergeants, one to superintend the cooking of the rations, and the other, (both are prisoners) the serving of them out. The camp being laid out in divisions of a thousand men each, is so arranged that each cook-house, as far as practicable, shall feed two divisions twice a day, and to avoid any confusion, each division furnishes to the cook-house where it gets its food daily, the number of men present, which must agree with the number stated on the morning the report is made to the Provost Marshal.

"Bread is delivered each noon for the twenty-four hours succeeding, to the sergeants in charge of companies of 100 men, who issue it to the men they have in charge. Each day at dinner the prisoners received a large cup of bean or pea soup, and in the morning received the ration of beef or pork, as stated. They are marched up by companies, to the number of five hundred at a time to each cook-house, and eat the rations prepared for them, and set on long tables, out of tin-ware, which is always kept clean and bright.

"Every care is taken to keep the cook-houses perfectly clean, and the food properly cooked and served. Once each week the Provost Marshal inspects the houses, and the medical officer of the day inspects the food daily. The Assistant Commissary of Subsistence of prison camp visits each house daily, and is strict in seeing that food, utensils, and houses, are kept clean, and that each of the employees attends to his duty.

"Sugar and coffee, or tea, are issued to the sick and wounded, in conformity to General Order No. 1, above referred to, in the manner therein specified.

"Prisoners employed on public works are allowed the following rations, viz:

"Pork or bacon, 12 ounces, (in lieu of beef;) salt or fresh beef, 16 ounces; flour or soft bread, 18 ounces; hard bread, 12 ounces, (in lieu of flour or soft bread;) corn meal, 18 ounces, (in lieu of flour or bread.)

"Per 100 rations: beans or peas, 15 pounds; rice or hominy, 10 pounds, (in lieu of beans or peas;) coffee, (ground) 5 pounds; coffee, (green) 7 pounds, (in lieu of ground coffee;) tea, 16 ounces, (in lieu of coffee;) sugar, 12 pounds; vinegar, 3 quarts; soap, 4 pounds; salt, 3¾ pounds; which they receive in the following manner: These prisoners receive daily, in the same way that other prisoners do at the cook-houses, the same rations that are issued to the bulk of the prisoners, and once every ten days the Assistant Commissary of Subsistence of the camp issues to the Sergeant of each detailed squad the difference between the ration already received and the allowance as above. The Sergeants in charge of details then divide this surplus equally between the men under them. There are about one thousand men employed on public works, viz: 350 on fortifications, and 650 by the Post Quartermaster.

"Soft bread is almost invariably furnished; in fact, hard bread has never been issued, except to prisoners arriving at this depot too late to have bread baked at the bakery on the Point. In all instances the rations are fresh and good, and are the same in quality as those issued to the United States troops. Every care is taken to have the rations (and they are) fairly served out, and especial care is taken to have them properly cooked and prepared. Rations are now issued to about 19,500 prisoners, exclusive of those in hospitals.

"Very respectfully, your obedient servant,
 "C. H. WHITTEMORE.
"Lieutenant and A. C. S. of Prisoners of War.
"Brigadier General JAMES K. BARNES,
Commanding District St. Mary's, Point Lookout, Md."

"PRISONERS' HOSPITAL,
"POINT LOOKOUT, MD., April 15, 1865.

"GENERAL: In compliance with your request, I have the honor to submit the following report, regarding the medical treatment of prisoners of war under your command:

"The camp is divided into divisions of one thousand men each; each division is under the charge of volunteer medical officers from among the prisoners, whose duty it is to treat those slightly sick in quarters, and report all serious cases to the United States medical officers in charge of all the divisions of camp, for examination, with reference to their admission into hospital.

"A daily sick call is held in each company, the same as in regiments of our own troops.

"The hospital proper consists of nine large wooden wards, each ward having sixty hospital beds, complete.

"In addition to these wards, there are sixty hospital tents, floored, and with beds.

"There are separate and detached wards for measles, erysipelas, and other contagious diseases. The hospital for small-pox is located one mile from the prisoners' camp and hospital.

"The medicines drawn for the use of the prisoners are of the same kind and quantity as issued to our own troops at military posts.

"The diet of the sick is the same as in United States general hospitals for the treatment of our own sick. The savings on the army rations constitute the hospital fund, and is expended the same as in other hospitals, in the purchase of articles of extra diet for the sick, such as butter, cheese, milk, corn starch, farina, vermicelli, macaroni, soda crackers, eggs, apples, onions, and such other vegetables as the market affords; the amount thus expended from July, 1864, to March, 1865, inclusive, being fourteen thousand, four hundred and forty-eight dollars and six cents.

"Large issues of clothing have been made to prisoners coming to the hospital in a destitute and suffering condition.

"A large per centage of the sick treated, have been those received from the front in a feeble condition, or coming from other parts. Especially is this true of scurvy, and diseases of scorbutic and malarial origin.

"Accompanying this report is a copy of the general summary of monthly report of sick and wounded, with a tabular list of the most common diseases and deaths, by which it will be seen that, with an average of nine thousand three hundred and seventy-four (9,374) prisoners per month, from July, 1864, to March, 1865, inclusive, there were one hundred and forty-seven deaths monthly, being a ratio of fifteen and seven-hundredths per one thousand men. From September 1863, to June 1864, inclusive, with an average of seven thousand four hundred and ninety-one (7,491) prisoners per month, there were sixty-two deaths, monthly, being a ratio of eight and four-tenths per one thousand men.

"The prevailing diseases are diarrhea, dysentery, remittent, intermittent and typhoid fevers, pneumonia and scurvy.

"I am, very respectfully your obedient servant,

"J. H. THOMPSON,
"Surgeon U. S. V. in charge.

"Brigadier General J. Barnes, Commanding."

Gross amount of articles purchased from Hospital Fund for extra diet, from July 1864, *to March,* 1865, *inclusive.*

Butter	lbs.	6,087
Cheese	lbs.	5,107
Con. milk	doz.	276
Eggs	doz.	2,976
Soda Crackers	bbls.	189
Apples	bbls.	50
Farina	lbs.	1,782
Corn Starch	doz.	177
Macaroni	lbs.	3,000
Vermicelli	lbs.	3,000
Pearl Barley	lbs.	2,498
Onions	bbls.	77
Turnips and other vegetables	bbls.	348

"I certify that the above is a true statement, complied from the monthly statement of hospital fund for the months included above.

"J. H. THOMPSON,
"Surgeon U. S. V. in charge."

"HEADQUARTERS DISTRICT OF ST. MARY'S
"PROVOST MARSHAL'S OFFICE,
"POINT LOOKOUT, MD., April 19, 1865.

GENERAL: In accordance with your instructions, I have the honor to report the manner in which the prisoners-of-war camps are conducted at this post:

The prisoners are divided into divisions of one thousand each, in charge of a non-commissioned officer detailed for that purpose from regiments doing duty at this post, and again divided into companies of one hundred each, in charge of a non-commissioned officer selected from the prisoners, who are held responsible for the cleanliness and good behavior of the prisoners under their charge. On the arrival of prisoners, they are required to deliver to the Provost Marshal, for safe-keeping, all moneys and valuables in their possession. Each package is marked with the owner's name, regiment and company, and is so registered and returned to them when leaving for exchange or discharge. Of the available currency a book is furnished them, upon which they are allowed to purchase from the sutler such articles as are allowed by the Commissary General of Prisoners. Any money sent them during their confinement is placed to their credit in the same manner. Letters are allowed to be written and received by the prisoners, and when examined, if found unexceptionable are immediately delivered. They are allowed to receive from their friends, "upon a permit from the Provost Marshal" such articles of clothing as they may require, provided that they are of the proper quality and color.

"The prisoners are comfortably quartered in Sibley tents, wedge tents, and wooden structures covered by shelter tents. The camps are thoroughly inspected every Sunday morning, and the prisoners paraded in by divisions, each man with his blanket, and any found in a filthy condition are required to bathe and wash themselves and clothing at once. For this purpose they are allowed free access to the shore, in rear of the camp on the Chesapeake Bay. The camps are thoroughly policed daily, and the sanitary condition is fully equal, if not superior, to any regiment of our own troops in the field.

"Very respectfully, your obedient servant,

"A. G. BRADY,

"Major and Provost Mar. in charge Prisoners of War.

"Brigadier General James Barnes, Commanding District St. Mary's, Point Lookout, Md."

The number of deaths per month for the eleven months, begining March 1st, 1864, and ending Feb. 1st, 1865, at Camp Sumter, Andersonville, was as follows:

March	278	First six days of Sept.	576
April	544	Balance of Sept. & Oct.	3,719
May	699	November	491
June	1,291	December	170
July	1,733	January, 1865	199
August	2,990		
		Total	12,633

Sixty-four of this number died of small pox.

From the 1st of July, 1864, to the 1st of January, 1865, the prisoners at Andersonville died at the rate of 12 per cent. per month. During my imprisonment at Danville, where some 4,000 men were confined, 470 died, making an average rate of about two-thirds per cent. per month. At Millen and Savannah, our prisoners died at the rate of 9 per cent. per month. The total number of deaths at Belle Island, for the quarter ending March 30, 1864, was 1,396. On the other hand, at Camps Chase and Douglas, there were about 18,000 men confined, out of which, it is said, 130, or about thirteen-eighteenths per cent., died per month, on an average. In one day, at Andersonville, 140 bodies were deposited in the dead house!

How is this enormous discrepancy in the lists of mortality to be accounted for? It cannot be on the ground that the Federal prisoners were of less robust constitution than the Rebels; for the system of non-exchange was not adopted till nearly all the regiments in our army had been in the field, for at least a year, during which time, those who were physically incapable of enduring the ordinary hardships of military life had been "weeded out" of the ranks, and sent home or detailed; neither was it because of the climate alone, although the malaria filling the atmosphere of the swamps in which we were placed, undoubtedly had a baleful influence on our health,—for in many districts as far South as Andersonville, where our troops were stationed, no such results followed. There can be but one answer to the question—disease induced by the poverty of the food—in short, starvation.

Above I have given data from three of the prisons; eleven more are yet to be accounted for. And when the great record is made up, there is no doubt it will show that from January, 1864, to January, 1865, 30,000 men were swept into the grave, and 20,000 more physically disabled for life by this atrocious treatment; men as brave and true as ever fought for sacred truth and justice, suffering martyrdom by the most horrible tortures ingenious human fiends could devise, for no crime, save that of striving to maintain the rights their fathers bequeathed them.

Those who were engaged in this wholesale slaughter of helpless men, will undoubtedly deny the charges presented in this and similar accounts. Official reports will be referred to, to show that the tale has been falsely colored. A little insight into the manner of keeping the medical reports, will show their fallacy as a basis upon which to found a correct opinion of the facts. Had the war closed by treaty, a final adjustment would have been made, by which the number of prisoners taken could have been compared with the number returned, when the terrible list of mortality would have been disclosed. But it will never be known how many brave men have paid the last penalty, through the barbarity of their captors, and a search for the truth among official records will be fruitless. The surgeon's report was made weekly, and returned to Richmond, showing the number under medical treatment, the number in hospital, the number in camp receiving medicine, the number discharged in camp, the number discharged from the hospital, and the number of the dead. A summary of these reports was occasionally made up and returned to the authorities at Washington. An order was issued by Capt. Wirz, requiring all who were sick to report daily at the sick call, or no medicines would be issued to them. Every one who reported at sick call, according to the previous rule, must be personally examined by the surgeon, before receiving his prescription. It had been the custom to require "standing" cases to be reported only occasionally, since the disease (scurvy) demanded the same treatment daily for months, or until it was cured. To these men the clerks had been accustomed to carry the proper medicine, as the patient needed it, both to save time and relieve the surgeons of a part of their herculean labors. It would have been impossible, under the new order, to examine all these cases personally in one day, (there were more than nine hundred obtaining medicine from the surgeon I attended,) and, if that had been possible, the same remedies would have been prescribed, day by day. Capt. Wirz knew this, and confidently anticipated the result which followed. Six hundred and fifty patients, who had daily received medicines at my surgeon's stand, were discharged, and their names struck from the list of the sick. They were returned on the surgeon's report as cured,—no other return could be made—when, in fact, the little medicine which they had been in the habit of receiving, had merely been the means of counteracting the effects of the disease, and not of eradicating it; as soon as the medicine was withdrawn they grew rapidly worse, and many of them died.

The awful reality of the torments inflicted upon the unfortunate victims of this war in rebel hands, can never be known, except by those who survived it. The constant craving of the appetite, from day to day and from month to month; the continued exposure to the scorching sun and drizzling rains, destitute of clothing and shelter; lying upon the wet ground, and inhaling the poisonous air arising from the swamp, infected as it was with the stench of decaying flesh that was dropping from living bodies by our side, as we slept; covered with vermin, that crawled in myriads over our persons, in spite of constant vigilance; the complete isolation; the absence of employment for mind or body; the same dismal recurrence of the horrible scenes day after day; the despair of release, or an improvement in our condition; the dreary sense of desertion and desolation; all these made up a picture of horror which no pen can describe, no pencil depict.

In the foregoing pages the half has not been told; indeed, my pen has tried to soften the dreadful picture as much as possible. But what is written is truth, every word, unyielding truth. The following description of the transfer of the prisoners from Millen and Andersonville, to the U. S. steamer "Star of the South" at the time I was exchanged was written by an employe of the Sanitary Commission, on board the vessel. Although the incidents there related did not come to my notice, others of similar character were known to me at the time, and I do not hesitate to say the account is in no particular overdrawn.

"No human tongue or pen can ever describe the horrible sufferings we have witnessed this day, (Nov. 20th). I was early at the landing, at half past eight o'clock in the morning, before the boat threw out her ropes for security. The first one brought two hundred bad cases, which the Naval Surgeon told me should properly go to the hospital near by, were it not that others were coming, every one of whom was in the most wretched condition imagable.

* * * * * * * *

"In a short time another boat-load drew near, and oh! such a scene of suffering humanity, I desire never to behold again. The whole deck was a bed of straw for our exhausted, starved, emaciated, dying fellow-creatures. Of the five hundred and fifty that left Savannah, the surgeon informed me not over two hundred would survive; fifty had died on the passage, three died while the boat was coming to the land of liberty. I saw five men dying as they were carried on stretchers from the boat to the Naval Hospital.

* * * * * * * *

"Some had become insane; their wild gaze and clenched teeth convinced the observer that reason had fled; others were idiotic; a few were lying in spasms; perhaps the realization of the hope long cherished, yet oft deferred, or the welcome sound of the music sent forth by the military band was more than their exhausted natures could bear. When blankets were thrown over them, no one would have supposed that a human form lay beneath, save for the small prominence which the bony head and feet indicated. O God of justice! what retribution awaits the perpetrators of such slow and awful murder.

"The hair of some was matted together, like beasts of the stall which lie down in their own filth. Vermin were over them in abundance. Nearly every man was darkened by scurvy, or black with rough scales, and with scorbutic sores. One in particular, was reduced to the merest skeleton; his face, neck and feet covered with thick green mould. A number who had Government clothes given them on the boat were too feeble to put them on; and were carried ashore partially dressed, hugging their clothing with a death-grasp that they could not be persuaded to yield. It was not unfrequent to hear a man feebly call as he was laid on a stretcher, "Don't take my clothes;" "O save my new shoes," "Don't let my socks go back to Andersonville." In their wild death struggle, with bony arms and hands extended, they would hold up their new socks, that could not be put on because of their swollen limbs, saying, "Save 'em till I get home." In a little while, however, the souls of many were released from their worn-out frames, and borne to that higher home where all things are registered for a great day of account."

Another gentlemen writing of the condition of the prisoners taken near Wilmington, North Carolina, who had been exchanged, says: "After nerving myself for the visit, and trying to picture all the horrors while riding slowly over the half mile to the house where they had been collected, my brain reeled for the moment, as the sickening reality burst upon me. Officers came in, and those who had never quailed on the field of death, whose cheeks had never blanched, there stood aghast, with tears in their eyes, grinding their teeth, clenching their hands and thanking God that there was a Hell. Pale, haggard and emaciated skeletons glared on us from glassy eyes, where the light of reason was just expiring With matted hair and skin blackened with pine smoke, scarcely covered with the filthiest shreds of cast-off rebel clothing, without blankets, and most of them without coats or shoes, they gazed at us with an almost idiotic stare, while the majority could with difficulty be roused from their listlessness. Many had forgotten their names; some could be aroused and their memories quickened by asking them of their homes, their wives and their children; these magic words bringing them back from the grave into which they were sinking so fast. Many were dying of starvation, with their hands clutching the bread our soldiers had brought them."

It is useless to multiply such scenes as these; they occurred at every exchange point, and at every arrival of a load of prisoners; Northern papers have circulated accounts of them over the entire country. But if the appearance of a few hundred was so terrible to an occasional witness, what must have been the emotions of those to whom for three months it was a daily occurrence to behold thousands in the same condition? And what must be the feelings of the survivors against the perpetrators of these enormities?

Greater crimes never lay at the door of any people, civilized or savage, than were perpetrated by the Confederate Government upon helpless prisoners of war. From the first battle of Bull Run till the last guerrilla fight of the war, it was their custom to rob their captives of their clothing, and when their cause grew hopeless under constant defeat, they turned their pitiless rage against their helpless foes. The great crime which sent our President to his bloody grave, whether by the sanction of the rebel rulers or not, was the legitimate offspring of the same spirit, as doomed us to slow and terrible death. Our condition must have been known to the Richmond authorities, for the medical reports revealed it; yet for fourteen months, we suffered, and were only relieved when fear of Sherman and his invincible army compelled them to move us. It seems useless to give trial to the subordinates in these fearful assassinations, and to allow the chief offenders to go unpunished, for they were only carrying out the orders of their superiors in command, in their full scope and spirit; rather let the infamous plotters of these deeds also suffer,—the men whose word alone, had it been spoken, could have changed our condition from death to life; the commanders of their armies, the head of their nation. These are the guilty parties; all others were but willing accessories.

The survivors of all these atrocities have returned,— a band of heroes and martyrs for Liberty's sake,— and it remains to be seen what adequate return will be made to them for their sufferings. Nobly have our soldiers fought and nobly died upon the bloody field, to save our beloved country from destruction. All honor to their holy memory. But these have sacrificed more than life, for they bear about them seeds of disease, which will render that life painful and wretched while it is prolonged, ekeing out a miserable existence through years, it may be, of physical torture, crippled and maimed, till the grave, most welcome, shall receive their "last of earth."

To memory of the illustrious dead, whose feebler bodies yielded to the dreadful tortures, let monuments of marble and granite rise, to record the holy sacrifice; to tell to the pilgrim as he visits those fields of blood where they lie interred, the horrid tale of barbarity to which they fell victims, and to teach to coming generations, the terrible sufferings, the heroic endurance, the unflinching fortitude, with which their ancestors met and vanquished the rebellious enemies of their great and noble and happy country."

Since the above narrative was placed in the hands of the printer, Capt. Wirz has been arrested and brought to trial for his crimes. It may not be without interest to the general reader, to notice briefly the circumstances attendant upon his arrest and the developments upon his trial, as far as they have been made, up to this time, (August 20th, 1865).

Sometime in May last, while I was acting as clerk in the office at Gen. Thomas' headquarters, a communication was sent there, by Gen. Wilson, commander of the cavalry forces of the army of the Cumberland, enclosing a letter addressed to that officer by Capt. Wirz, requesting protection for himself and family, against former prisoners, who "were disposed to wreak their vengeance upon him, for what they had suffered," in the Andersonville prison. Accompanying the letter, were the statements of several men of Wilson's command, who had suffered under Capt. Wirz's tyranny, relative to the treatment themselves and others had received at his hands. Immediately on the receipt of these papers, I made a statement to Gen. Whipple, Chief of Staff and A. A. G. to Gen. Thomas, setting forth some of the facts embodied in this book. The result was that Capt. Wirz, instead of being protected by a guard at home, as he requested, was taken into custody and forwarded to Washington, to await an investigation of the charges made against him.

Capt. Wirz claims, in his letter, that he was forced into the rebellion by the excitement of the times; that, being badly wounded in the early part of the war, he was incapacitated for further active service in the field, and in February, 1864, he was ordered to report to Gen. J. H. Winder, by whom he was placed in command of the prison interior at Andersonville. He complains that his duties there were "arduous and unpleasant"; that he was not responsible for shortness of rations, over crowded state of the prison, inadequate supply of clothing, want of shelter, &c.; and asserts that as soon as he can make arrangements he intends to return to Switzerland,—his native country—with his family. He further states himself to have been the "medium, and may better say tool," in the hands of his superiors.

Without stopping here to reiterate the charge of

cowadice, which I have already made, against him,—for who will doubt it, when Capt. Wirz attempts to conceal himself under the flimsy pretext of "orders," which he could at any time have avoided by throwing up his commission,—I pass on to consider briefly how far he was responsible for the treatment of prisoners in his hands.

He was responsible for the "over-crowded state of the prison," because he had the power to enlarge its limits at any time; he was responsible for the "want of shelter," because he had the control, by his own confession, of the prison interior, and he could have allowed the prisoners the privilege of providing themselves with the necessary materials for protection against the climate; he was responsible for the terrible punishments of the stocks and chain-gang or Lieut. Davis, who was in command during the illness of Capt. Wirz, expressly prohibited those punishments; thus proving that there were no order from Richmond, or from any "superior officer," for inflicting them.

It is well known that orders, given from a superior officer to his subordinate, are general in their nature; and especially are they such, when they are given to one having command of an important post, like that at Andersonville, while great discretionary powers are allowed to carry out a general plan. This is so patent to any one having the least knowledge of military affairs, that it needs no comment. There is no doubt that there was a general plan on the part of the Confederate Government to murder the Federal prisoners, nor that Capt. Wirz was selected as a fit and willing instrument, in furtherance of it; but the details of the torture were all his own. No order was ever given him to load men with balls and chains, and keep them wearing them for four or five weeks; no order was given him to place a sick man in the chain-gang and retain him there till he died; no order was given him to shoot defenceless sick men, or to murder those whom his brutality had rendered insane and irresponsible; but he did all these things.

There seems to be a feeling, among a certain class of philanthropists, that the United States Government has no right to punish this man for his crimes; and a great cry of horror goes out against his trial. Men say he was acting under orders; but they forget that, even if that were true, the fact does not protect him. No man has a right to do anything unlawful, even though he is ordered by his superior to do so. Men argue in favor of Wirz, as if he were a subordinate of a foreign power, and irresponsible to any Government except his own; but, even in that view, would it be consonant with the dignity and self respect of the United States, to make peace with a foreign power whose subordinates had treated its prisoners of war with such barbarity, without making a demand that the criminals be surrendered for punishment, or that suitable punishment be inflicted upon them by the home authorities?—and is it to be supposed that peace would ever be made between the contending parties, until such demand was fully complied with? If such a course is just and right, between two sovereign states, it is certainly just and right to adopt it between the Government and its rebellious subjects.

It is a false philanthropy to consider rebels as anything but rebels; no government ever succeeded in asserting its power in any other way. It may be policy to pardon them; if so, they should be treated as pardoned men, whose immunity from punishment for the future, depends upon their own conduct. But there are crimes which do not deserve pardon, and if the deliberate starvation of thousands of helpless men, is not one of these, then should all punitive laws be abolished, and society resolved into its original elements, owning no law but that which endows every individual with the right to use any means, necessary for self-preservation.

The whole nation, the civilized world, right, justice and humanity, demand the punishment of the perpetrators of these astounding crimes; that men may know that even war with all its attendant horrors, does not permit them to indulge their gust for blood, unrestrained; that it is not a cloak with which they can cover their fiendish atrocities, and that its sanction will not protect them in the practice of private vengence, or in the gratification of their lust for the sight of misery. Whoever the criminals may be, whether Capt. Wirz, the instrument, or Davis and Lee the originators, each and all should be made to undergo an extreme penalty for their great guilt, to suffer tortures not less terrible than those they inflicted upon innocent and unoffending men.

From the homes made desolate by their hands; from the deserted firesides, whose ashes have long been cold; from mothers, wives and kindred, whose loved ones come no more to greet them; from every hamlet and crowded town, throughout the land; from the bloody graves of twelve thousand victims, cut down in the pride of manhood, and wasted by famine and torture, such as never earth witnessed before, there comes a cry for retribution; and the voices of those murdered men, pleading for justice, will haunt these homicides, carrying their appeal from an earthly tribunal, to that higher Court, where a merciful, but an avenging Judge shall set the seal of right at last.

Names of Ohio Soldiers

WHO HAVE DIED AT ANDERSONVILLE, GA., AND SALISBURY, N. C.

[And., Andersonville; Salis., Salisbury.]

Name.	Co.	Place of Death.		Name.	Co.	Place of Death.
1st INFANTRY.			Priv	R S Fires	G	And.
Sergt T P Simonds	A	And.		H B Lever	C	
Corp J W Allen	G			H H Liver	G	
C Mitchell	K			E H Barnes	D	
J B Smith	B			W S McHugh	D	
Priv C Copeland	A			P Regman	D	
R Twadle	A			O F Stuart	D	
H Brouser	B			M Cline	E	
D Hinly	B			J B Johnston	E	
F Miller	B			J Salp	E	
G W Halloway	C			S Stouts	F	
J E Harris	E			E Church	G	
H Gordon	G			B Hymeio	G	
N H Smith	H			W Rhotin	G	
C Blight	I			Wm Smith	G	
M Dessender	I			I Montgomery	G	
A Ervin	I			J P Dumas	H	
H Kelly	I			C W Chard	H	
F McGinlkin	I			I Linway	H	
P F Prouse	I			—— Dodge	I	
C Gardner	K			Wm Hazlett	K	
2d INFANTRY.				J Hastmat	K	
				Wm McHenry	K	Salis.
Sergt Thos J Moore	D	And.		G Skeddy	K	And.
James Frasier	E			J Steward	K	
W P McCormic	G			**3d INFANTRY.**		
Corp J H Shepard	E		Priv	G Perrin	B	
J Lawson	E			J Bumgardner	C	
H Fulkison	I			John O'Brien	D	
D Smith	I			A J Caldwell	D	
Priv D D Moore	A			**4th INFANTRY.**		
C Finch	B			J Diver	A	
—— Eckhart	B			J Sutton	A	
John Bowman	C			E Wilson	A	
R E Colts	C					

	Name.	Co.	Place of Death.		Name.	Co.	Place of Death.
Priv	G Gaston	C	Salis.	Priv	J Hicks	D	And.
	James Snider	C	And.		H McKnight	G	
	F. Miller	E			W H Boyle	H	
	A Maloney	H			C E Morris	H	
	S E Scott	I			J Brinker	K	
	5th INFANTRY.				G W Smith	K	
	D Hubber	A			12th INFANTRY.		
	W C Kimble	I			P Maxwell	A	
	6th INFANTRY.				S Decker	C	
	J Singer	B			M Ferballeger	C	
	A T Vatier	C			L Grove	C	
	N Bright	E			H Halchelt	C	
	A Cummings	E			H McKabe	C	
	C Boutrelle	G			J Hughes	E	
	G W Gilbert	G			J D Scarrell	E	
	J Rourk	G			S Uchre	E	
	W Young	G			S N Leohnard	H	
	A Vandevier	H			N Vale	K	
	J H Cohagan	K			13th INFANTRY.		
	7th INFANTRY.				D Greesling	A	
	George Arthur	B			J Hamilton	A	
	G M Vale	D			J Master	A	
	A A Shoufer	E			M Fensley	B	
	John Young	E			W R Foroman	E	
	H I Boyd	H			A G Graff	E	
	H E Davis	H			F Hood	F	
	D Smith	H			H Gates	G	
	John Brownlee	I			C Rogers	H	
	M McKinsley	I			A Curr	I	
	B Heyt	K			H Hartman	K	
	A Lepe	K			G Pepenbring	K	
	8th INFANTRY.				14th INFANTRY.		
	John Arnold	B	Salis.	Sergt	G E Church	C	
	Henry Ringer	D		Corp	Wm Gaunt	I	
	C Shoemaker	F	And.	Priv	O Halbert	A	
	Jas McKeever	G			H Waldron	A	
	9th INFANTRY.				M Lutz	C	
Sergt	Thos Snider	G			J Warner	C	
Priv	J S Goodrich	A			F Spegle	D	
	F Walters	B			Eli Burchfield	G	
	Jas Russell	E			C Bruhning	G	
	L Harmon	F			Wm Samse	H	
	C Blessing	F			J Cepp	I	
	— Young	F			H Vanfleet	I	
	John Bogart	G			S McComb	K	
	F K Hennell	G			15th INFANTRY.		
	W Manson	G					
	J Shaffer	G		Sergt	N Jarett	A	
	J H Weibrick	G			J Caldwell	D	
	10th INFANTRY.			Corp	A G Craven	C	
				Priv	N Martin	A	
	Geo R Coules	S S	Salis.		James Wood	B	
	P Freeley	G	And.		J C Chambers	C	
	E Hart	G			J Kellar	D	
	11th INFANTRY.				R N White	D	
	W Cost	D			G Kelley	E	
					John Brandon	F	

Name.	Co.	Place of Death.
Priv C Hurley	F	And.
S R Wingrose	F	
G Stull	G	
W H Doughty	H	
I Collins	I	
W Shaw	I	

16th INFANTRY.

Name	Co.	Place of Death
Priv R Bryan	C	

17th INFANTRY.

Name	Co.	
Sergt J L Vail	C	
Priv John Stover	A	
James Mitchell	D	
Frank Briggs	G	
Sam'l Masters	I	

18th INFANTRY.

Name	Co.	
Corp W Fullerstine	K	
Priv J Eastman	C	
P Kinkade	C	
L Younker	F	
James Finlan	K	
J Haver	K	

19th INFANTRY.

Name	Co.	
J Gilbert	B	
J S Seward	B	
M Lemmons	E	
J Mick	E	
D Balcomb	F	
O Hendrickson	F	
C Moore	H	
J Balunt	I	
P E Goff	K	

20th INFANTRY.

Name	Co.	Place
Sergt W H Barrum	B	
W H Tapp	E	
E M Evans	I	
Corp W Elliott	F	
Priv H Rapp	F	
Peter Wolf	F	Salis.
F G Hiles	G	And.

21st INFANTRY.

Name	Co.	
Sergt Geo McMurray	G	
L W Brown	E	
S Hull	E	
G Smith	I	
Corp P L Gingeri	E	
S Marshal	G	
Priv A Cary	A	
H M Clark	A	
H G Watson	A	
G Caswell	C	
F Pinert	C	
A Arnewbrish	D	
Wm Hibbett	D	
E Kelley	D	
J Lindsey	D	

Name.	Co.	Place of Death.
Priv A T Manahan	D	And.
W Patten	D	
M Fanaman	E	
J Night	E	
G Pratt	G	
G H Morrison	H	
A H Foenix	H	
G H Reid	H	
H Riggs	H	
Ira Ward	H	
J Harrison	I	
C Myer	I	
P S Davidson	K	
Wm Forrest	K	
G Jolly	K	
J Powers	K	
E Whiting	K	

22d INFANTRY.

Name	Co.	
J F McMillen	A	
W Lehigh	B	
J Collyer	G	
B Davis	—	

23d INFANTRY.

Name	Co.	Place
Sergt Wm McIntosh	I	
Priv Wm Hubbell	A	
E A Piper	B	
Charles Brown	D	
Samuel Hall	D	Salis.
John Ridgway	D	And.
J A Holebaugh	E	
James Ludely	E	Salis.
Wm Bartels	I	
Charles Dille	I	And.
C Crumbarger	I	
O C Johnson	I	Salis.

24th INFANTRY.

Name	Co.	Place
Corp J Jennings	K	And.
Priv Edmond Gerry	D	Salis.
W Douglas	F	And.
E Shoulder	F	
J Endermill	K	

25th INFANTRY.

Name	Co.	
R Beeman	E	

26th INFANTRY.

Name	Co.	
Sergt J Cochran	G	
Corp H Jacobs	F	
Priv V B Thompson	C	
J Townsend	C	
S C Barrett	F	
W Brown	G	
C Diccy	G	
A Wiley	I	
A P Clanyan	K	

27th INFANTRY.

Name	Co.	
P M McLaine	A	

Name.	Co.	Place of Death.
Priv A Gilland	F	And.

28th INFANTRY.

Jacob Selb	C	
A Ehmann	F	
C Goodbraith	G	
D Keanskoff	I	
C Miller	I	

29th INFANTRY.

H B White	A	

30th INFANTRY.

Jas Gallagher	F	

31st INFANTRY.

Sergt J C Clark	H	
Priv W F Longstreet	A	
T L Barnes	B	
L Shieber	B	
W Ingler	C	
W H Mitchell	D	
L H Burch	H	

32d INFANTRY.

Sergt A Taner	G	
Corp J H Humes	I	
Priv B Horerlin	B	
W Simpson	F	

33d INFANTRY.

Corp U A Copen	C	
W Pile	F	
Priv H Hughes	A	
J C Massie	A	
E Rear	A	
W H Radabaugh	A	
Samuel Evans	B	
R Hazerman	B	
Samuel Pullen	B	
W V Richards	B	
C W Aldridge	C	
T Daily	D	
W H Davis	D	
J Fip	E	
J W E McCormic	E	
A B Whitehead	F	
J W Knidler	H	
H Phillips	I	
C N Dearth	K	
John Dilldine	K	
C S Steward	K	

34th INFANTRY.

Wm Elcook	A	Salis.
A Alown	B	And.
H T Bean	B	
W Preston	B	
Joshua Baker	C	Salis.
H Callihan	C	And.
G W Davidson	C	Salis.

Name.	Co.	Place of Death.
Priv J Shepherd	D	And.
G Hitchcock	G	
George Elder	H	Salis.
A Hendrick	H	And.
J Vollis	H	

35th INFANTRY.

Sergt J M Fenton	I	
Priv F Cattlchock	A	
E Shannon	A	
F J Wisser	A	
J W Higgins	D	
B F Warner	E	
C B Livingood	G	
A McCloud	G	
W S Cummings	I	

36th INFANTRY.

E F Parks	D	
Jas H Yeager	D	Salis.
W Yoager	D	And.
J Weazon	F	
A Barnes	G	
J Heckler	G	
H Jeffries	I	
J Gilliman	K	

39th INFANTRY.

J Baughman	C	

40th INFANTRY.

Sergt R I Malone	H	
Priv E P Fitch	G	
C Gibson	H	
R Gibson	H	
T W Henderson	H	
F Hicks	H	
J Porter	H	
W C Porter	H	
Wm Trimmer	H	

41st INFANTRY.

Corp H H Brown	H	
Priv L E Doty	H	

43d INFANTRY.

D Johnston	B	
D C Brewer	K	

44th INFANTRY.

Sergt T S Boden	—	
Priv Jas Thomas	C	
J Imboden	E	
E B Rutan	E	
John Way	I	

45th INFANTRY.

Sergt R Dayman	B	
Corp G A Smith	F	
A S Johnston	I	
Priv A Beers	A	

IN SOUTHERN PRISONS. 387

Name.	Co.	Place of Death.
Priv W F Hanna	A	And.
A W Lance	A	
J Bird	A	
W Allen	B	
E Baker	B	
W Gordon	B	
Geo W Justice	B	
Jack Horner	B	
I Laughessy	B	
George Musser	B	
C D Nash	B	
S B Turner	B	
John Wooley	B	
G Duffy	C	
N Hockingburgh	C	
W Humphreys	C	
R Jones	C	
J Kelley	C	
R Minishall	C	
John Neal	C	
J Staneli	C	
W J Buldy	D	
N Curtis	D	
J Hendershot	D	
J Mason	D	
L Werts	D	
G W Davis	E	
Geo Downing	E	
W A Gutterlee	E	
P O Jacobs	E	
S Rollins	E	
A Spangler	E	
W J Botken	F	
A S Bothkins	F	
P Steets	F	
A Godfrey	G	
H Jones	G	
G Ridler	G	
W H H Vinning	G	
W R Arrows	H	
S J B Kannady	H	
John Long	H	
James Pussey	H	
Wm E Parker	H	
A Ross	H	
W Brookhart	I	
O Batch	I	
Chas Shannon	I	
Wm Bodkin	K	
F Leasure	K	
Charles Laine	K	
George Shriver	K	

46th INFANTRY.

| William Kelly | C | |

47th INFANTRY.

| Sergt J Shoemaker | E | |
| Priv A Ryan | A | |

49th INFANTRY.

Sergt Maj J W Clokie		And.
M Sweet	F	
J Cregg	K	
Priv L Cover	B	
Thomas Squires	C	
J Davine	D	
G W Sheldton	E	
D McSorley	F	
James Lowry	I	
S Bishop	K	
A Duncan	K	

50th INFANTRY.

| D McIntosh | D | |
| James Mooney | D | |

51st INFANTRY.

Jas Buckbier	A	
Wm Cahill	A	
John Ditto	A	
J Johnson	A	
James McKerr	A	
D Alinger	C	
C Ott	C	
I Rogers	C	
L Coultright	F	
J D Stonehicks	F	
W Evans	I	
A Sickles	I	
B Mahin	I	
S Bowman	K	

52d INFANTRY.

| A P Downer | B | |

53d INFANTRY.

| Sergt Charles Dick | G | |

54th INFANTRY.

Priv W L Hill	A	
J D Masters	B	
C Bender	C	
J Knapp	E	
A Myers	I	

55th INFANTRY.

| J H Griffith | C | |

57th INFANTRY.

| David Coons | C | |

59th INFANTRY.

J Ross	A	
J H Moore	C	
A Penny	C	
M Drake	D	
R Reese	D	
W H Wood	E	

Name.	Co.	Place of Death.
Priv M Donly	G	And.
W H Cromwell	H	
N Elleman	K	

60th INFANTRY.

Name	Co.	Place of Death.
George Black	A	Salis.
James Doran	A	And.
L Garroll	A	
S Maulag	A	
A Norton	A	Salis.
John Shumme	A	
Geo Williams	A	
J Cuvere	B	
J Ginther	B	
C W Albrook	C	
Albert Brock	C	Salis.
G W Clark	D	And.
Edw'd Harkins	D	Salis.
John W Green	D	
M Harkins	D	And.
J H Moore	D	
Orien Holcomb	F	Salis.
N Bremer	F	And.
Thos Jenkins	F	Salis.
G W Mills	F	And.
Charles Wolfe	F	Salis.
J W Wagnan	F	
S M Williams	F	And.
Thos Watson	F	Salis.
N Shipman	H	
T W Carpenter	H	
H Harper	I	And.
James Pease	I	Salis.

61st INFANTRY.

F Bower	I	And.

62d INFANTRY.

H S Clarke	E	
S Starbuck	E	

63d INFANTRY.

A Lanson	D	
J Olinger	F	
J R Anderson	K	
T Sharp	K	

64th INFANTRY.

J Arni	D	
A Foreman	E	

65th INFANTRY.

Sergt G Peasley	H	
Priv G Bunkhorner	C	
J Robinson	D	
G Carnahan	F	
C Waller	I	
J Mullin	K	

66th INFANTRY.

Priv J McKnabe	G	And.

67th INFANTRY.

Corp J Kenny	E	

68th INFANTRY.

Priv R Maymene	D	
A Coleman	K	

69th INFANTRY.

H Cameron	B	
J W Wearan	F	Salis.
Joseph Harris	I	
J Arthur	K	And.

70th INFANTRY.

A Bell	B	
S Blangy	B	
J McCabe	C	
Mus. J Howard	D	
Priv P Winder	D	
H Copeheart	I	

71st INFANTRY.

Geo Sponscular	B	

72d INFANTRY.

Corp N S Hains	C	
F Stodler	E	
Priv A Almond	A	
William Hinton	A	
M Perrin	A	
H Sturdevant	A	
L Wentworth	A	
O Hadwell	C	
G H Lowe	C	
John Pursell	D	
S Jackson	E	
M Lockner	E	
H Potter	E	
N J Zink	E	
H Shook	F	
M J Sanner	F	
S Backman	G	
C Frankinburg	G	
P Sopser	G	
J Ross	H	
M Weaver	H	
P Donahue	K	

73d INFANTRY.

D Wickhames	D	
E A Hausbury	E	
J White	E	

74th INFANTRY.

Sergt Saml Campbell	G	
Priv Wm Hudson	G	

IN SOUTHERN PRISONS. 389

Name.	Co.	Place of Death.		Name.	Co.	Place of Death.
75th INFANTRY.			Priv	Wm McDill	C	And.
Priv G Chapman	A	And.		J M Ralston	C	
Wm Pearce	H			L Snyder	C	
J Roman	H			W B Thomas	C	
76th INFANTRY.				Geo M Coyner	D	
T Sullivan	C			Sam'l Eppert	D	
Charles Harvey	E			C Sampson	D	
77th INFANTRY.				A Seymour	D	
J Gullendick	E			O Scurbens	D	
80th INFANTRY.				J S Wright	E	
A Ruce	C			F Logan	F	
A Steel	H			E P Hill	G	
81st INFANTRY.				W B Perkins	G	
Wm Sheets	A			F Sly	G	
82d INFANTRY.				J M Vanmalley	G	
Corp W Carpenter	D			L G Wainwright	G	
Priv B Cole	A			R S Chambers	H	
H B Smith	B			J W Johnston	H	
W Falks	D			Wm H Latter	H	
J Bramugan	F			J Lucas	H	
J H Feehes	F			A J McDonnald	H	
A Talman	H			L Wrotin	H	
G Richardson	—			J D Clark	I	
84th INFANTRY.				J B Carter	I	
Corp Wm Jones	B			D Fisher	I	
85th INFANTRY.				J B Sawyer	I	
Priv Greenbaugh	E			S Nelder	I	
86th INFANTRY.				D B Robins	I	
G Hofner	G			P Smith	I	
89th INFANTRY.				W Christy	K	
Sergt J C Arthur	A			W R Houser	K	
T J Barre	A			**90th INFANTRY.**		
W J McKeel	D			Joseph Wyatt	B	
W J Rolstan	D			D Williamson	D	
E N Townsley	E			J C Beery	E	
T Augustis	K			**91st INFANTRY.**		
A Willis	A			D Lane	D	
Corp Wm L Riley	B			J C Allen	F	
L C Cornelius	C			H Hartley	F	Salis.
W Wilkinson	D			**92d INFANTRY.**		
S M Spencer	E		Corp	L C Hardee	E	And.
Priv James Bomers	A			V H Barnes	H	
James Lambert	A			J M Crooks	K	
G Staley	A		Priv	J McElroy	B	
Wm Wood	A			J Blackwood	I	
J J Cordray	B			**93d INFANTRY.**		
O Hull	B			R Anderson	C	
J Payne	B			J Stiver	C	
J P West	B			P Tinway	C	
Wm Crust	C			A Smock	D	
B F Harry	C			A Schmats	E	
				J Wagner	F	
				94th INFANTRY.		
				G W Police	C	
				W C Baker	E	

27

Name.	Co.	Place of Death.	Name.	Co.	Place of Death.
Priv A A Akers	F	And.	103d INFANTRY.		
Samuel D Rush	F		Corp N Hawkins	G	And.
M Biddinger	K		Priv J Conway	A	
95th INFANTRY.			W Thomas	B	
D J Cutsdapner	D		F O'Connor	E	
B Durant	D		Wm Smith	F	
G W Henry	E		A Jordon	G	
W P Fike	H		Geo Hind	H	
R Neff	H		H Vangilder	H	
96th INFANTRY.			S J Harrington	I	
John Love	E		A Miller	I	
98th INFANTRY.			**104th INFANTRY.**		
Corp Thos Rees	C		B C Entortin	K	
Priv S Kinnible	A		**105th INFANTRY.**		
J B McCoy	A		J Morris	A	
J H Johnson	D		G W Shaw	A	
D Lagrace	D		E Bartholomew	C	
J Hillyard	F		F Belding	D	
99th INFANTRY.			J L Jones	D	
Sergt E D Harris	I		G Martin	F	
Corp E Ham	K		**109th INFANTRY.**		
Priv G W Black	F		Corp W H Bonesline	I	
Jas Fry	I		**110th INFANTRY.**		
Daniel Frayer	I		Sergt H H Robinson	H	
100th INFANTRY.			Corp M Brown	F	
Sergt P H Hally	B		Priv C Honick	F	
Corp H Price	A		P H Riper	G	
Priv R M Foster	A		**111th INFANTRY.**		
C Fowler	A		Corp W Demming	B	
C Smith	A		J Hudison	B	
A M Towns	B	Salis.	Priv G L Brown	A	
J M Zuber	B	And.	K Cline	B	
Geo Beaver	C		D V Clark	B	
H Benor	E		J Decker	B	
M R Metcalf	E		S Jones	B	
H Stephens	E		A K Raney	B	
E W Ostrander	H		L T Russell	B	
M Still	H		D Stevenson	B	
Geo Ames	K		J Stevenson	B	
John Lovely	K		J W Swinebeart	B	
Jos Wentling	K		Wm Wickham	B	
101st INFANTRY.			N Crasser	C	
Sergt F E Struchion	A		Wm Facar	K	
Priv A Bradley	A		R Moek	K	
G Coleman	A		**112th INFANTRY.**		
B F Decker	B		G Boles	H	
R F Moore	C		**113th INFANTRY.**		
D Bush	H		Corp F Peterson	G	
F Dibble	H		Priv P Gaffy	G	
G W Stephens	H		W H Hunt	G	
P Schaffer	I				
J Schein	K		**114th INFANTRY.**		
102d INFANTRY.			A G Hatfield	E	
G Beckley	F				

Name.	Co.	Place of Death.	Name.	Co.	Place of Death.
Priv S E Irving	H	And.	Priv J M Gould	A	And.
J H Scott	H		J C Horney	C	
J Skiver	H		M Chandler	E	
115th INFANTRY.			Z Parker	E	
			S S Law	I	
Dan'l Harboldt	F		J Rei	K	
116th INFANTRY.			**125th INFANTRY.**		
R Hoit	B		J Pearson	B	
A G Preshale	C		J Wric	B	
J Worte	C		A E Hayford	C	
W F Flowers	D		A Sell	E	
A Forshay	F		B Vaughn	F	
R G Russell	G		B H Bretton	H	
			J Brooks	I	
118th INFANTRY.			G W Lamphue	K	
R W James	F		**126th INFANTRY.**		
120th INFANTRY.			J G Buckley	A	
R Robertson	D		J Hurtis	C	
J Mitchell	F		M Johnson	C	
121st INFANTRY.			Isaac Weaver	C	Salis.
			J J Benkle	E	And.
Corp A B Allen	C		S Hall	F	
Priv P D Doxter	D		J O'Neal	F	
N Smith	H		W A Jewell	G	
J M Burna	K		J J Brocker	H	
123d INFANTRY.			H Grager	H	
J Dunbar	B		G W Hatfield	K	
D Worthen	B		**128th INFANTRY.**		
J R Briace	C		O Dipper	I	
J H Kerr	C				
J Oliver	C		**130th INFANTRY.**		
O Clay	D		Geo Wickliffe	D	Salis.
A G Cromblet	E		**135th INFANTRY.**		
R L Franks	E				
James Potts	E		Sergt A M Pror	B	And.
D Henderson	H		Corp J Rochelle	F	
C Redd	H		Priv A Alward	A	
P C Robins	H		G W Hutchins	A	
J Spiger	H		B Hayner	A	
J Adams	I		H Boyle	B	
J Lasiere	K		James Bell	B	
			Geo Brookover	B	
123d INFANTRY.			W B Crooks	B	
G Pfiffer	A		H Licklighter	B	
S Wood	A		S H Myers	B	
S F Bond	B		J Mark	B	
J B Hayward	C		G Vankirk	B	
Wm O Forrey	D		E Ewong	D	
F Shultz	E		W A Benner	F	
J Durr	H		G H Barstow	F	
W L Fry	H		J A Chappin	F	
C Valentine	H		J R Clarke	F	
John Lay	K		J Diver	F	
			W Ensley	F	
124th INFANTRY.			M B Firgrave	F	
Corp N Plunket	E		W Holmes	F	
W Parker	H		R Harmon	F	

	Name.	Co.	Place of Death.		Name.	Co.	Place of Death.
Priv	S D Jones	F	And.		**2d CAVALRY.**		
	Samuel Miller	F					
	Wm Morris	F		Sergt	P W Stanford	A	And.
	S Palmer	F			D Craig	D	
	J Sullivan	F			T Hull	H	
	R Talbert	F			A Glisson	M	
	J M Woodruff	F		Priv	A A Smith	A	
	J F Drake	G			M R Hickox	B	
	J Miller	I			E Adams	C	
					S B Cook	C	
	144th INFANTRY.				F G Palmer	D	
					H Reeker	E	
	James Grover	B	Salis.		Sam'l Sears	F	
	H Guise	B			J Bessel	G	
	John McCombs	B			C J Robinson	G	
	Isaac H Price	B			U S Turner	G	
	Walter Wood	B			R Coales	H	
	Hiram White	E			Jos Ferris	H	
	C E Henry	H			Wm Rie	K	
	F Barton	I			D Shingle	L	
	Wm Brown	I			S R Bickel	M	
	W Brown	I			F Wing	M	
	Adam Bovil	K					
	Israel Burns	K			**3d CAVALRY.**		
	C A Bryant	K					
	B Ensminger	K			H Furguson	D	
	F H C Fresbie	K			Ed Niver	I	
	J A Mars	K			J W Rex	K	
	John Morgan	K			J B Jones	M	
	John Rubale	K					
	Oran Sage	K			**4th CAVALRY.**		
	L Talmer	K					
					A Malsbray	A	
	145th INFANTRY.				F Mitler	A	
					A Kerby	A	
	W H Danton	E	And.		E Green	D	
	George Winters	K			Wm Earles	G	
					Wm Herbert	L	
	149h INFANTRY.						
					5th CAVALRY.		
	Preston Sawyer	F	Salis.				
	H Benner	H			F Dyke	K	
					J Moreart	K	
	153d INFANTRY.						
					6th CAVALRY.		
	J W Hutchens	A	And.				
	G G B'Hymer	A		Corp	S Groscaust	G	
	B Futtimon	C		Priv	G Brabham	B	
	J Poistian	F			E Knowlton	B	
	J Mott	H			R J Green	C	
					H Logan	E	
	1st LT. ARTILLERY.				V Ferinan	G	
					J W Parks	G	
	Geo Crocker	A			J Shepple	G	
					W L Sprague	K	
	1st CAVALRY.						
					7th CAVALRY.		
	L B Bates	A					
	Thos Dugan	B		Sergt	A Idold	C	
	John Hugel	C			J Davis	F	
	Thos Nelson	E			J Hill	L	
	James Donley	F		Corp	R L Hudsonpiller	L	
	C Gamer	K		Priv	Sam'l Leisure	A	
	F Nelson	K			J Murphy	B	
Blacksmith,	L Myers	—			J Yager	E	

	Name.	Co.	Place of Death.		Name.	Co.	Place of Death.
Priv	J E Smith	K	And.	Priv	J D Clayton	D	And.
	N Huming	D			N Baldwin	F	
	John Denton	E			Charles Arnold	G	
	Wm Holloway	F			Wm Smith	G	
	John Smith	F			N Wistman	G	
	Saml Sweeney	G					
	E Dodson	H					

10th CAVALRY.

	Name	Co.
	M Hurring	I
	B McClung	I
	O Williams	K
	B Gillingham	L
	G D Hank	L
	Joseph Henry	L
	George Shields	L
	J Manley	M

	T Martin	A
	R C Mitchell	B
	B Barber	D
	E Brutsche	I
	G E Pease	I
	E Evall	M
	Wm Thomas	M

8th CAVALRY.

James Dunham M

12th CAVALRY.

Corp L Dorson I
Priv R G Morgan H

9th CAVALRY.

S Vanhorn C

3d OHIO IND'P'T CAVALRY.

Priv T Dandelion —

Total list of deaths in Andersonville........................879
   "   "   "   in Salisbury............................. 62

www.ingramcontent.com/pod-product-compliance
Lightning Source LLC
Chambersburg PA
CBHW032012220426
43664CB00006B/221